THE INFLUENCE AND ANXIETY OF
THE BRITISH ROMANTICS

Front Cover: John William Waterhouse, 'La Belle Dame Sans Merci'. 1893.
Hessisches Landesmuseum Darmstadt

Back Cover: photo © Gavin Ruston

THE INFLUENCE AND ANXIETY OF THE BRITISH ROMANTICS
Spectres of Romanticism

Edited by
Sharon Ruston

With Assistance by
Lidia Garbin

Salzburg Studies in English Literature
Romantic Reassessment
Volume 153

The Edwin Mellen Press
Lewiston•Queenston•Lampeter

Library of Congress Cataloging-in-Publication Data

The influence and anxiety of the British romantics : spectres of romanticism / [compiled by] Sharon Ruston ; with assistance by Lidia Garbin.
      p. cm. -- {Salzburg studies in English literature. Romantic reassessment ; v. 153)
  The essays in this volume had their origin in an inaugural postgraduate conference at the University of Liverpool in the summer of 1998 under the aegis of the British Association for Romantic Studies.
  Includes bibliographical references and index.
  ISBN 0-7734-7999-6
  1. English literature--19th century--History and criticism Congresses. 2. Influence (Literary, artistic, etc.) Congresses. 3. Romanticism--Great Britain Congresses. 4. Anxiety in literature Congresses. 5. Ghosts in literature Congresses. I. Ruston, Sharon. II. Garbin, Lidia. III. Series: Salzburg studies in English literature. Romantic reassessment ; 153.
PR457.I55   1999
820.9' 145--DC21
                                                      99-16083
                                                          CIP

This is volume 153 in the continuing series
Salzburg Studies in English Literature
Romantic Reassessment
Volume 153 ISBN 0-7734-7999-6
SSRR Series ISBN 0-7734-4176-X

A CIP catalog record for this book is available from the British Library.

Copyright © 1999 The Edwin Mellen Press

All rights reserved. For information contact

   The Edwin Mellen Press   The Edwin Mellen Press
        Box 450   Box 67
    Lewiston, New York   Queenston, Ontario
       USA 14092   CANADA L0S 1L0

Edwin Mellen Press, Ltd.
Lampeter, Ceredigion, Wales
UNITED KINGDOM SA48 8LT

Printed in the United States of America

Table of Contents

List of Illustrations vii

Preface *John Whale* ix

Acknowledgements xii

Introduction *Sharon Ruston* xv

1. Terror, Transcendence and Control in Charlotte Dacre's *Zofloya, or The Moor*

   Sue Chaplin (University of Sheffield) 1

2. William Blake and the Spectre of Anatomy

   Tristanne Connolly (King's College, Cambridge) 19

3. 'The moving accident is not my trade': Wordsworth, *Lyrical Ballads*, and the Anxiety of German Borrowings

   Peter Mortensen (Johns Hopkins University) 43

4. 'A new species of humorous writing': Thomas Love Peacock and the Renegotiation of Genre

   Jerome de Groot (University of Newcastle) 67

5. Shelley's 'The Triumph of Life': A Resistance to History and the Art of Forgetting

   Rieko Suzuki (University of Newcastle) 89

6. 'You'll pardon me for being jocular': *La Belle Dame sans Merci* and Keats's Light Verse
James Kidd (University College, London) 109

7. Resurrecting Thomas Lovell Beddoes
Michael Bradshaw (Japan Woman's University) 139

8. Ghastly Visualities : Keats and Victorian Art
Sarah Wootton (University of Sheffield) 159

9. Sinister Romance: A Twist of the Tale in *The Turn of the Screw*
Hazel Hutchison (University of Aberdeen) 181

10. Mediumistic Shelley Sonnets in the Netherlands
Kris Steyaert (University College, London) 199

Bibliography 225

Index 241

List of Illustrations

Plate 1. William Cowper, *Myotomia Reformata*, p. 8. Reproduced by permission of the Syndics of Cambridge University Library.

Plate 2. William Blake, *Jerusalem*, plate 47. Reproduced by permission of the William Blake Trust.

Plate 3. William Cowper, *Anatomy of Humane Bodies*, Table 45. Reproduced by permission of the Syndics of Cambridge University Library.

Plate 4. William Cowper, *Anatomy of Humane Bodies*, Appendix 3. Reproduced by permission of the Syndics of Cambridge University Library.

Plate 5. William Blake, *Jerusalem*, plate 25. Reproduced by permission of the William Blake Trust.

Plate 6. William Blake, *Jerusalem*, plate 85. Reproduced by permission of the William Blake Trust.

Plate 7. William Blake, *Jerusalem*, plate 24. Reproduced by permission of the William Blake Trust.

Plate 8. William Cowper, *Anatomy of Humane Bodies*, Table 40. Reproduced by permission of the Syndics of Cambridge University Library.

Plate 9. William Cowper, *Anatomy of Humane Bodies*, Table 60. Reproduced by permission of the Syndics of Cambridge University Library.

Plate 10. William Cowper, *Anatomy of Humane Bodies*, Table 62. Reproduced by permission of the Syndics of Cambridge University Library.

Plate 11. Dante Gabriel Rossetti, 'Mnemosyne'. 1881. Reproduced by permission of the Delaware Art Museum

Plate 12. Dante Gabriel Rossetti, 'La Belle Dame Sans Merci'. Circa 1855. Reproduced by permission of the British Museum

Plate 13. John William Waterhouse, 'La Belle Dame Sans Merci'. 1893. Reproduced by permission of the Hessisches Landesmuseum Darmstadt

Plate 14. Sir Frank Dicksee, 'La Belle Dame Sans Merci', Exh. 1902. Reproduced by permission of the City of Bristol Museum and Art Gallery and the Bridgeman Art Library, London/New York

Plate 15. Frank Cadogan Cowper, La Belle Dame Sans Merci. Private collection and Bridgeman Art Library, London/New York

Plate 16. William Russell Flint, 'La Belle Dame Sans Merci'. 1908. Reproduced by permission of the Board of Trustees of the National Museums and Galleries on Merseyside (Walker Art Gallery, Liverpool)

Preface

The essays in this volume had their origin in the highly successful inaugural postgraduate conference which took place at the University of Liverpool in the summer of 1998 under the aegis of the British Association for Romantic Studies. Its theme of 'Romantic Spectres' provided ample opportunity for new scholars to explore some of the key aspects of Romantic texts and the critical formulations of Romanticism inherent in such dialectical relationships as the material and the metaphysical, body and soul, at the same time as investigating new configurations of literary history, influences, and omissions. As a result, a great range of topics was explored: from the more expected links with canonical Victorian literature through to the popular culture of the 1960s and 1970s, and to the present day. Those of us present who'd been working slightly longer in this field could not be anything but impressed by the range and intensity of intellectual activity which took place. The organization of such an event clearly met a pressing need in the postgraduate community at large and there were scholars here from a wide range of historical periods and specialisms who were prepared to share their research and generously engage with new ideas in the area of Romantic studies. There was a wonderful atmosphere of enthusiastic and shared intellectual commitment which, it has to be said, is not always to be met with at academic conferences.

From the specialist perspective of Romantic studies one of the most noticeable — and most refreshing — aspects of the conference was the apparent freedom with which speakers addressed aspects of Romanticism and the Romantic canon. The old monuments and monoliths were still very much present and still attracted a high level of intellectual curiosity, but it was clear that the superstitious awe which they had generated in the past did not have the same transfixing hold on the new generation. Boy George, Coleridge, Tony Harrison, and William Blake, if they were not exactly on speaking terms with each other, at least were made to communicate in new ways across a literary terrain which was inhabited, but not necessarily haunted, by the ghosts of the past.

The following ten essays which have been selected and developed from the conference papers reflect some of the excitement of the original event. They also demonstrate most forcibly the intellectual quality which was present. The old Romantic canon is much in evidence here in the figures of Keats, Shelley, and Blake, but the inclusion of essays on Charlotte Dacre and Thomas Lovell Beddoes signals a rewriting of the canon which is a recurrent and sustained feature of the volume in its focus on the mutually defining nature of genre and gender. As befits a volume on the subject of spectres, there is throughout a welcome sense of the unsettling potential to be found within the canonical: the capacity for re-negotiating meaning and for re-writing the familiar stories of literary and historical development. In keeping with current trends in Romantic studies, the body in its different guises and as the subject of different intellectual and material practices — such as anatomy, painting, the sublime, and laughter — also haunts these pages with its uncanny presence and its material intractability. This unsettling figure is studied to great effect as it makes its presence felt at the heart of the creative process. If such attention to the 'body' of Romantic texts is now a familiar and important aspect of Romantic criticism, the origin and afterlife of such texts in other languages and cultures is still often underplayed and unexamined. Here we have the opportunity to see the pyschic transformation of Percy Shelley's sonnets in the work of Dutch poet Willem Kloos; and to explore further the anxious engagement with German romances in some of Wordsworth's contributions to Lyrical Ballads.

The volume offers a valuable and refreshing return to the anxieties of influence, but it balances this with the sound of laughter. One of its more unusual, and certainly one of its most welcome, aspects is its attention, in the two essays on Keats and Peacock, to the humour of Romantic period texts. This laughter is not only, as it should be, a haunting and often uncanny presence for the literary historian and critic, but also a fitting reminder of the original event.

John Whale
President of B. A. R. S.

Acknowledgements

I would like to thank everyone involved in the production of this book, particularly the individual contributors for their commitment and enthusiasm. Especial thanks are due to Jerome de Groot for his generous help and eternal optimism, Lidia Garbin for her proficient and meticulous assistance, and George, Bernadette and Gavin Ruston for their patience and confidence. Thanks to everyone who attended and helped organize the 'Spectres of Romanticism' conference and made it the success it was.

The following have given advice and support to myself and the contributing authors: Peter Ainsworth, Paul Baines, Jonathan Bate, Bernard Beatty, John Bleasdale, James Cannon, Jerome Christensen, Richard Clemens, Rose Dawson, Kelvin Everest, Judith Higgens, Avril Horner, Hamish, Dors and Nick Kidd, Angela Keane, Jacqueline M. Labbe, Clark Lawlor, Desdemona McCannon, Lenore Messick, Andrew Moor, Brian Nellist, Ralph Pite, Michael Rossington, Peter Swaab, S. A. J. van Faassen, Timothy Webb, John Whale, David Worrall, Hisaaki Yamanouchi.

A number of organisations have supported this project. The editor and contributors would like to thank: William Blake Trust, Thomas Lovell Beddoes Society, Bridgeman Art Library, City of Bristol Art Museum, British Museum, Cambridge University Library, Commonwealth Scholarship Commission,

Delaware Art Museum, Danish Council for Research in the Humanities, Dutch Literary Museum and Documentation Centre in The Hague, Department of English (University of Sheffield), European Studies Research Institute (University of Salford), Fitzwilliam Museum, Folio Society, Heissisches Landesmuseum, Darmstadt, Humanities Graduate School (University of Liverpool), Keats-Shelley Society, King's College (University of Cambridge), National Chapter of Canada IODE, Social Sciences and Humanities Research Council of Canada, Walker Art Gallery.

S. R.
University of Liverpool

Introduction

Sharon Ruston

These essays were first read as conference papers at the 'Spectres of Romanticism' conference, held by the British Association for Romantic Studies, at the University of Liverpool in June 1998. The conference testified to the fact that the array of spectres haunting Romanticism and Romanticists are many and varied and the concept of haunting was used and defined in a number of different ways. Significant presences and absences in individual texts and within the canon itself were the subject of many papers, with speakers introducing or re-assessing evidence of intertextuality. Other papers considered the ghosts and phantoms of Gothic literature: stories of corpses and grave robbers, resurrections and resurrectionists. The conference offered a stimulating and exciting environment within which to consider these various aspects of the Romantic spectre. The essays included in this volume give a taste of both the diverse interpretation of, and shared response to, the title of both the conference and book.

Though coined in the seventeenth century, the word 'spectre' became increasingly popular around the turn of the nineteenth. The word was often used with reference to its etymological history, specifically its derivation from the

Latin *'specere'*, to look or see. A spectre is an apparition; it is visible. Strange visual phenomena, caused by combinations of light and reflection, were called spectres. It was a word used to suggest illusion and deception, natural and supernatural tricks on the eye and imagination. Scientifically, the epithets 'spectre' or 'spectral' were appropriated to describe certain insects and animals, particularly those with highly emphasised exoskeletons. There was a spectre-bat, -mantis, -lemur, -shrimp, and -tarsier. Some were popular names: the 'spectre-bat' was another name for the Vampire bat; the 'spectre-shrimp' was also known as the 'Skeleton shrimp'. Comparative anatomists classified a species, which had been known as the genus *Phasmidae*, 'spectre-insects'.[1]

Between 1790 and 1830 there were a number of texts that used the words 'spectre', or 'spectres', in their title: M. G. Lewis's *The Castle Spectre* (1798) was partly responsible for this: the play was very successful and ran into a number of editions.[2] Subsequently, many authors consciously referred to Lewis's play in their own titles. In some literary contexts spectre could be synonymous with ghost, ghoul or phantom, a reincarnation of the dead. In others there is a clear demarcation of its individual sense. William Blake's 'Spectre of Urthona', in *Jerusalem* and *The Four Zoas*, might well be another kind of spectre altogether, an Epicurean notion of spectre as a material emanation from corporeal beings. With this definition another comes into play, the idea that a spectre is an imitation or likeness. Southey in *The Doctor, &c* referred to this usage: 'The old anatomists supposed that the likenesses or spectres of corporeal things [...] assail the soul when she ought to be at rest'.[3] This idea might be at the heart of P. B. Shelley's 'phantasms' that inhabit the world of the dead in *Prometheus Unbound*; they are the 'shadows of all forms that think and live'.[4] Everyone has their own 'phantasm'; from which they are separate whilst they live but join after death. The only living man ever to have 'met his own apparition' was the Magus Zoroaster (I. 192). The phantasms are doppelgangers of their earthly counterparts and though they are described as 'frail and empty forms' (I. 241), they have a material self.

The 'Spectre' has been useful for the Romantic critic as well as the Romantic writer. Since Harold Bloom's 1973 book, *The Anxiety of Influence*, the influence of an earlier poet on one of a later generation has been seen as an uncomfortable spectral haunting.[5] Each new poet and critic has to cope with what Walter Jackson Bate called the 'burden' of the past, and their condition of 'belatedness'.[6] Bloom argues that the younger poet has to take on his father figure precursor, wrestling him even to the death by creatively misreading his work. The only poets to survive this encounter emerge as 'strong poets' and they themselves figure as threatening forces to the next generation of writers. Chapter six of Bloom's book is called '*Apophrades*, or The Return of the Dead'. The title refers to the Athenian belief that there were certain days 'upon which the dead returned to reinhabit the houses in which they lived' (15). The dead repossess what was once theirs, not without some discomfort for those who have taken their place; Bloom writes that 'the strong dead return, in poems as in our lives, and they do not come back without darkening the living' (139). Living poets have to acknowledge and confront the presence of their precursors.

Binding all the essays in this collection together is the recognition of a Bloomian precursor that haunts a later poet's work. The authors of these essays do not, however, accept blindly that which Bloom put forward but instead challenge his notions of the purpose and effects of influence. Some explore the anxiety in the younger poet's awareness of the spectral presence of their precursor poet. Others, the apparently unproblematic constructive use, and appropriation of, earlier texts and writers. However, all these essays first have to confront the precursor critic, Bloom himself, before establishing their own position in relation to him. The essays are arranged roughly in chronological order but there are a number of links between them. Some deal explicitly with the status of the spectral precursor. For example, Sarah Wootton's essay re-examines the relationship between Rossetti and his beloved Keats, Kris Steyaert's the re-invention of Shelley by the Dutch poet Willem Kloos. Wootton considers the different relationships between the Pre-

Raphelite and *fin de siècle* artists who treated Keatsian subjects. Rossetti's anxious and fraught emulation resulted in the inability to finish Keatsian compositions. In contrast, Hunt's comfortable relationship with Keats produced a highly marketable and successful partnership.

There are two essays on Keats and two on Shelley, one on Blake and one on Wordsworth; while this might seem to reinforce the Romantic canon, all these essays investigate the nature of such canonicity. The contributors to this volume examine the efforts of their subjects to sanitise, depoliticize and dehistoricize earlier writers in order to control the precursor's posthumous reputation. The rank and standing of text and author within Romantic studies is questioned throughout. For some this means the hierarchical and canonical relationship between writers and their 'forbears', whilst others consider the influence and appropriation of other literatures, cultures and genres. Several essays consider fragmented texts; they examine the status of editorial policies and provisions, the connection between unfinished 'versions' of texts, and the state of the text itself.

Sue Chaplin's essay considers the neglected Gothic novel Charlotte Dacre's *Zofloya, or The Moor*. Using models of the sublime from Burke, Wordsworth and Keats, and critical responses to these ideas, Chaplin considers *Zofloya* an unusual example of the Gothic tradition exemplified by Ann Radcliffe. Dacre's novel refuses to conform to the gendered stereotypes of female submission to, and male control of, the sublime. The notion of 'blockage' is as important here as for Wootton's discussion of Rossetti's painter's block. Both are created by a source of dread, whether the sexual threat of 'chaotic femininity' (Chaplin, 4), or the anxiety caused by the influence of another artist. Chaplin also looks at the prevalence of eighteenth-century medical tracts on female hysteria and the relevance of these representations for Gothic writing. Chaplin considers the effects of the growing fascination with the biological make-up of the female body and an attempt through medical practice to explain and control female moral and psychological characteristics.

Tristanne Connolly's essay considers the influence of anatomical illustrations on William Blake. As with the subject of Michael Bradshaw's essay, Thomas Lovell Beddoes, and also James Kidd's essay on Keats, an established biographical connection with the medical world provides interesting and relevant ways in which to re-consider the ideas of the text itself. Connolly finds that anatomical theories and images are pertinent to Blakes's own artistic output. The act of engraving is likened to the operations of anatomy and surgery. Blake's spectre is a material being and some of the unusual images in Blake's illustrations are shown to have their source in anatomical representations of the body. The scientific illustration, Connolly argues, can serve to avert the viewer's attention from the horror and disgust of the subject matter. As with Chaplin's essay, the 'gaze' can rob the subject of its horror, impose control over it, and even transcend it. The medical influences on Blake's work also provide us with possible sources for his idiosyncratic notion of body and spirit. Bradshaw assesses the use of medical language to discuss the project Beddoes set himself: Beddoes's own appropriation of metaphors from anatomy enabled him to represent his relationship to his past and present literary world. Beddoes's recognition of his identity as a third generation Romantic sharpens his acute sense of 'belatedness', of inheritance, and of the need to revive and resurrect the glorious past.

The role of the critic has been likened, not always positively, to that of an anatomist or even an exhumer. The connection between literature and medicine is a growing area of criticism, and proves a successful approach to Romantic writing in the essays by Chaplin, Connolly and Bradshaw.[7] The difficulties that the medical world encountered before the Anatomy Act of 1832 presented Romantic writers with a problematic moral and intellectual dilemma; these circumstances provided the stimulus for Mary Shelley's *Frankenstein*.[8] Surgeons were unable to get the number of bodies they needed to carry out anatomy courses in flourishing medical schools and turned to the underground world of resurrectionists to provide them with the corpses they required. The much documented cases of grave-robbing during the period were eventually eclipsed by the hanging of William Burke in 1829, who, with William Hare, murdered their victims to deliver corpses for dissection. Anatomy literature provides a whole new language for critics: the dissection or anatomization of precursor texts; their resurrection to satisfy a scientific curiosity and to find out how they work; the discovery of both beautiful and loathed images among the parts of the body. Connolly looks at the influence of eminent surgeons and anatomists William and John Hunter on the circle of artists who attended lectures at the Royal Academy. Thomas Lovell Beddoes's medical training provides metaphors of dissection and reanimation for Bradshaw's discussion of Beddoes.

Many of the essays deal with the by now familiar problem of the posthumous image of the Romantics. Rieko Suzuki looks at the part that Mary Shelley played as editor of Shelley's work, considering the personal and political ideas that characterised her editorial role in the first publications of 'The Triumph of Life'. Shelley and Keats, in particular, suffered at the hands of acolytes who idolised a constructed idea of these poets that had little to do with their true historical and political selves. Kidd looks at the recent spate of biographies of Keats, historicized studies that attempt to rescue the poet from this fate. Kidd has similar motives, but rather than emphasise the image of Keats as a political figure he considers his neglected identity as the creator of light and comic verse. The Keats that emerges from Kidd's study is a human, robust and even healthy figure, as unlike the youth who 'grows pale, and spectre-thin and dies' as could be imagined.[9] Steyaert looks at one of the most devoted of Shelley's admirers, and his attempts to possess exclusive rights over him. The Shelleyana Kloos collected became instrumental in his immersion in the character of Shelley. He believed that a psychic communion was made possible through the material once owned by the poet and that this relationship endowed him with an authority over Shelley's poetic and historical reputation. Steyaert places Kloos within a context of the depoliticization of Shelley attempted by contemporaries such as Joseph Severn, and the later Shelley Society. The flagrantly disrespectful Larkin, in Kidd's essay, is a breath of fresh air; conversely, there is a greater connection between Larkin and Keats, with their similar experiences of disappointed sexual relations, than Larkin would care to admit. Kidd finds that it is the creative writers, Larkin and Burgess among them, who are more ready to accept Keats's lighter side.

Peter Mortensen discusses the Romantic view of German texts and ideas as an infection that proved contagious to those who came into contact with it. Periodical writers denounced German supernatural tales as 'low culture', dangerous to poets and readers alike. They spread an image of German writing as a racial and cultural disease that could infect those receptive to its seductive wiles. Wordsworth, in this context, made efforts to carefully control the influence Bürger exercised on his poetry. Transplanting Bürger's 'The Chase' to a safe English environment, and removing signs of Bürger's social message, Wordsworth used the tale to his own ends in 'Hart-Leap Well'. Similarly, Jerome de Groot considers the political significance behind Thomas Love Peacock's orchestrated display of allusion, echo, quotation and misquotation. Peacock confronts the issue of inheritance in his novels, but is not weighed down or suffocated by the presence of the dead; instead he constructs a newly operational text from his pickings. De Groot examines the political motivation behind Peacock's manipulation of genre and his creation of a new mode of humorous writing. This essay can be read with Kidd's: both contribute new research to the underdeveloped study of Romantic comic writing. Peacock's social and literary levelling muse and Keats's manipulation of gender roles expose the overtly political purpose behind humour.

The spectre has proved a useful metaphor for critics other than Bloom: Jacques Derrida defines a spectre as a 'paradoxical incorporation, the becoming-body, a certain phenomenal and carnal form of the spirit'.[10] In his *Specters of Marx*, Derrida alludes to the famous opening of *The Manifesto of the Communist Party*: 'A spectre is haunting Europe — the spectre of communism' (Derrida, 4). Appropriately, Derrida tells us that he had chosen the title of the lecture first before re-reading the *Manifesto* and re-discovering this reference. The echo is the ghost waiting in the text to be discovered, haunting the critic (4). Marx himself echoes Thomas Carlyle's *French Revolution*: 'That same cloud-capt, fire-breathing Spectre of Democracy'.[11] The spectre threatens with an apocalyptic inevitability. Derrida makes use of one of the most famous of spectres, Hamlet's father. Peacock also explores the ideas of inheritance that Shakespeare discusses in *Hamlet*. De Groot considers Peacock's relationship with his own texts, as author and father, and his decision to publish them anonymously.

Derridean critics are content to live with the presence of ghosts in the text. There is no drive for supremacy over the spectre and therefore no privileging of one presence over another. Hazel Hutchison's essay is written in this tradition, using the Derridean concept of '*supplement*' to discuss the relationship between Henry James's precursor texts, his own preface, and *The Turn of the Screw*. Hutchison is happy to acknowledge the influence of *Northanger Abbey* and *Jane Eyre* on James's novel but refuses to accept that these influences in any way explain the text. These and James's own attempts to explain his work merely add to or supplement the number of readings possible. These supplements playfully work alongside the text itself, undermining the manifold attempts to explain the nature of the ghosts and governess in psychological terms.

Efforts to create whole and complete texts are discussed by Bradshaw and Suzuki. Bradshaw, contextualises the state of Beddoes's corpus of work with its unfinished and fragmented condition. Anatomy provides Beddoes with a language that can describe the ways, both positive and negative, in which a text can be brought back to life. Bradshaw examines the editorial accidents and decisions which have rendered Beddoes the ultimate 'Romantic poet of fragments' (152). The impossibility of building a complete Beddoes *oeuvre* is integrated into Bradshaw's conception of the author's work: his uncertain place in the Romantic canon and his preferred method of composition are related through images of the body in disarray. Suzuki considers the notoriously unfinished text of Shelley's 'The

Triumph of Life' and adds Rousseau's previously neglected study of the origin of languages to the extensive list of source texts. Suzuki uses this work to argue a persuasive case for a more systematic composition and editorial arrangement of the text. Breaks in the manuscript to compose the lyrics addressed to Jane Williams are incorporated into Shelley's discourse on the historical and temporal in the 'Triumph'. Editions of the poem have substantially privileged one side of this confrontation over another. The tessellation of manuscript evidence and published versions Suzuki presents contribute to a dialogue dramatised within the poem itself.

Connolly, Wootton, and Steyaert explore the interface between literature and the visual arts. Wootton charts the appropriation of Keats's texts through the paintings of the Pre-Raphelites and into *fin de siècle* art. Concentrating on representations of *La Belle Dame sans Merci*, both Wootton and Kidd discuss new and alternative impressions of the knight and lady. The knight's spectral and unsubstantial presence is contrasted with the recognition of the lady's place in the context of Keatsian strong women. In Kidd's essay this is a source of pathos, the knight is a pathetic figure, a source of laughter as well as sympathy. Wootton however, examines the appearance of the knight at specific historical points and traces the emergence of a female franchise within the changing portrayal of the Keatsian subject.

This volume demonstrates that issues of Romantic inheritance and influence continue to affect literary studies today. As these essays testify, Romanticism has influenced writers across geographical and historical boundaries, as well as extending to other cultural and artistic mediums. The collection offers an illuminating reassessment of the relationship between Romantics and their predecessors and successors. The use of anatomy and laughter present the reader with a fresh look at canonical critical concepts.

[1] The 'spectre-insects' were distinguished by the five joints in their tarsus (the part of the leg that lies distal to the tibia), *OED*.

[2] *The Castle Spectre: A Drama in Five Acts, Performed at Theatres of London and Dublin with Uncommon Applause* (London: J.Bell, 1798). The play went through eight editions within the first year of publication.

[3] Robert Southey, *The Doctor, &c*, 7 vols (London: Longmann, Rees, Orme, 1834–47), V, 11.

[4] *Shelley's Poetry and Prose* ed. by D. H. Reiman and Sharon B. Powers (London and NY: W. W. Norton, 1977), I.198.

[5] *The Anxiety of Influence: A Theory of Poetry* (NY: Oxford University Press, 1973).

[6] *The Burden of the Past and the English Poet* (London: Chatto and Windus, 1971).

[7] For general comments on the interface of literature and medicine, see G. S. Rousseau, 'Literature and Medicine: The State of the Field', *Isis*, 72 (1981), 263–424; Susan Sontag, *Illness and Metaphor* (Harmondsworth: Penguin, 1983); *The Body and The Text*, ed. by Bruce Clark and Wendell Aycock (Texas: Texas Tech University, 1990).

[8] See Ruth Richardson, *Death, Dissection and the Destitute* (London and NY: Routledge and Kegan Paul, 1987) and Tim Marshall, *Murdering to Dissect: Grave Robbing, Frankenstein and the Anatomy Literature* (Manchester and NY: Manchester University Press, 1995).

[9] 'Ode to a Nightingale', ll. 26, in *Complete Poems*, ed. by Jack Stillinger (Cambridge, MA and London: Harvard University Press, 1978).

[10] Jacques Derrida *Specters of Marx: The State of the Debt, The Work of Mourning, and The New International*, trans. by Peggy Kamuf (NY and London: Routledge, 1994), p. 6.

[11] Thomas Carlyle, *The French Revolution: A History in Three Parts*, 3 vols (NY and London: Methuen, 1902), I. 1. iv.

Terror, Transcendence and Control in Charlotte Dacre's *Zofloya, or, The Moor*

Sue Chaplin

> Darkness and gloomy solitude reigned around when the eyes of Victoria opened to the sense of life and perception. She found herself reclining on the bare earth; the thunder rolled aloud over her head and flashes of flame now and then displayed the terrific sublimity of surrounding objects — immense mountains piled upon one another appeared to encompass her and to include within their inaccessible bosoms the whole of the universe. Beyond their towering walls, the imagination suddenly thrown back and staggered at its own conceptions, could not presume to penetrate. Mighty rocks and dizzying precipices at their base in which water falling from an immeasurable height battled gloomy caverns which seemed the entrance to pandemonium. Alpine cliffs, that in their fierce projection menaced ruin to the wretch beneath. Such was the scene that, as the blue lightening flashed, struck upon her view. Amidst these awful horrors, with folded arms and a majestic air, stood the towering Zofloya.[1]

The embodiment of virtue and eighteenth-century conceptualizations of sensibility and the sublime are intimately related. It is possible to identify an approach to the sublime whereby the subject seeks empowerment via the mastery of terror and to demonstrate that an appreciation of the implications of this response is vital to an understanding of Dacre's *Zofloya* and its influence.

Contemporary theorists have tended to view the sublime in terms of a crisis of subjectivity and of epistemological faith which generates dread. Indeed, the sublime experience has been posited as the post-modern experience par excellence. In Thomas Huhn's words, it is related to 'the problematic of a subjectivity not just unable to make a presentation to itself, but unable to present *itself* at all'; as such it is comprised of a radical loss of agency which finds its equivalent within the eighteenth century and which is crucial to an understanding of the formation of Romantic self-identity through transcendence.[2] What is more, the act of transcendence designed to guarantee self-identity in the face of chaos is, as Huhn points out in his appraisal of the Kantian sublime, fundamentally an act of violence. Terror, transcendence and control are intimately associated in terms of the eighteenth-century sublime. In *The Romantic Sublime,* Thomas Weiskel contends that the sublime 'plays a critical role within the semiotic economy of the eighteenth century', an economy within which there emerges a discontinuity between word and idea and between idea and sensation which produces moments of anxiety.[3] It is possible to isolate from Weiskel's complex psychological account of the sublime two varieties of sublime experience based upon such moments. On the one hand, there is the Kantian, 'negative' sublime, which is the consequence of an attempt by the imagination to grapple with infinity. The result is a recognition of the limits of imagination and its willing submission to a greater force. On the other hand, there is that which Weiskel terms the 'positive', or, following Keats, the 'egotistical' or 'Wordsworthian' sublime. The ego seeks here to identify itself with the sublime so as to recognize within itself a source of comparable power. This variant of the sublime is thoroughly transcendental and is bound up with the formulation of an ideal self-identity, an identity which is, for Weiskel, 'an infinitely repeatable "I am"' (139). With certain modifications, this 'positive' sublime finds expression within the Gothic novel as it does within Romanticism, particularly at the juncture between 'male' and 'female' Gothic, a point of interface which it may be said partially to define.

There may appear to be little to relate Weiskel with Robert Miles. Nevertheless, Miles's reworking of the dichotomy between 'male' and 'female' Gothic may be used in order firstly to indicate how Weiskel's account of the sublime may be interpreted as gendered and secondly to emphasize certain aspects of eighteenth-century responses to the sublime. Miles presents evidence of the gendered nature of the eighteenth-century sublime and the consequent inscription of sexual difference into Gothic writing. This inscription has produced a fissure between masculine and feminine subject positions implicit within 'male' and 'female' Gothic which is symptomatic of a more fundamental schism between the sublime stimulus and the response it is deemed to provoke. Within 'male' Gothic, woman is frequently stigmatized as man's 'other'; she is a threat to masculine self-identity. Within 'female' Gothic, the sublime has as its stimulus that which is powerful, awe-inspiring and 'habitually masculine'.[4] The response to it is seen to be feminine where the feminine is understood to correspond to the eighteenth-century ideal of the submissive woman of feeling. This translates into a concern on the one hand with the attainment of power, and on the other, with the problematics of a response to the sublime based upon terror and a 'paradoxical delight' (Miles, 66). This analysis of the feminine subject position implicit within Gothic writing may be likened to Weiskel's conceptualization of the negative sublime. Both Miles and Weiskel recognize the masochism inherent within what for Weiskel may be seen as a facet of the sublime and for Miles as a response to it. An alternative response to the sublime, however, involves neither transcendence nor submission but control. The subject seeks to control the origin of the sublime, whether that origin lies with God, infinity, nature or with difference. This is an attempt at empowerment, not through an identification with the sublime, but through an opposition to it and a mastery of it and, if one source of the sublime is sexual difference, then this response is likely to have significant implications for 'male' and 'female' Gothic. This is so particularly if one accepts that in the eighteenth century a newly constructed ideal of femininity became a possible source of the sublime owing to the location of virtue within the female body. Virtue was a quality still associated theologically, if not philosophically, with the transcendental power of God. What is more, the sublime power of the virtuous woman acquired additional force on account of the cultural association between man's fear of social and epistemological chaos and the traditional conception of woman's nature as at least in part corrupt. Neil Hertz's reading of the sublime illuminates this point. Examining the notion of 'blockage' in relation to the sublime experience, Hertz reads Weiskel's psychoanalytic approach to Kant alongside Samuel Holt Monk's association of the sublime with, amongst other things, the 'woman not fit to be seen'.[5] He argues that, for both Weiskel and Monk, the disordered woman is a source of dread who, in Barbara Freeman's words, 'becomes a metaphor for the obstacle or blocking agent' which facilitates the sublime experience.[6] Hertz observes that in the eighteenth century the political threat of revolution came to be represented as a sexual threat through the evocation of images of chaotic femininity as, for example, the figure of Medusa was used by Burke to convey the full horror of the French revolution.

The embodiment of virtue in the eighteenth century owed something to David Hume's sceptical challenge to philosophical rationalism. Hume deprived reason of its privileged epistemological and ethical status and replaced it with the imagination, a gesture which, to revert to the theme of epistemological crisis and its relation to the sublime, generated in Hume himself a sense of dreadful uncertainty.[7] Even virtue was seen to be dependent upon the operation of a 'moral sense' finely tuned by the imagination acting in response to sensory experience. It became to some degree a matter of physiology. Indeed, it is interesting in this context to observe the extent of correlation between Hume's findings and those of his contemporaries working within the field of physiology. Robert Whytt concluded that the entity referred to as the soul was in fact diffused throughout the entire nervous system and that reason was inseparable from physical sensibility.[8] Jerome Gaub likewise anticipated Hume with his assertion that 'the human virtues arise from the emotions'.[9] A highly refined sensibility, defined in terms of an extreme delicacy of nerves, thus became the guarantee of the proper operation of the moral sense and the key to spiritual grace. A number of critics have explored this theme, particularly the extent to which biology became woman's destiny as never before in the eighteenth century. In *Making Sex,* Thomas Laqueur relates the development of the physiological 'two sex model' to the idealization, in moral terms, of female sexual difference.[10] Michel Foucault has spoken of a female body organized 'wholly in terms of the reproductive function which kept it in a constant state of agitation'.[11] Ludmilla Jordanova has explored the gendering of physiological attributes in eighteenth-century medical discourse in terms of masculine muscle and feminine nerves.[12] If this is so, and if woman is defined thus at a time when morality is deemed to be rooted within the body, then her relation to the moral order must undergo a radical change. In a reversal of the traditional order of things, woman moves closer to God than to the devil, or, to paraphrase Barker-Benfield, the eighteenth century perhaps witnesses the transformation of God into a *woman* of feeling.[13]

The cult of the woman of feeling created a discourse of femininity whereby it became possible to regard woman no longer as essentially corrupt, although her potential for corruption remained, but as almost Christ-like in her compassion, her bodily suffering and her powers of salvation. She was thought capable of reforming male manners and even of inspiring religious devotion in men and of rehabilitating the spiritual and sexual transgressor. Clarissa Harlowe in Richardson's *Clarissa* is one of the most potent examples of female integrity and acceptance of suffering in the face of persecution. Her virtue leaves Lovelace defeated and reforms a social order which was in danger of becoming wholly corrupted by male greed and ambition. Clarissa becomes 'an angel and no woman'; this suggests the continuing theological association between virtue and transcendental divinity.[14] It may be argued, however, that there is still nothing awe-inspiring about this model of female virtue; the heroine of sensibility is so acutely vulnerable that she is almost inevitably a victim of fear and not a source of it. What is significant, however, is that the moral superiority of the eighteenth-century woman rests upon a physiological excess of feeling. In his analysis of the place of hysteria within the cult of sensibility, John Mullan speaks of hysteria as marking 'a rupture of the relations between head and heart, the ensuing gap opening up a way for the dark, the weird and the demonic'.[15] Sensibility, if virtuous, is also hysterical; virtue is thus tainted with the stigma of madness and disease. The symptoms of virtue are never far removed from the symptoms of mental and physical disorder and virtue thus becomes in a sense a malfunctioning of the body, or, one might say, a *proper* functioning of a *female* body which is 'constituted as disordered, inconsistent, precarious' (207). A negative image of the ideal woman thus appears at the heart of the eighteenth-century reformulation of virtue. The casting of virtue onto a hysterical female body undermined, perhaps as much as Humean scepticism, an ethical tradition based upon a clear demarcation between order and disorder, good and evil. The heroine of sensibility is the embodiment of virtue yet she remains close to madness, threatening the emergence of 'the dark, the weird, the demonic' (202). Her status justifies the point made by Gilbert and Gubar:

> For every glowing portrait of submissive women enshrined in domesticity, there exists an equally important negative image that embodies the sacrilegious fiendishness of what Blake called the 'female will'. Thus, while male writers traditionally praise the simplicity of the dove, they invariably castigate the cunning of the serpent. Similarly, assertiveness, aggressiveness — all characteristic of a male life of significant action — are monstrous in women.[16]

Ambrosio, in M. G. Lewis's *The Monk*, contemplates what he takes to be a painting of the Virgin Mary; his voyeuristic gaze reduces the body of this female spiritual ideal to the status of sexual object. Ironically, however, it is not a representation of the Virgin which he contemplates but that of a demonic female who is poised to bring about his damnation. The power relation established by

Ambrosio's gaze is thus subverted and it is this controlling, voyeuristic gaze which facilitates a response to the sublime comprised of a quest for the mastery of dread.

Annie Van Sant has discussed the extent to which the emphasis placed upon the scientific gaze in the mid to late eighteenth century encouraged an investigative approach not only to science but to sensibility and human virtue.[17] The body, and in particular the female body, could be scrutinized for evidence of virtuous sensibility such as blushing, fainting and weeping. As Markman Ellis observes, the nervous body turned into something akin to a 'signifying system'.[18] The desire on the part of the investigator to penetrate the female body, either literally with the scalpel, or figuratively with the gaze, resulted in its scientific and sexual objectification. Jordanova contends that even the practice of dissection showed signs of becoming morbidly erotic by the end of the century through its use of passive and highly sexualized representations of the female body (87–110). In this respect, it is extremely interesting to note the extent to which de Sade's *Justine* borrows from the language of medical discourse to the point of using whole passages from Bienville's treatise on the nervous system.[19] The doctor may be likened, then, to the voyeur of female sensibility who interprets the symptoms of virtue manifested by the hysterical female body. Virtue becomes a spectacle in the eighteenth century, written on the body of the woman of feeling, and subjected to penetrating visual analysis. This development is a prelude to the sexual objectification of the virtuous woman in Gothic and Romantic writing whereby feminine virtue is subordinated to the gaze of the sexual and spiritual voyeur. To gaze upon the sublime, here in the form of a deeply ambivalent, semi-divine, semi-demonic woman, is to control it. To look unflinchingly into the abyss is to obviate its horror and this is relevant to the wider phenomena of 'horror' Gothic. The horror writer appears to issue a challenge to his, or her, readers along the following lines: 'Look hard at this. I have the stomach for it. Do you? Can you fix your gaze on it? Or are you overawed?' Dacre, unusually for a female writer of her time, issues precisely this challenge to her readers.

Given the nature of the heroine of sensibility, it would seem to follow that her response to the sublime would be one of submission. Indeed, one finds just such a response on the part of Emily in Radcliffe's *The Mysteries of Udolpho*. Yet one finds evidence also of Weiskel's egotistical, or Wordsworthian, sublime; there are points at which Emily seeks empowerment through an imaginative association with the power of God or nature. In addition, the text refuses to make a spectacle out of Emily. She is never made to stand disempowered in the direct line of the reader's voyeuristic gaze. The text instead displays a variety of responses to the sublime whilst denying the reader the opportunity of objectifying and controlling an ambivalent, embodied virtue. It is a similar complexity of approach to the sublime which is present within Dacre's work, one which resists explanation in terms of the paradigm of 'male' and 'female' Gothic. A struggle takes place between transcendence, submission and control; a struggle often mediated through the power of the gaze and anticipating issues which were to perplex the Romantics. It is a struggle which threatens to destroy the coherence of the text and which is resolved ultimately at the expense of terror and transcendence and in favour of control.

To summarize the plot of *Zofloya*, the novel is set in late fifteenth-century Venice and the protagonist, Victoria, is the daughter of an aristocratic Italian family. In the opening chapters, Victoria's mother, Laurina, elopes with her lover, Ardolphe, who then slays Victoria's father. Victoria meanwhile forms an attachment with one Count Berenza. She inherits her mother's sexual appetite yet, in the first half of the novel at least, is exceptionally strong-willed and ruthless. She is not in love with Berenza but is flattered by his attention. To save her from disgrace and to make amends for the bad example she has set for her daughter, Laurina sends Victoria into isolation at the home of her cousin, the Signora di Modena. Victoria escapes and seeks refuge with Berenza whom she eventually marries. She is deeply dissatisfied in marriage, however, and after five years develops an intense passion for Berenza's brother, Henrique. Henrique is engaged to a young girl named Lilla. His servant, Zofloya, offers to help Victoria realize her ambition to take Lilla's place. With his help, she poisons her husband, murders Lilla and secures one night of passion with Henrique who, by means of a potion prepared by Zofloya, has been deluded into thinking that Victoria is Lilla. When he discovers his error, he takes his life. Victoria and Zofloya flee into the mountains where Victoria becomes increasingly enamoured of, and dependent upon, Zofloya. The strength of mind which marked her character in the first half of the novel disappears as she submits herself entirely to his protection. Her damnation is assured, however, when Zofloya reveals his demonic identity and Victoria suffers the same fate as Lewis's Ambrosio: she is cast into the abyss.

The text can be split into two parts, divided by Victoria's first encounter with Zofloya. This marks, not only a turning point for Victoria, but a shift in the novel's treatment of sensibility and the sublime. In the first half of the novel, Victoria is distanced from the conventional heroine of sensibility and her responses to the sublime may be seen as a part of that distancing process. They mark her as unfeminine. She is sharp-witted, rational, physically strong and courageous and her cynical manipulation of Berenza contrasts sharply with her mother's pathetic dotage upon her lover, Ardolphe. Victoria lacks sufficient sensibility to be moved by the sublime. At the beginning of her period of imprisonment by Signora di Modena, when she looks out upon a typically Radcliffean scene from her bedroom window, she does not fall into worshipful contemplation of sublime nature; instead she takes out her pencils and sketches the view to pass the time, an act which hints at the controlling power of her gaze. She appears to have no need either of transcendence or of submission and throughout her confinement with the Signora, refuses to learn the lessons of sensibility. She defies the Signora's attempts to teach her 'softness, humility and obedience' and instead calmly contemplates her predicament and plans her escape, nurturing a fantasy of revenge which lends to her character 'an additional shade of harshness'; 'she became like the untameable hyena which confinement renders only more fierce' (*Zofloya*, 50, 49).

Indeed, if Victoria resorts to the language and gestures of sensibility in the first half of the novel, it is purely for the purpose of dissemblance. Seeking to inspire Berenza's devotion, she mimes a delicate and melancholy femininity:

> Her plan arranged she entered upon it gradually: her eyes no longer, full of a wild and beautiful animation, were taught to languish, or to fix for hours with a musing air upon the ground; her gait, no longer firm and elevated, became hesitating and despondent. She no longer engrossed the conversation; she became silent, apparently absent and plunged in thought (78).

Ironically, it is Berenza who is reduced by this display to a state of blushing inarticulacy. He begins to idolize Victoria and abandons his original, Rousseauean aim to mould her according to his own vision of ideal femininity. It is, in fact, men in this novel who are more often seen to be victims of excessive feeling and who are overawed by female power. Victoria's brother, Leonardo, is smitten by the sexually predatory Magalena and in the following passage is subjected to objectification by her sexually assertive gaze:

> While unconsciously he thus reposed, a female chanced to wander near the spot. She had quitted her house for the purpose of enjoying more freely the fresco of the evening, and to stroll along the banks of the lake; the young Leonardo, however, arrested her attention and she softly approached to contemplate him — his hands were clasped over his head and on his cheek, where the hand of health had planted its brown red rose, the pearly gems of his tears still hung — his auburn hair sported in curls about his forehead and temples, agitated by the passing breeze — his vermeil lips were half open and disclosed his polished teeth — his bosom, which he uncovered to admit the refreshing air, remained disclosed and contrasted by its snowy whiteness the animated hue of his complexion (103).

This is the language of sexual voyeurism whereby vulnerable, 'snow white', flesh is exposed to a powerful onlooker whose gaze the victim cannot meet. Like

Berenza in the presence of Victoria, Leonardo is reduced to confusion by the appearance of Magalena. He adopts the gestures and language of the heroine of sensibility:

> His cheeks became suffused with deepening blushes and his eyes, with which he longed to gaze upon her, were yet cast bashfully towards the earth. In faltering voice he replied, while every consideration but of the object before him vanished from his mind (104).

Leonardo is terrified of Magalena. She has 'an unlimited power' over him, a power which is expressed frequently in terms of the strength of her gaze (119). Consider the following account of Magalena's discovery of her lover in the arms of another:

> With a look, wherein was depicted the blackest rage, the deepest vengeance and the bitterest scorn, without advancing a step, she continued to contemplate them; then firmly and deliberately approaching Leonardo, she seized him by the arm. So unimpaired was her power over his soul, such was the awe, almost the terror, which he involuntarily felt while sinking abashed beneath the powerful glance of her eye, that he had no power to resist the decisiveness of her action (112).

Both Victoria and Magalena, far from embodying virtue, appear to personify the negative image of ideal femininity. Through these women, femininity is associated in the first half of the novel with the sublime in the sense that it inspires fear. Dacre's use of the sublime is in this respect strikingly original. In a reversal of the power relation deemed fundamental to 'female' Gothic, there is seen to be a *feminine* stimulus to the sublime which provokes a submissive *masculine* response. Moreover, Victoria is allowed a response to the sublime which thus far has been posited as masculine; she seeks to dominate rather than to submit.

This starts to change following Victoria's initial encounter with Zofloya. She begins to lose control. The turning point is marked by the first dream Victoria has of Zofloya in which he appears as the facilitator of her adulterous and murderous desires. He is a figure of immense power whom Victoria regards with admiration and awe. Her waking response to this dream is interesting; she finds herself in a state of extreme agitation from which she struggles to 'resume her usual firmness' (137). Eventually, she regains sufficient composure to take control of her dream, subjecting it to rational interpretation. Within a few pages, however, she is seen again to be losing precisely this ability to interpret rationally her own thoughts and actions. 'Inconceivably to herself', she is deeply distressed by news of Zofloya's sudden and mysterious departure and, though she 'knows not why', she rushes to find out the cause. On hearing of his apparent death, 'she found it impossible to account for the feeling which affected her' (140). There follows a further dream in which Zofloya is seen to guide Victoria through sublime landscapes to which she would earlier have been largely indifferent. Her response now, however, is more in keeping with that of the traditional heroine of sensibility; she is overawed by the spectacle. This is further evidence that Victoria is losing her ability to rationalize terror. At this juncture, she has to struggle enormously to control her imagination:

> Scarcely had her head reclined upon the pillow than the image of Zofloya swam in her sight; she slumbered and he haunted her dreams; sometimes she wandered with him over beds of flowers, sometimes over craggy rocks, sometimes in fields of brightest verdure, sometimes over burning sands, tottering on the ridge of some huge precipice, while the angry waters waved below. Often the circumstances were so strong that the bounds of fancy could contain them no longer and, hastily awakening, scarcely could she assure herself that Zofloya stood not at the side of her bed (143).

What is more, as Victoria becomes increasingly susceptible to Zofloya's influence, so she begins to adopt the language of sensibility. Frequently in his presence she is reduced to a state of trembling, blushing speechlessness:

> Victoria felt surprise; she lifted her eyes to the countenance of the Moor but they fell beneath his fiery glances — she would have spoken; she knew not what conflicting emotion chained her tongue (181).

Similarly, following the death of Berenza:

> The frame of Victoria trembled and she retreated towards the door. Horror and awe at the inexplicable character of the Moor so wholly possessed her that though she longed, she durst not require any explanation of intentions with respect to the body of Berenza. His dark but brilliant eyes pursued her to the threshold of the door; she stooped, hesitated and attempted to speak, but the effort was in vain (191).

The extent to which this power relationship is played out through the medium of the gaze is apparent here. The culmination of the power struggle is that vivid evocation of the interaction between sensibility and the sublime which takes place in the passage at the beginning of this essay. The passage marks a full reversal of the power relations established in the first half of the novel between a masculine sensibility and female sublime power; Victoria encounters Zofloya at last 'in his proper sphere' (232).

Victoria's downfall is occasioned at least partly by her growing sensibility, which results in the failure of any response to the sublime which would stress empowerment over submission. Sensibility is given a pivotal role in the annihilation of Victoria and yet nothing in the first half of the text prepares the reader for the feminization of Victoria in the second. Her transformation threatens the coherence of the text and perhaps the only means of addressing this is to examine Dacre's implicit criticism of the female subject position at the heart of the 'negative' sublime.

Throughout this text, sensibility is a concept associated with weakness. The chief representative of sensibility, Lilla, is a virtuous but pathetic figure whom Dacre almost ridicules. Ultimately, the tenuous alignment of sensibility with virtue is ruptured by the fact that Victoria ironically becomes a *villain* of sensibility, displaying several of the symptoms of virtue whilst possessing none of its graces. The sole characteristic of sensibility is a pernicious ineffectuality which submits Leonardo to Magalena, Lilla to Victoria and Victoria to Zofloya. What is more, sensibility guarantees a response to the sublime which is one of self abasement; it is the conventional response of the female subject disciplined by male power. It is a response Victoria initially scorns but which destroys her once she does succumb to it. Dacre abandons her villain of sensibility to the abyss and challenges the reader to gaze upon the horrors within it. The powerful individual who dominates the first half of the text and who, even as her will weakens, still believes that she controls her own destiny, is annihilated. In this gesture, it is possible to recognize what Kim Michasiw has referred to as Dacre's 'challenge to the myths of romantic selfhood'.[20] With regard to Shelley's *St. Irvine*, he observes how 'this revelatory attack upon the self made self sufficiency of the Romantic male echoes moments in Dacre' (25). It is possible to argue also that, whilst the Romantic male subject frequently does seek aggrandizement through his engagement with the sublime, this by no means eliminates the presence within Romanticism of alternative modes of reacting to the sublime. What often emerges is an uneasy relationship between terror, transcendence and control of the sort which troubles *Zofloya*. David Haney, for example, has recently discussed the crisis of perception in Wordsworth in terms of a shift away from a transcendence facilitated by the 'tyranny of the eye' and towards a prioritization of sound.[21] The Romantic fascination with dreadful female power, meanwhile, echoes Dacre's concern with the same theme and with the relation between terror and control that is fundamental to it.

The Medusa of Shelley's poem *On the Medusa of Leonardo Da Vinci* is a dreadful creature who controls through the power of her 'brazen glare'.[22] Her strange beauty mesmerizes the poet. Yet, whilst Shelley appears to mix fear and adoration in his submission to the 'tempestuous loveliness of terror', his response to the Medusa is ambivalent (32). The poet clearly relishes the tormented beauty of this severed female head generating the possibility that what appears to be a surrender may in fact be a strategy of control. The Sadean treatment of Beatrice in *The Cenci* is less ambivalent. Exposing the heroine to the public gaze, the poem makes a horrific spectacle of her:

> I will drag her, step by step,
> Through infamies unheard of among men:
> She shall stand shelterless in the broad noon
> Of public scorn, for acts blazoned abroad [...]
> Her spirit shall approach the throne of God
> Plague-spotted with my curses. I will make
> Body and soul a monstrous lump of ruin.[23]

Mario Praz has explored the influence of Sade on Shelley but the above is reminiscent also of Dacre's treatment of Lilla and Victoria, her heroine and her villain of sensibility.[24] Moreover, the association of female beauty with death which Shelley draws upon here, and which was to persist throughout the nineteenth century, recalls that negative image of ideal womanhood which haunted the acceptable face of femininity in the eighteenth century. It calls to mind the subversive reverse side of sensibility with which the hysterical woman of feeling was associated. It was on account of these conflicting associations that the woman of feeling became sublime in the eighteenth century and Dacre's response is to seek to master this sublime female. Like Lewis's *The Monk*, and Shelley's *The Cenci*, Dacre's *Zofloya, or, The Moor* abandons terror and transcendence in favour of control and in so doing frustrates a straightforward evaluation of the novel in terms of the paradigm of 'male' and 'female' Gothic.

---

[1] Charlotte Dacre, *Zofloya, or, The Moor* (Oxford: Oxford University Press, 1997), p. 232. All quotations from the novel are taken from this edition.

[2] Thomas Huhn, 'The Kantian Sublime and the Nostalgia for Violence', *The Journal of Aesthetics and Art Criticism*, 53 (1995), 269–75 (p. 270).

[3] Thomas Weiskel, *The Romantic Sublime* (Baltimore: Johns Hopkins University Press, 1976), p. 16.

[4] Robert Miles, *Gothic Writing: A Genealogy, 1750–1820* (London: Routledge, 1993), p. 16.

[5] Neil Hertz, *The End of the Line: Essays in Psychoanalysis and the Sublime* (NY: Columbia University Press, 1985), p. 52.

[6] Barbara Freeman, *The Feminine Sublime: Gender and Excess in Women's Fiction* (Berkeley: University of California Press, 1995), p. 22.

[7] It has been suggested that Hume suffered what may have been a nervous breakdown in the writing of the *Treatise*. See Alisdair MacIntyre, *After Virtue* (Indiana: University of Notre Dame Press, 1981), p. 55.

[8] For Whytt see J. Sambrook, *The Intellectual and Cultural Context of English Literature, 1700–1789* (London: Longman, 1993), p. 78.

[9] Quoted in L. J. Rather, *Mind and Body in Eighteenth-Century Medicine* (Berkeley: University of California Press, 1965), p. 78.

[10] Thomas Laqueur, *Making Sex: Body and Gender from the Greeks to Freud* (London: Harvard University Press, 1990), p. 153.

[11] Michel Foucault, *The History of Sexuality: Volume Two* (London: Penguin, 1990), p. 104.

[12] Ludmilla Jordanova, *Sexual Visions: Images of Gender in Science between the Eighteenth and Twentieth Centuries* (London: Harvester Wheatsheaf, 1989), p. 60.

[13] J. Barker-Benfield, *The Culture of Sensibility* (Chicago: Chicago University Press, 1992), p. 266.

[14] Samuel Richardson, *Clarissa* (London: Penguin, 1985), p. 725.

[15] John Mullan, *Sentiment and Sociability: The Language of Feeling in the Eighteenth Century* (Oxford: Oxford University Press, 1988), p. 202.

[16] S. M. Gilbert and S. Gubar, *The Madwoman in the Attic: The Woman Writer and the Nineteenth-Century Literary Imagination* (London: Yale University Press, 1979), p. 28.

[17] Ann Van Sant, *Sensibility and the Novel: The Senses in Social Context* (Cambridge: Cambridge University Press, 1993).

[18] Markman Ellis, *The Politics of Sensibility: Race, Gender and Commerce in the Sentimental Novel* (Cambridge: Cambridge University Press, 1996), p. 43.

[19] See G. S. Rousseau, 'Nymphomania and the Rise of Erotic Sensibility', in *Sexuality in Eighteenth-Century Britain*, ed. by P. G. Boucle (Manchester: Manchester University Press, 1982), pp. 96–120 (p. 110).

[20] Kim Ian Michasiw, introduction to *Zofloya, or, The Moor* (Oxford: Oxford University Press, 1997), p. 25.

[21] David P. Hanney, 'Eye and Ear in Wordsworth', *Studies in Romanticism*, 36 (1997), 173–99 (p. 182).

[22] P. B. Shelley, *On The Medusa of Leonardo Da Vinci in the Florentine Gallery*, in *Shelley: Poetical Works*, ed. by Thomas Hutchinson, corrected by G. M. Matthews (Oxford and NY: Oxford University Press, 1971), l. 34.

[23] *Shelley's Poetry and Prose*, ed. by Donald H. Reiman and Sharon B. Powers, (NY: Norton, 1977), IV. I. 80–83, 93–95.

[24] Mario Praz, *The Romantic Agony* (Oxford: Oxford University Press, 1933), p. 133.

William Blake and the Spectre of Anatomy

Tristanne J. Connolly

William Blake, in *The Marriage of Heaven and Hell*, described one purpose of his illuminated books:

> the notion that man has a body distinct from his soul, is to be expunged; this I shall do, by printing in the infernal method, by corrosives, which in Hell are salutary and medicinal, melting apparent surfaces away, and displaying the infinite which was hid.[1]

Blake suggests that engraving can disclose the mysterious link between body and soul. In relation to engraving, and to removing surfaces, the word 'medicinal' recalls anatomy literature. The revelatory aspect of Blake's work, and its preoccupation with the human body, bears comparison with dissection and its depiction in art. The often frightening aspect of Blake's poetic and graphic bodies, in their muscularity and viscerality, brings into play the idea of the spectre. They are terrifying, contorted visions, seemingly unreal despite their fleshiness. Blake's use of anatomical imagery is critical, transformational, even antagonistic, all of which is to be expected from his devilishly polemical tone above. Blake questions the relationship between surface and depth, and asks, what is truly spectral, the material or the immaterial body? In his association with the Royal Academy, Blake confronted the problem of the artist's relationship to nature, at the same time as he witnessed powerful examples of the interaction of art and anatomy. Blake's subversive use of anatomy does not merely assert the primacy of the spirit and the imagination over the body and nature. It suggests a complex and fascinating relationship between these and other contraries.

The spectre is a central concept in William Blake's poetry: a troublesome but necessary aspect of the psyche, which can become personified, and physically separate from the individual. The character Los, often a persona of Blake, is the creative blacksmith praised because he 'kept the Divine Vision in time of trouble'.[2] Yet, he is also referred to as the spectre of Urthona (another of Blake's characters: one of the four Zoas, who are each different elements of the eternal man) (*Jerusalem*, plate 95). Though Los spends much of *Jerusalem* trying to subdue his own unruly spectre, Los himself is a spectre. This doubling is an example of Blake's intriguing, purposeful inconsistency which multiplies possible meanings. On plate 53 of *Jerusalem* Los is referred to as the 'vehicular form' of Urthona. Being a spectre, then, involves providing the possibility of movement and action. Los's own spectre works at his forge (when Los is able to force him to). Similarly, Los could be the working form of the Zoa Urthona. The nature of this working form is suggested by another line from *Jerusalem*. In an address 'To the Deists', Blake accuses deism of teaching 'that Man is Righteous in his Vegetated Spectre' (*Jerusalem*, plate 52). The 'Natural Religion' of the deists does not see beyond the material world; the 'vegetated spectre' here is the material body. Los is the material embodiment of Urthona. Los's spectre in his Caliban-like brutality is a more physicalized embodiment of Los, and suited for the dirty work of the forge.

It might seem strange to consider a spectre, an unreal, ghostly apparition, to be a fleshy embodiment. However, Blake perpetrates this reversal as a matter of conviction. In his *Descriptive Catalogue* he asserts:

> A Spirit and a Vision are not, as the modern philosophy supposes, a cloudy vapour or a nothing: they are organized and minutely articulated beyond all that the mortal and perishing nature can produce. He who does not imagine in stronger and better lineaments, and in stronger and better light than his perishing mortal eye can see does not imagine at all.[3]

Blake takes materiality's strongest argument for reality, its definite substantiality, and claims it for the spiritual; the supposed intangibility of the spiritual is attached to the illusion of matter. In this light, coming into a body is not necessarily coming into being. In fact, in *The First Book of Urizen* the Genesis creation story is parodied, and Blake writes,

> Six days they shrunk up from existence
> And on the seventh day they rested.
> And they bless'd the seventh day, in sick hope
> And forgot their eternal life.[4]

The First Book of Urizen depicts the embodiment of Urizen, Los, Enitharmon and their children in sickeningly biological terms. In *Jerusalem* the emphasis is on pain, horror, and even a labour like childbirth, as Los's spectre separates from his back, while his emanation separates from his breast:

> his Emanation divided in pain,
> Eastward toward the Starry Wheels. But Westward, a black Horror.
> His spectre driv'n by the Starry Wheels of Albions sons, black and
> Opake divided from his back; he labours and he mourns!
>
> For as his Emanation divided, his Spectre also divided
> In terror of those starry wheels: and the Spectre stood over Los
> Howling in pain: a blackning Shadow, blackning dark & opake
> (*Jerusalem*, plates 5–6).[5]

Albion also has a spectre who separates from him; the fleshiness of the division is evident. He is seen by Los to be 'spreading in bloody veins in torments over Europe & Asia; / Not yet formed but a wretched torment unformed & abyssal' (*Jerusalem*, plate 60). Los, trying to control his own spectre, works his body in the forge. He

> Smit[es] the Spectre on his Anvil & the integuments of his Eye
> And Ear unbinding in dire pain, with many blows,
> Of strict severity self-subduing, & with many tears labouring (*Jerusalem*, plate 91).

A passage which deals with embodiment generally, might also be applicable to the emanation and spectre, since they are usually female and male:

> The Feminine separates from the Masculine & both from Man.
> Ceasing to be His Emanations, Life to Themselves assuming:
> And while they circumscribe his Brain. & while they circumscribe
> His Heart, & while they circumscribe his Loins! a Veil & Net
> Of Veins of red Blood grows around them like a scarlet robe.
> Covering them from the sight of Man like the woven Veil of Sleep
> Such as the Flowers of Beulah weave to be their Funeral Mantles
> But dark: opake! tender to touch & painful: & agonizing
> To the embrace of love, & to the mingling of soft fibres
> Of tender affection (*Jerusalem*, plate 90).

Blake again associates the formation of the physical body with pain and opacity. The images of the body's interior, such as the brain and the heart, veins, blood and fibres, are used to create a sickening and alienating effect. These interior parts grow into a covering; in a transformation from interior to exterior they evolve into a veil impenetrable to sight. The body is portrayed as a nauseating and uncontrollable 'Incrustation over [the] Immortal / Spirit'.[6] Yet Blake also manages to undermine this excessively physical imagery and call its material reality into question. He attaches it to invented, mythological figures who dwell in cosmic landscapes and personify mental processes. In his illustrations and his verses he depicts these gross, fleshy beings in postures and actions which surpass the restrictions of the flesh. They defy gravity; their positions would strain sinew and break bone. Blake is in the difficult position of having to portray, in his designs and poetry, the material as insubstantial, and the immaterial as strongly limned.

The problems Blake encountered in his efforts to be graphically true to his visions of the human body are apparent in another passage from *A Descriptive Catalogue*. Blake describes a painting (now lost) entitled *The Ancient Britons*:

> The flush of health in flesh, exposed to the open air, nourished by the spirits of forests and floods, in that ancient happy period, which history has recorded, cannot be like the sickly daubs of Titian or Rubens. Where will the copier of nature, as it now is, find a civilized man, who has been accustomed to go naked. Imagination only, can furnish us with colouring appropriate, such as is found in the Frescos of Rafael and Michael Angelo: the disposition of forms always directs colouring in works of true art. As to a modern Man stripped from his load of clothing, he is like a dead corpse. Hence Rubens, Titian, Correggio, and all of that class, are like leather and chalk; their men are like leather, and their women like chalk, for the disposition of their forms will not admit of grand colouring; in Mr. B's Britons, the blood is seen to circulate in their limbs; he defies competition in colouring (545).

There is an interesting valuation of translucence in Blake's description of his painting. Opacity is associated with the modern naked man, as it is with the spectre in the above quotations, but in relation to *The Ancient Britons* it is explicitly condemned. The ancient man is transparent: his life, the blood circulating in his limbs, is visible. In order to witness the circulation of the corpse-like modern man, the violence of incision is usually necessary, but Blake argues that the imagination can provide the x-ray vision which was common in the golden age. An idealization of the pellucid is well suited to Blake's vision of Eternity, where interpenetration is essential: 'When in Eternity Man converses with Man they enter into each others Bosom', explains Los on plate 88 of *Jerusalem*. Various personified aspects of the individual are involved in this process: 'first their Emanations meet / Surrounded by their children. if they embrace & comingle / The Human Four-fold Forms mingle also in thunders of

Intellect' (88). Elsewhere, Blake uses the word 'Cominglings' to describe ideal sexual intercourse (*Jerusalem*, plate 69), adding another dimension to this physicalization of spiritual activity, emphasising the permeability of the body. The flesh of the modern man becomes opaque because he is shielded from 'the spirits of forests and floods' and his fellow humans by his heavy clothing. He is as pale as a corpse and is impenetrable to communication and to sight.

Like Blake's visionary art, anatomical art reveals the hidden human interior. It combines the nauseatingly real with the uncannily impossible: skin folded back to reveal internal organs; systems of nerves and veins standing separate from other body components; babies in the womb; flayed bodies posing in landscapes. These images were present in anatomical art from the Renaissance.[7] Blake's own encounter with the role of anatomy in art, as with all of his early influences, can be traced through his association with the Royal Academy. David Bindman writes, 'It is difficult to penetrate the obscurity of Blake's apprentice days, but with his entry into the Royal Academy in 1779 he emerges more clearly; he now became acquainted with more readily identifiable artistic figures and we begin to discern something like a Blake circle'.[8] In this circle of people, there were many whose work shows an interest in anatomy. Hogarth's *Stages of Cruelty* culminates in the depiction of an executed criminal's dissection for the advancement of scientific and artistic knowledge.[9] Flaxman made muscular and skeletal studies which were posthumously published in a book for the use of artists.[10] George Stubbs was an engraver who produced comparative anatomical drawings of animals as well as humans.[11] He was patronized by John and William Hunter, who were dominant forces in the scientific study of anatomy; both of their individual medical interests crossed over into the arts. Robert Knox, writing in the 1850s about *Great Artists and Great Anatomists*, went so far as to name the British academic painters of Blake's time the 'Anatomical School'.[12] Even James Barry, whose stylized portrayals of the human form recall Blake's, especially in the similarity of his King Lear to Blake's Urizen, also created works which represent the body with accurate anatomical knowledge and even imitate the form of anatomical drawings.[13] Henry Fuseli's artistic relationship to nature seems as tenuous as Blake's, and his work shares so many elements with Blake's that critics find it difficult to decide who influenced whom.[14] Yet Fuseli practiced dissection, and despite his common interests with Fuseli, and fanatical admiration of Michelangelo, Blake did not follow their examples and practice dissection for the sake of his art.[15] His devaluation of the mortal body gave him a distaste even for life drawing (Bindman, 19).

Blake did not produce anatomical drawings as a commercial engraver, even though he was associated with James Basire, and later Joseph Johnson, both of whom dealt with medical publications. The closest Blake came was the work he did on James Earle's *Practical Observations on the Operation for the Stone*. The plates in this book portray urinary tract stones, and the tools used to extricate them. These tools could be compared to engraving tools: they are long and thin, with an elongated penlike slice taken from the end, and they are used for scraping unwanted material away.[16] Blake engraved plates for two other medical books, John Brown's *Elements of Medicine* and Thomas Henry's *Memoirs of Albert de Haller*, but they were merely the portraits of the physicians; the books contained no other plates.[17]

A strong anatomical influence on Blake, which occurred early enough in his life to influence his images of the body, was his acquaintance with the Hunters. John Hunter appears, with his name scored out and changed to 'Jack Tearguts', in Blake's satirical manuscript, *An Island in the Moon*. Erdman points out that Hunter's house, where his comparative anatomy museum was also located, was not far from Blake's residence at the time, nor was it far from the houses of Hogarth and Reynolds.[18] Carmen Kreiter argues that the imagery of *The First Book of Urizen* is influenced by John Hunter's theories and his displays of comparative anatomy, which he sees as an early suggestion of evolution (114). Both John and William Hunter occasionally enlisted the assistance of Basire,

Blake's engraving master until 1779 (Kreiter, 113). William Hunter was Professor of Anatomy at the Royal Academy from 1768 to 1783; Blake joined in 1779.[19] Hunter's influence there is shown to be extensive in Martin Kemp's study, *Dr. William Hunter at the Royal Academy of Arts*. Two paintings by Johann Zoffany made at the time show William Hunter 'performing his statutory duties' as Professor of Anatomy, 'demonstrating the muscles of the human body to a mixed audience of students and Academicians' (Kemp, 13). As a student of the Royal Academy (though soon disaffected) Blake would have attended at least some of the lectures and demonstrations offered.

A note found by Kemp in the Academy's council minutes gives the date and time for Hunter's lecture on the skeleton, but as for 'the other lectures on the muscles,' they are 'to be at such times as a body can be procured from the sheriffs to whom he recommended that application should be made' (Kemp, 18). From the paintings previously mentioned, it is known that Hunter did not always use real cadavers for his demonstrations. He also used écorchés: models of skinned human bodies which show the muscles for the use of artists. Écorchés are often realistically coloured, having a reddish tinge; Blake's colouring of skin, as well as his muscle emphasis, strongly recall their appearance.[20] Hunter tried to perfect the techniques of making casts from real skinned bodies, and Kemp finds evidence that more than one écorché in use at the Royal Academy in Blake's time was made from a real body (16).

Contact with the Hunters acquainted Blake with some of the intersections of art and anatomy, and with various other aspects of physiology. The influence of physiology on Blake's art and verse includes the proto-evolutionism which Kreiter sees in *The First Book of Urizen*; the inquiry into the composition of blood to which David Worrall calls attention in his notes to the same poem; and the controversy over the form and function of nerves which, according to Nelson Hilton, informs Blake's fibre imagery (Kreiter, 110–18; Worrall, 137–38).[21] The Hunters did not produce any general guides to anatomy, nor medical books for the use of artists. Their books focussed on more specific issues. Because John Hunter's interests lay largely in comparative anatomy, many works he commissioned are of animal anatomy.[22] About the human body, John Hunter wrote treatises on the blood and gunshot wounds, and on venereal disease.[23] William Hunter is best known for his *Anatomy of the Human Gravid Uterus*.[24] The strange births which pervade Blake's prophecies may have been influenced by theories developed by the Hunters, such as their explanation of how blood circulates between the mother and the unborn child through the placenta. However, the majority of images in the *Gravid Uterus* are of babies in the womb. It is very rare that Blake depicts such an ordinary form of birth. To imbibe many features of anatomical art not found in books written by the Hunters, such as flayed figures in landscapes, Blake would have had to look at additional sources.

The anatomy books whose illustrations have the most in common with Blake's visual art and poetic imagery, are those of William Cowper.[25] Cowper was born in Hampshire and was admitted as a 'Barber-Surgeon' in London in 1691. He was a Fellow of the Royal Society, and his work reflects the emphasis on experimental science associated with that group.[26] As K. B. Roberts and J. D. W. Tomlinson find, Cowper is 'best remembered as a plagiarist, and as the anatomist whose name has been applied to the male urethral glands' (412). Though Cowper had artistic skills, and included some of his own drawings in an appendix to the book, he borrowed the plates for his *Anatomy of Humane Bodies* from an earlier publication by the Dutch anatomist Govard Bidloo. The illustrations were by Lairesse. Cowper simply wrote new text to accompany the old plates. Bidloo was enraged and vilified Cowper in writing; Cowper added an admission of his borrowings in the second edition (412–13). Lairesse's drawings are of two varieties. In some, 'the anatomical figures are given life, a skeleton, for example, emerges from a grave set in the midst of classical tomb architecture'; in others, the subjects are decidedly cadavers, and even 'the pins and blocks that prop up the dissected parts' are included (311). Cowper's *Myotomia Reformata* (which, unlike *Anatomy of Humane Bodies,* is wholly original) also combines visceral realism with classicism, only in the same figure. Cowper claims,

> The outlines of some of the figures are drawn after Rafael, Sir Peter Paul Rubens, Guido Reni, Mons. Le Fage; but the muscling is done after several human subjects, and not copied from any anatomical book whatever (416).

Hogarth mentions Cowper in *The Analysis of Beauty*, referring to him as 'the famous anatomist'.[27] Blake was familiar with Hogarth and his *Analysis*, and may have followed this recommendation.[28] In fact, Cowper is recommended in reference to the torsion of muscles, a feature which pervades Blake's depictions of the human form. One of Cowper's illustrations is copied by Hogarth to demonstrate how muscles wrap in a serpentine fashion around the ideal human leg. Both of Cowper's books, where they depict full figures, follow the convention of placing them in landscapes, or at least in the surroundings in which they were dissected. The presence of complete human forms follows from the purpose of Cowper's books, as indicated in their titles: one is a general guide to anatomy, the other is a guide to musculature. Roberts and Tomlinson explain, Cowper 'thought the figures of the more superficial muscles would be of use not only to surgeons but also to "those who bend their studies to the admirable arts of sculpture and painting", arts which Cowper had studied, and in which he was proficient' (417). However, this is no ideal marriage between science and art, from a Blakean point of view, due to Cowper's empiricism. Cowper complains that a belief in the senses as 'gross and ignoble' results in shadowy knowledge rather than substantial truth (414). This is in stark opposition to Blake's descriptions of the material body's feeble sense organs, such as 'The Eye of Man' as 'a little narrow orb, closd up & dark. / Scarcely beholding the Great Light; conversing with the ground' (*Jerusalem*, plate 49) and his assertion that imagination, not ordinary perception, has a better claim to perceiving the real and definite. Cowper's anatomical studies rely on narrow, empirical sense perception, and are caught in what Blake would call 'Single vision & Newtons sleep' (*Complete Poetry and Prose*, 722). This is implied by the presence of an essay on the physics of muscular motion (complete with mathematical diagrams) written by Henry Pemberton, editor of Newton's *Principia*, in the 1724 edition of *Myotomia Reformata* (416).

In Cowper's *Myotomia Reformata* and *Anatomy of Humane Bodies* there are recurring images in the drawings which strongly recall Blake's visual and poetic themes. Recurring throughout *Myotomia Reformata* as section headpieces are images of flayed bodies in positions of suffering, muscles strained, surrounded by rugged rocks (plate 1). The contortion, and the muscle emphasis, are shared with Blake (plate 2). The surroundings recall Blake's repeated comparison of the material body to a cavern (for example, *Marriage*, plate 14), and also the rock where the dying giant Albion sits (*Jerusalem*, plate 15). The book, like Blake's, takes advantage of the relationship between text and picture. There are fascinating initial letters to each section which illustrate the subject to follow. For the initial letter A of the section 'of the Muscles of the Penis', a flayed body reclines, his hand grasps the crossbar of the A, and either leg curls around either leg of the letter (plate 1).

In the *Anatomy of Humane Bodies,* illustrations which recall Blake's image of vegetative fibres are present throughout. The vegetable associations of bodily fibres are made explicit by Cowper who often refers to veins as 'Arboreous' (*Anatomy*, 10th table). It is not only the nerves and veins which are fibrous; many other organs, including parts of the reproductive system, are represented in this tree-like form (plate 3, figure 2). The culmination comes with the illustration of the 'Arteries injected with Wax, and free'd from the Body of an Infant Six Months Old' (plate 4). Cowper, from his own dissection experience, disagrees with Lairesse's portrayal and provides his own drawing in an appendix (*Anatomy*, 23rd table). Not only does this bring to light the spectral relationship of mixed dependence and antagonism between Cowper's edition and Bidloo's book, from which he took the majority of plates for his *Anatomy*; it also calls into question Cowper's confidence in his own senses. Roberts and Tomlinson do not consider

Cowper's diagram to be an improvement on Lairesse's: 'One fears that considerable artistic licence was involved in producing such a diagram from a cast'. From a medical point of view, 'errors and misinterpretations abound', which spur Roberts and Tomlinson to make such comments as 'how could this not be noticed?' (418). Cowper claims to have 'freed' arteries from infants and adults many times; this would involve injecting the vessels with wax and removing them by dissection. The complex process of extricating anatomical features from the body they are entangled in, and necessary to, does not seem suitably described by the verb 'free'. When Blake presents one figure drawing out veins from another in *Jerusalem* 25, the emphasis is on enclosure as the veins form a sinister canopy (plate 5). In *Jerusalem* 85 also, the vegetative fibres of one figure are being drawn out by another; they are spread out, impossibly independent of the body they came from (plate 6). A psychological and moral dimension is added to this strange imagery in Jerusalem's cry to Albion, 'Why wilt thou number every little fibre of my Soul / Spreading them out before the Sun like stalks of flax to dry?' (*Jerusalem*, plate 22). There is a cruel exactitude, whether the incisive analysis pulls out for display the fibres of the body or the fibres of the soul (if these are indeed separate). Being a scientific diagram, Cowper's plate numbers the infant's veins.

Another anatomical motif in Blake's designs is that of the intestine. Clouds, worms, and chains of human bodies, are portrayed in intestinal shapes in a number of *Jerusalem* designs, for instance on plate 24 (plate 7). The same shape also appears in Cowper's plates in unexpected organs. The small intestine itself can be seen in table 40 of Cowper's *Anatomy* (plate 8). In table 45 (plate 3) figure 3 the *vas deferens* has the cloud-like, tubular shape, and table 60 presents the umbilical cord in a similar form (plate 9). Organs particularly involved in the conception and growth of the child reflect the cloud shapes found in *Jerusalem*. Along with fibres, images of the material which humans are formed by and consist of, decorate the pages of the prophecy. By depicting clouds which ambiguously reflect body parts, Blake visually insists on the point he made in his *Descriptive Catalogue*: 'A Spirit and a Vision are not, as the modern philosophy supposes, a cloudy vapour or a nothing' (541). In fact, clouds themselves, the way Blake portrays them here, may be not vaporous but visceral.

Cowper's table 62 is a particularly affecting example of the intestinal cloud shape (plate 10). In order 'to show the Progress of the Umbilical Vessels towards its Navel', Cowper has found a 'seven month female' and cut open her belly. He has taken the 'umbilical rope' and suspended it, tying and nailing it to the wall behind the table where the child lies. Otherwise it looks like a normal baby, sleeping perhaps, lying with its head to one side and legs slightly curled up: it is not in the stiff position of a corpse. The depiction of the infant's extricated veins is too alien to be shocking. The parts are removed from the body; one could imagine they were not really human. However, the juxtaposition of a recognizable infant's form, looking almost alive and healthy, with its innards displayed so mechanically, is so moving that it verges on eliciting a physical as well as emotional reaction. As Blake says, in the two lines following the ones quoted above on numbering fibres, 'The Infant Joy is beautiful, but its anatomy / Horrible ghast & deadly!' (*Jerusalem*, plate 22).[29]

The ghastliness and deadliness Blake associates with anatomy are not purely related to the violence and pain of bodily incision. His own works are full of violence and pain, and he often emphasizes that they are created by burning acid and gouging needles. Blake does not reject but rather borrows the shock value carried by the exposure of the human interior. What is 'ghast & deadly' is a preoccupation with the material body unconnected to the spiritual: numbering fibres, anatomizing an 'infant joy' whether a child or a newborn emotion. The scientific detachment with which William Hunter, for example, treated his anatomical subjects can be seen in the preface to his *Anatomy of the Human Gravid Uterus*. Hunter emphasizes his great good fortune in being provided with so many excellent examples of the human gravid uterus. These examples are provided by the bodies of women who died during pregnancy; their unborn children also died; these women were not given Christian burial by loved ones but subjected to the undesirable fate of dissection. Blake's insistence that an empirical approach reduces one's perception may seem to be a narrow-minded, anti-scientific cliché. Yet, examples such as this show the dangers of 'Single vision & Newton's sleep'. In the concentration of attention which is perhaps necessary to medical study, the humanity of the subject is forgotten; the ghastliness of anatomization is a matter of perception.

The perception of the body, and of any natural object, is as crucial for Blake's art theory as for his contemporaries. For Blake, the human body is the most important of all natural objects. Considered as more than its physical husk, it is the Human Form Divine which comprises all other forms, and is the embodiment not only of God but also of Imagination. As Martin Kemp finds, William Hunter, though not an artist, propounded his ideas on art as well as anatomy in his Royal Academy lectures (Kemp, 14). Believing Nature to be the best of all artists, Hunter argued that to imitate nature as faithfully and minutely as possible was the only way to achieve the same compelling, empathic response that nature elicits. The artist must work from knowledge rather than intuition because the slightest deviation from nature, though seemingly undetectable, will alter the combination of elements which affect the viewer. The viewer's response is intuitive, but the artist cannot afford to be intuitive in creating an effective illusion (Kemp, 18–19). It would seem that an anatomical artist would be more constrained to imitate nature strictly, but this is not always the case. In the preface to his *Anatomy of the Human Gravid Uterus*, Hunter insists that 'anatomical figures are made in two very different ways; one is the simple portrait, in which the object is represented exactly as it is seen; the other is a representation of the object under such circumstances as were not actually seen, but conceived in the imagination'.[30] Interestingly, the example Hunter gives of the first variety of illustration is Bidloo, the anatomist whose plates Cowper employed in his

Anatomy of Humane Bodies. Cowper, in his insistence on 'sense and experiment', has been seen as a precursor of John Hunter, but he also presages William Hunter, who also equates unembellished sense data with substantial truth (415). L. J. Jordanova, in an essay on Hunter's *Gravid Uterus*, questions the possibility of representing anything 'exactly as it was seen'. She identifies in that book 'an attempt to create the illusion that there need be no mediations between nature and the human mind'.[31]

There were oppositions to Hunter's extreme naturalism: Kemp supposes that Sir Joshua Reynolds's third 'Discourse' may have been intended 'to shoot down Hunter's creed' (Kemp, 22). To counter the ideas of the strict imitation of nature which Hunter was advocating to the Academy students and members, Reynolds cautioned that ideal beauty could not be found in any individual in nature, but had to be abstracted:

> The power of discovering what is deformed in nature, or in other words, what is particular and uncommon, can be acquired only by experience; and the whole beauty and grandeur of the art consists, in my opinion, in being able to get above all singular forms, local customs, particularities, and details of every kind [...] [the artist's] eye being enabled to distinguish the accidental deficiencies, excrescences, and deformities of things, from their general figures, he makes out an abstract idea of their forms more perfect than any one original; and what may seem a paradox, he learns to design naturally by drawing his figures unlike to any one object.[32]

Hunter associates the second kind of anatomical illustration mentioned above with the generalizing impulse:

> A figure of fancy, made up perhaps from a variety of studies after *NATURE*, may exhibit in one view, what could only be seen in several objects; and it admits of a better arrangement, of abridgement, and of greater precision.

One reason an anatomical artist might have for conceiving figures in the imagination was practical: Hunter explains that 'much time must be lost, and the parts must be considerably injured by long exposure to the air before the painter'.

In fact, this problem worsens 'if the work be conducted by an anatomist who will not allow the artist to paint from memory or imagination, but only from immediate observation'. Imagination could supplement the parts which had been rotted by time. However, Hunter argues that this 'only describes, or gives an idea' while accurate representation 'shews the object, or gives perception [...] it represents what was actually seen, it carries the mark of truth, and becomes almost as infallible as the object itself'. The object described as 'infallible' is a decaying body; the project Hunter gave his artist (Jan van Riemsdyck) was doomed by putrefaction. Jordanova insists that the illustrations in the *Gravid Uterus* do not strictly follow the prescriptions set out by Hunter himself, for the very reason of decay:

> [They] did not reflect nature but fabricated it. For example, the bodies from which the pictures were drawn were dead, and had often been so for a long time. The plates strive to give an impression of vitality, as in the way the umbilical cord seems to gleam as if it were still wet (Jordanova, 394).

The plates are studies of the origin of life, but this life could only be studied and depicted in death. Naturalism, here, means drawing a subject which is quickly transforming into putridity, yet attempting to capture its fleeting undecayed state. The illustration becomes like a spectre: a representation of a body both undead and unreal.

Hunter admits to some of the difficulties of accurate portrayal: 'The figure which is a close representation of nature, and which is furnished from a view of one subject, will often be, unavoidably, somewhat indistinct or defective in some parts.' Anatomical practices, such as injection with wax, alter the appearance of the innards to make invisible vessels visible, as Hunter explains in his preface (Jordanova, 394). The word 'defective' conjures up the argument with Reynolds about ideal forms, and connects an artistic problem with a scientific problem. Anatomical knowledge comes from generalizations made from a variety of examples, because not every human interior is the same. Jonathan Sawday quotes a medical examiner's experience: 'individuality stamps its mark on every part of the anatomy: no two hearts are entirely alike; the shapes of livers are never quite the same; branching vessels always ramify in a unique way'.[33] Where, then, does one draw the line between individual variation and deformity?

In a comment on the introduction to Reynolds's 'Discourses', Blake leaves no doubt as to his position on this matter: 'To Generalize is to be an Idiot'.[34] His annotations to 'Discourse III' provide more specific arguments against Reynolds's ideal abstraction: 'One Central Form Composed of all other Forms being Granted it does not therefore follow that all other Forms are Deformity' (*Annotations*, 648). Blake perceives that on Reynolds's terms, everything that is not abstract is deformed. However, Blake does not react to this by championing individual nature; Reynolds's correction of Hunter's excess naturalism is not a great improvement, from a Blakean point of view. Reynolds does not replace nature as the central preoccupation of the artist, he merely adds abstraction to nature. Since for Blake the natural world is insubstantial illusion, abstracting it takes it another step further away from reality. Blake corrects both Reynolds and Hunter in two other comments on 'Discourse III'. Against each of these sentences Blake has written 'A Lie' (*Annotations*, 647):

> This great ideal perfection and beauty are not to be sought in the heavens, but upon the earth. They are about us, and upon every side of us. But the power of discovering what is deformed in nature, or in other words, what is particular and uncommon, can be acquired only by experience (Reynolds, 44).

Reynolds tries to transcend nature's imperfections through abstraction, yet wishes to bar the artist from seeking beauty in the heavens. Blake sidesteps both nature and abstraction when he explains his view: 'All Forms are Perfect in the Poets Mind. but these are not Abstracted nor Compounded from Nature but are from Imagination' (*Annotations*, 648).

Blake does not go to the extreme of arguing that all an artist requires is Imagination. In opposition to Reynolds, who in 'Discourse II' discourages too much copying, Blake writes, 'no one can ever Design till he has learnd the Language of Art by making many Finishd Copies both of Nature & Art & of whatever comes in his way from Earliest Childhood' (*Annotations*, 645). Blake also says that 'Servile Copying is the Great Merit of Copying' (*Annotations*, 645); however, the servility of Blake's own copies is questionable.[35] Critics such as John Harvey and Christopher Heppner find it difficult to reconcile Blake's insistence on attention to minute particulars in art with his seeming carelessness in anatomy and perspective.[36] A possible explanation for Blake's various inconsistencies lies in other comments, also on Reynolds's second 'Discourse': Blake claims, 'Every Eye Sees differently As the Eye — Such the Object' (*Annotations*, 645). Near the end of the second 'Discourse', Blake writes, 'the Man who asserts [...] that every thing in Art is Definite & Determinate has not been told this by Practise but by Inspiration & Vision because Vision is Determinate & Perfect & he Copies That without Fatigue' (*Annotations*, 646). Going one step further, in his *Public Address* Blake claims that exact copying of nature is a doomed task:

> Men think they can Copy Nature as Correctly as I copy Imagination this they will find Impossible. & all the Copies or Pretended Copiers of Nature from Rembrat to Reynolds Prove that Nature becomes [tame] to its Victim nothing but Blots & Blurs. Why are Copiers of Nature Incorrect while Copiers of Imagination are Correct this is manifest to all (*Annotations*, 574–75).[37]

Nature victimizes its copiers by relegating them to the constant production of blots and blurs, which is only to be expected, considering the indistinctness of non-visionary reality. Even Hunter admits that indistinctness is often unavoidable in close representations of nature. For Blake, the superior reality of imagination makes it the only 'correct' thing to copy. Blake copies determinate and perfect vision without fatigue. Perhaps when copying servilely from nature or art, he is being servile to the vision: not an abstraction from what is seen, but a revelation of the true form. Blake's 'medicinal' engraving project was to reveal the 'infinite which was hid'. He also sought to depict the ideal Ancient Briton, the model for whom cannot be found by 'the copier of nature, as it now is,' but 'Imagination only can furnish' (*Descriptive Catalogue*, 545).

Blake's method of acquainting himself with, and portraying, the bodily interior may be akin to a recommendation made by Hogarth. In the introduction to *The Analysis of Beauty*, a work obsessed by shapes and lines, just as Blake is preoccupied with forms and outlines, Hogarth explains how best to gain intimate knowledge of a shape:

> Let every object under our consideration, be imagined to have its inward contents scoop'd out so nicely, as to have nothing of it left but a thin shell, exactly corresponding both in its inner and outer surface, to the shape of the object itself: and let us likewise suppose this thin shell to be made up of very fine threads, closely connected together, and equally perceptible, whether the eye is supposed to observe them from without, or within; [...] the imagination will naturally enter into the vacant space within this shell, and there at once, as from a center, view the whole form within, and mark the opposite corresponding parts so strongly, as to retain the idea of the whole, and make us masters of the meaning of every view of the object, as we walk round it, and view it from without (26–28).

Hogarth advocates investigating objects from the inside, but in a different way from the invasive techniques of anatomization which, by cutting and revealing, merely render the inside a new outside. Hogarth offers a view from within which provides a more perfect knowledge of the whole, from every possible perspective. The multiple outlines of an object, because Hogarth describes them as 'threads', are akin to Blake's 'fibres', discussed above. When thought of as a multiple outline, fibres become an element which defines identity, an identity which is manifold and permeable.

Barbara Stafford, in her book *Body Criticism*, spins out the anatomical implications of Hogarth's 'ingenious scheme for getting inside forms'. It is, she writes, 'a kind of mental dissection' akin to the type of anatomical drawing which considers the skin, muscles, *et cetera*, as so many layers which can be peeled away in turn to reveal the lower layer, right down to the skeleton.[38] The mind, in Hogarth's system, replaces the doctor's tools, scoops out the body's interiors and 'probe[s] its vacancies or densities'.[39] She later likens the doctor's tools to the engraver's tools, which also gouge and seek to reveal the shapes beneath the surface. The gouges (the engraved lines which will constitute the work of art) are compared by Stafford to veins, filled with blood-like ink (70). The ink which fills the veins of copy E of *Jerusalem* and gives life to its depictions of the human interior, is a bloody vermilion.

Los the visionary blacksmith works on the body of his spectre, as though it were a piece of metal, to expand its narrow senses. Similarly, Blake the visionary engraver shapes his body of work. By using, and transforming, the revelatory force of anatomical literature, with all its connections to engraving, Blake melts surfaces away. Using imaginative x-ray vision, Blake displays the circulation of the human body's lifeblood and the pain of its tender fibres. Blake practices anatomization and dissection with the 'medicinal' tools of engraving, not in the realm of the perishing mortal body, but in that of the imagination, which is more real. Through a symbolic rather than a literal use of anatomical conventions and imagery, Blake is able to psychologize and spiritualize the physical body. Against the nature- and sense-based values of major artists (like Reynolds) and major medical thinkers (like Hunter and Cowper), Blake does not merely champion a disembodied spirit. Rather, he calls attention to the aspects unseen by natural, single vision and abstraction alike. As he set out to do, Blake reveals through his engravings that the body is a spectral part of the soul, the apparition of soul that moves in this world: 'Man has no Body distinct from his Soul for that calld Body is a portion of Soul discernd by the five Senses, the chief inlets of Soul in this age' (*Marriage*, plate 14).

[1] William Blake, *The Marriage of Heaven and Hell*, in William Blake, *The Early Illuminated Books*, ed. by Morris Eaves, Robert N. Essick and Joseph Viscomi, Blake's Illuminated Books, (London: Tate Gallery and William Blake Trust, 1993), III, 113–224 (plate 14).

[2] William Blake, *Jerusalem*, ed. by Morton D. Paley, Blake's Illuminated Books (London: Tate Gallery and William Blake Trust, 1991), I, plate 95.

[3] William Blake, *A Descriptive Catalogue*, in *The Complete Poetry and Prose of William Blake*, rev. edn, ed. by David V. Erdman (NY: Anchor and Doubleday, 1988), pp. 529–50 (p. 541).

[4] William Blake, *The First Book of Urizen*, in *The Urizen Books*, ed. by David Worrall, Blake's Illuminated Books (London: Tate Gallery and William Blake Trust, 1995), VI, 19–152 (plate 23).

[5] The spectre and the emanation are respectively male and female aspects of the greater (male) personality (though there is one briefly mentioned emanation who is male, *Jerusalem*, plate 49). What is true of the spectre is also true of the emanation: ideally, they are subordinate personality aspects who assist human creativity. However, if separate and out of control, they both can mar work rather than aid it. As can be seen by the front/back and east/west oppositions in the passage quoted, the spectre and the emanation are almost like mirror images: similar yet different. They have different ways of assisting with labour (at the forge and the loom respectively) and different ways of sabotaging it (through doubt and malice, and stubbornness and sexual wiles, respectively).

[6] William Blake, *Milton: A Poem*, ed. by Robert N. Essick and Joseph Viscomi, Blake's Illuminated Books (London: Tate Gallery and William Blake Trust, 1993), V, plate 42.

[7] See Jonathan Sawday, *The Body Emblazoned* (London: Routledge, 1995) for examples of Renaissance anatomical art.

[8] David Bindman, *Blake as an Artist* (Oxford: Phaidon, 1977), p. 19.

[9] Ronald Paulson, *Hogarth's Graphic Works*, 3rd edn (London: The Print Room, 1989), plate 190a.

[10] An example from Flaxman's *Anatomical Studies of the Bones and Muscles for the Use of Artists* can be seen in David Irwin, *John Flaxman 1755–1826: Sculptor, Illustrator, Designer* (London: Studio Vista and Christie's, 1979), p. 119. Irwin claims that Flaxman practiced anatomy drawing throughout his life, and kept a skeleton in his studio; he also mentions that Flaxman would have been taught anatomy at the Royal Academy by William Hunter (pp. 118–19).

[11] Examples of Stubbs's human anatomy drawings, from his *Comparative Anatomical Exposition of the Structure of the Human Body with that of a Tiger and a Common Fowl* can be seen in Judy Egerton, *George Stubbs 1724–1806* (London: Tate Gallery, 1984), plates 139–51. They include,

in positions of action and of rest, whole bodies, muscle-men (with layers of muscle of different depths), and skeletons.

[12] Cited by Martin Kemp, *Dr. William Hunter at the Royal Academy of Arts* (Glasgow: University of Glasgow Press, 1975), p. 25.

[13] See Jean Hagstrum, *William Blake, Poet and Painter* (Chicago: University of Chicago Press, 1964), pp. 64–65; Kemp, p. 25.

[14] Eudo C. Mason, *The Mind of Henry Fuseli* (London: Routledge and Kegan Paul, 1951), pp. 49–50.

[15] Carmen S. Kreiter, 'Evolution and William Blake', *Studies in Romanticism*, 4 (1965), 110–18 (p. 115).

[16] Robert N. Essick in *William Blake: Printmaker* (Princeton: Princeton University Press, 1980), pp. 15–21, describes various engraving tools. They were all cut at an angle at the end, though none were hollow like the tools pictured in Earle's book. Though most gravers were straight (unlike modern ones), a stipple burin apparently had a curved shaft, like the medical instruments in question.

[17] Robert N. Essick, *William Blake's Commercial Book Illustrations* (Oxford: Clarendon, 1991), pp. 33–34.

[18] David V. Erdman, *Prophet Against Empire*, rev. edn (Princeton: Princeton University Press, 1969), pp. 101–102n. Kreiter explains that John Hunter's museum 'contained hundreds of species of mammals, birds, reptiles, and fish dissected and arranged to portray the series of changes in the development of the embryo' (p. 114).

[19] Sidney C. Hutchison, *The History of the Royal Academy 1768–1968* (London: Chapman and Hall, 1968), p. 235. Blake joined the Royal Academy as a student in 1779; he exhibited there in 1780, 1784, 1785, 1799 and 1808; he returned as late as 1815 to sketch the Laocoön. See the chronology in William Blake, *Blake's Poetry and Designs*, ed. by Mary Lynn Johnson and John E. Grant (NY: Norton, 1979), pp. xxviii–xxxviii.

[20] See, for example, a late eighteenth-century écorché trunk, in Deanna Petherbridge, *The Quick and the Dead* (London: National Touring Exhibitions, 1997), p. 95.

[21] Nelson Hilton, *Literal Imagination* (Berkeley: University of California Press, 1983), p. 83.

[22] See, for example, the drawings of the incubation of the chick and the gosling, made for John Hunter by two different artists (William Bell and Saint Aubin), in Petherbridge, p. 103.

[23] John Hunter, *A Treatise on the Blood, Inflammation, and Gun-Shot Wounds* (London: J. Richardson for G. Nicol, 1794); *A Treatise on the Venereal Disease* (London: G. Nicol, 1786).

[24] William Hunter, *Anatomy of the Human Gravid Uterus* (Birmingham: John Baskerville, 1774).

[25] This is William Cowper the surgeon, 1666–1709, after whom Cowper's gland, a part of the male reproductive system, is named. He was not related to William Cowper the poet, 1731–1800. The texts referred to in this essay are William Cowper, *The Anatomy of Humane Bodies* (Oxford: [no pub.], 1698) and *Myotomia Reformata* (London: [no pub.], 1724).

[26] K. B. Roberts and J. D. W. Tomlinson, *The Fabric of the Body* (Oxford: Clarendon, 1992), pp. 412, 415. Unless otherwise stated references to Cowper's works are taken from this text.

[27] William Hogarth, *The Analysis of Beauty*, ed. by Joseph Burke (Oxford: Clarendon, 1955), p. 72.

[28] In his *Public Address*, Blake refers to Hogarth's concept of the 'line of beauty' (*Complete Poetry and Prose*, p. 575).

[29] This is the only time Blake uses the word 'anatomy'. Along with the lines quoted above on numbering the fibres of the soul, these lines also appear in 'Night the First' of *The Four Zoas*. There they are spoken by Tharmas, and unchanged except for the word 'number' which *in The Four Zoas* reads 'Examine' (*Complete Poetry and Prose*, p. 302).

[30] Hunter, 1774, preface, no page numbers. Unless otherwise indicated, all quotations from William Hunter are from this short preface to *Anatomy of the Human Gravid Uterus*.

[31] L. J. Jordanova, 'Gender, Generation and Science: William Hunter's Obstetrical Atlas', in *William Hunter and the Eighteenth-Century Medical World*, ed. by W.F. Bynum and Roy Porter (Cambridge: Cambridge University Press, 1985), pp. 385–412 (pp. 393–94).

[32] Joshua Reynolds, *Discourses on Art*, ed. by Robert R. Wark (San Marino: Huntington Library, 1959), p. 44.

[33] From F. Gonzalez-Crussi, *Notes of an Anatomist*, on the work of Milton Helpern, former chief medical examiner for NY (in Sawday, p. 7).

[34] *Annotations to the Works of Sir Joshua Reynolds*, in *Complete Poetry and Prose*, pp. 635–62 (p. 641).

[35] For example, Blake's copies of Michelangelo involve crucial changes. See Jenijoy LaBelle, 'Blake's Visions and Re-Visions of Michelangelo', in *Blake in his Time*, ed. by Robert N. Essick and Donald Pearce (Bloomington: Indiana University Press), pp. 13–22 (p. 19).

[36] John Harvey, 'Blake's Art', *Cambridge Quarterly* 7.2 (1977), 129–150 (p. 139); Christopher Heppner, *Reading Blake's Designs* (Cambridge: Cambridge University Press, 1995), pp. 53–54, 220.

[37] Blake deleted the word 'tame'.

[38] An example of layer anatomy can be seen in Cowper's *Myotomia Reformata*. On pages 117 and following, the same figure in a landscape is depicted with its 'external Teguments removed',

then with some external muscles lifted or removed, then 'farther denuded' of muscle, then as a skeleton. The same process is then repeated from the side and back views.

[39] Barbara Maria Stafford, *Body Criticism* (Cambridge, MA: The MIT Press, 1991), p. 55.

'The moving accident is not my trade': Wordsworth, *Lyrical Ballads*, and the Anxiety of German Borrowing

Peter Mortensen

I

During the last decade of the eighteenth and the first decade of the nineteenth century, British culture experienced a sudden, unexpected, and dramatic influx of texts translated and adapted from the German. The generic category of 'German romance' consisted primarily of texts rich in supernatural pageantry, heavy on violent spectacle, and rife with titillating melodrama. 'As represented by the work that found its way into England', writes J. M. S. Tompkins in *The English Popular Novel, 1770–1800*, 'German taste [...] came to connote wild extravagance of sentiment and incident, passion wound up to the highest pitch, horror, grotesqueness, and the expression of all these qualities in inflated language'.[1] While German sensationalism was enthusiastically received and avidly devoured by ordinary readers, it was also widely and vehemently opposed by Britain's outspoken and influential periodical press reviewers. From around 1795, literary and cultural commentators routinely spoke of a frightful northern 'invasion', 'incursion', 'inundation', or 'deluge'. According to one anonymous contributor to the Tory *Anti-Jacobin Review*, for example, closer attention to the 'passion for German Literature' that was currently spreading throughout Great Britain revealed 'a kind of systematic plan for corrupting the public taste and national morality of Englishmen'.[2] The conservative conduct book writer Hannah More used her *Strictures on the Modern System of Female Education* (1799) to call upon respectable British gentlewomen 'to oppose, with the whole weight of their influence, the irruption of those swarms of Publications now daily issuing from the banks of the Danube, which, like their ravaging predecessors of the darker ages, though with far other and more fatal arms, are overrunning civilized society'.[3] More's contemporary William Preston figured the dispersion of German melodrama in similar, almost apocalyptic terms, as a 'torrent', 'tribe', 'horde', or 'swarming host of writings', threatening Britain with an imminent 'irruption of Gothic barbarism and ferocity'. 'An extraordinary revolution', Preston writes, 'seems to be taking place in the republic of letters, as well as in other states; and the muses, in the more southern parts of Europe, appear to be menaced with subjection, if not with extirpation, by invading swarms from the northern hive'.[4] With a consensus uncharacteristic of a press known above all for its political factionalism, British critics fashioning themselves as protectors of the reading public aggressively branded the popular German literature a Jacobinical disease or infection, which possessed an uncanny ability to disseminate itself, and which already threatened to inflame Britain's entire body politic. Imagining a jaded readership addicted to, and surfeited with, toxic novelties, the Romantic reviewers also denounced the domestic culprits disseminating the German contagion: circulating library owners pushing sordid luxuries to inexperienced readers; unpatriotic theatre managers bent on demolishing the institutions of the national drama; and unscrupulous copyists seeking only to make a quick profit on the latest foreign fashion.

'At the turn of the nineteenth century', as David Simpson writes, '"Germany" was clearly established as the new evil empire in Europe, even more urgently demonized than France'.[5] The British Romantic writers were influenced by, and participated in, the anti-Jacobin establishment's revulsion against German romance and its shocking popularity within the cultural marketplace. Several of Romanticism's best-known literary manifestos and programmatic declarations, including Wordsworth's preface to *Lyrical Ballads* (1800) and Coleridge's *Biographia Literaria* (1817), contain paradigmatic passages in which the poets anathematize the flood of translations that made Germany the land of violence and turbulence during the 1790s and 1800s.[6] In spite of this, the Romantic writers experimented freely with German techniques, and they borrowed liberally from popular yet controversial writers such as Goethe, Schiller, Bürger, and Kotzebue. It is surely no coincidence that Coleridge englished Schiller's *Wallenstein* and *The Death of Wallenstein*, that Scott paraphrased Bürger's 'Lenore' and 'Der Wilde Jäger', that P. B. Shelley anglicized lengthy scenes from Goethe's *Werther* and *Faust*, and that De Quincey kept up a steady supply of texts from the German.[7] Yet even these German transcriptions and transliterations on the margin of the Romantic canon do not exhaust the full significance of the British writers' sustained traffic in foreign merchandise. With the possible exception of Blake, in fact, all the six 'Great Romantics', at various points in their careers and with varying degrees of success, chose to include and subsume the types and stereotypes of German formula fiction within their own publications, assimilating them even as they sought to reformulate them for their own purposes.[8]

As a powerful and conspicuous precursor genre, the German romance and melodrama provided tools of narrative, character, and metaphor to British writers: literary methods and strategies which the Romantics poets used as knowingly as, if more ambivalently than, contemporary novelists such as Ann Radcliffe, Matthew Gregory 'Monk' Lewis, William Godwin, and Mary Shelley. The Romantics' compulsive *pas de deux* with German romance must be viewed as a carefully calculated bid to assimilate and co-opt continental tales of wonder and excess, capitalizing on their sensational popularity while also converting them to the different and altogether healthier ends of a unified British literature and national identity. In its own right, the Romantics acknowledged, German-style sentimentalism represented a crude, intrusive, and essentially unhealthy form of entertainment: a potentially disruptive yet also attractive and ultimately redeemable presence within 'the otherwise well-ordered island of Great Britain'.[9] German romance's trademark features were labelled by Wordsworth 'gross and violent stimulants', and its cardinal effect Coleridge called 'a moral and intellectual *Jacobinism* of the most dangerous kind [...] [namely] the confusion and subversion of the natural order of things' (*Prose*, I, 128; *Biographia Literaria*, II, 190). Yet by absorbing German paraphernalia into their own poetry, the Romantic writers could tap strength and vitality from the very same forms that they also thereby attempted to master. Containing German romance's symbols, plots, and imaginative repertoires within their own works, in other words, furnished the Romantics with a way of exploiting this alien genre's spectacular success, while also bringing it under aesthetic and ideological control.

This essay follows a new direction in considering Wordsworth's intertextual conversation with the German balladeer Gottfried August Bürger. In several poems from *Lyrical Ballads*, and most remarkably in 'Hart-Leap Well' (1800), Wordsworth can be seen struggling to yoke the power of Bürger's extravagant and extravagantly popular verse narratives to British Romanticism's culturally and politically revisionist agenda. As Wordsworth understood, the German Gothic ballad could, when 'tinctured' by the colours of the imagination, be transformed into cultural capital for the British Romantic movement.[10] If this errant form was at once domesticated and enriched, it could be given a new meaning, endowed with a new literary value, and turned to ideological advantage for British literature and the new generation of poets. Yet, at the same time, Wordsworth is also haunted by a problematic consciousness of the impropriety of entangling himself publicly with Germany's scandalous formula fiction. Constant drawing from polluted continental sources, after all, does not sit well with Wordsworth's declared wish to establish himself firmly among the English poets, as *primus inter pares* in the literary pantheon with Chaucer, Spenser, Shakespeare, and Milton. Throughout his sophisticated anti-literary negotiations with Bürger's supernatural ballad, Wordsworth remains uncomfortably aware, as does his collaborator Coleridge, that the frequent use of German pretexts in their experimental compositions ultimately jeopardizes the Lake Poets' project of seeking cultural legitimacy for themselves and their publications.

II

Over a period beginning in 1796 and culminating with the publication of M. G. Lewis's *Tales of Wonder* (1801), British literary culture saw the appearance, in broadsides, in popular magazines, and in separate anthologies, of numerous marvellous ballads imported from Germany, or from the region more vaguely described as 'the North'. Spawning a veritable plethora of British translations, adaptations, imitations, and parodies, G. A. Bürger's 'Lenore' (1773–96) stands out as the most celebrated poem in the short-lived but intense craze for German balladry. Translated by William Taylor (in two versions), J. T. Stanley, H. J. Pye, W. R. Spencer, and Walter Scott, 'Lenore' (1773) appeared in no less than six different English versions, several of them lavishly illustrated, within the same year, 1796. 'Lenore' has long been recognized as an important influence on British Romantic ballad experiments.[11] This essay, however, dwells instead on the Romantic response to another of Bürger's startling tales, 'Der Wilde Jäger' (1778).

First translated by Walter Scott, 'The Chase' was published, along with his translation of 'Lenore', in a slim volume entitled *'The Chase' and 'William and Helen': Two Ballads from the German of Gottfried Augustus Bürger* (1796). During the same year, excerpts of the poem also appeared in the *Critical Review* — the same periodical that employed Coleridge as a reviewer of Gothic romances between 1794 and 1798. Written in traditional ballad stanzas, and characterized throughout by an evident relish for ghastly narrative effects and spectacular rhetorical devices, 'The Chase' concerns the fate of an aristocratic huntsman (the Wildgrave) who decides to go out hunting one Sunday morning, ignoring the village church-bells that toll and call him to service. The huntsman soon catches sight of a 'stag more white than mountain snow' and sets off in pursuit of it.[12] But as the ride progresses and the hunter gathers speed, two additional horsemen, one dressed in white and the other in black, appear at his side. The first rider tries to appeal to the huntsman's better instincts, urging him to return home and warning him about the consequences of his uncontrollable fury:

> 'To-day, the ill-omened chase forbear,
> Yon bell yet summons to the fane;
> To-day the Warning Spirit hear,
> To-morrow thou mayst mourn in vain' (33–36).

The other rider, however, encourages the Wildgrave to continue in his current course and fully savour the pleasures of the chase:

> 'Away, and sweep the glades along!'
> The Sable Hunter hoarse replies;
> 'To muttering monks leave matin-song,
> And bells, and books, and mysteries' (37–40).

Not surprisingly, the noble hunter heeds the latter horseman's advice rather than the former's; he continues his relentless assault on the stag, rather than turning back to observe his religious duties. Throughout the remainder of the run, the Wildgrave repeatedly and wilfully disobeys the voice of reason and morality, proceeding to level the fields of a poor farmer, butcher the sheep of a penniless shepherd, and invade the sacred territory of a peaceful sylvan hermit. But suddenly, when the climax of the race seems close at hand, the sky darkens and the sounds of the hustle disappear, as if time and place were suspended:

> Wild gazed the affrighted Earl around;
> He strove in vain to wake his horn,
> In vain to call: for not a sound
> Could from his anxious lips be borne (157–60).

Gradually, as the huntsman hears from afar the ferocious barking of 'the misbegotten dogs of hell', the terrible irony of his fate begins to dawn upon him:

> What ghastly Huntsman next arose,
> Well may I guess, but dare not tell;
> His eye like midnight lightning glows,

> His steed, the swarthy hue of hell.
>
> The Wildgrave flies o'er bush and thorn
> With many a shriek of helpless woe;
> Behind him hound, and horse, and horn,
> And, "Hark away, and holla, ho!"
>
> With wild despair's reverted eye,
> Close, close behind, he marks the throng,
> With bloody fangs and eager cry;
> In frantic fear he scours along (184–96).

The once-so-proud huntsman has himself become the prey of a terrifying, endless, unhallowed pursuit. From now until eternity, he will haunt the earth, a frightening example of human insolence and obstinacy to everyone who crosses his path or hears the sounds of the infernal chase.

Critics have shown that there is a close intertextual connection between Bürger's 'The Chase' and Wordsworth's 'Hart-Leap Well', and that the two poems are linked by striking parallels of situation, narrative, and character.[13] The poetry of *Lyrical Ballads*, as Wordsworth writes in the 1800 preface, is dominated by figures selected from 'low and rustic life', characters such as Betty Foy, Goody Blake, Harry Gill, and the anonymous narrator of 'The Thorn' (*Prose*, I, 124). Yet 'Hart-Leap Well', like 'The Chase', has at its centre a brash and arrogant hunting squire, and this unusual choice of an aristocratic protagonist suffices to make probable, if not to prove, Wordsworth's indebtedness to Bürger. The beginning lines of 'Hart-Leap Well' evoke the tension and excitement preceding the hunt, and Wordsworth's Sir Walter, like Bürger's Wildgrave, is shown abusing and bullying his servants in preparation:

> 'Another horse' — That shout the vassal heard,
> And saddled his best steed, a comely grey;
> Sir Walter mounted him; he was the third
> Which he had mounted on that glorious day.[14]

Then Sir Walter sets off, and Wordsworth's poem follows the huntsman's pitiless pursuit of a white stag, in an impetuous, ongoing chase set in a solitary, mountainous landscape:

> A rout this morning left Sir Walter's hall,
> That as they galloped made the echoes roar;
> But horse and man are vanished, one and all;
> Such race, I think, was never seen before.
>
> Sir Walter, restless as a veering wind,
> Calls to the few tired dogs that yet remain:
> Brach, Swift, and Music, noblest of their kind,
> Follow, and up the weary mountain strain.
>
> The Knight hallooed, he chid and cheered them on
> With suppliant gestures and upbraidings stern;
> But breath and eyesight fail; and, one by one,
> The dogs are stretched among the mountain fern.
>
> Where is the throng, the tumult of the race?
> The bugles that so joyfully were blown? —
> The chase it looks not like an earthly chase;
> Sir Walter and the Hart are left alone (13-28).

Even as he interpolates virtually every structural component (chase, huntsman, stag, horse, dogs) of Bürger's well known romance narrative into the poetry of 'Hart-Leap Well', Wordsworth also departs from his textual antecedent in various important ways. Almost as though to signal to the reader that he has transplanted 'The Chase' onto British territory, Wordsworth adds to his ballad a prefatory note that anchors the action in a familiar landscape: 'Hart-Leap Well', Wordsworth writes, 'is a small spring of water, about five miles from Richmond in Yorkshire, and near the side of the road which leads from Richmond to Askrigg. Its name is derived from a remarkable chase, the memory of which is preserved by the monuments spoken of in the second part of the following poem, which monuments do now exist as I have there described them' (133). Spoken in a new context and assimilated into English poetry, the elements of 'The Chase' no longer carry the same meaning which they had in the original version. In capturing and carefully modifying the fashionable German ballad narrative, the British Romantic poet has also lent it a new significance, re-routing it towards a different cultural destiny. We are presented with a paradigmatic instance of that ability to harness other people's thoughts and writings which Keats in one of his letters called 'the wordsworthian or egotistical sublime'.[15]

'Der Wilde Jäger' politicizes the chase motif. Bürger's German tale, characteristically, combines Christian moralism, Gothic supernaturalism, and anti-aristocratic propaganda in a highly explosive cocktail. The sin for which the huntsman is punished is not just the moral transgression of hunting on a Sunday in defiance of religious edict; it is also, and surely more importantly, the worldly crime of brazenly disrespecting and mistreating fellow members of society. 'The Chase' places considerable ideological emphasis on the substantial economic injury that the blue-blooded hunter inflicts on those lower-class countrymen and women who prowl the margins of the poem, eking out a meagre living in the barren countryside which the hunter treats as his private pleasure-ground. When a 'husbandman with toil embrown'd' appeals to the Wildgrave to '"Spare the poor's pittance [...] / Earn'd by the sweat these brows have pour'd / In scorching hour of fierce July"', his plea draws an unfeeling response from the patrician horseman: '"Away thou hound! So basely born, / Or dread the scourge's echoing blow"' (66–68, 73–74). Later the hunter encounters a grizzled shepherd who addresses him in equally pathetic terms: '"O spare, thou noble Baron, spare / These herds, a widow's little all, / These flocks, an orphan's fleecy care"' (98–100). But once again the Baron's reply is cold-hearted almost to the point of inhumanity, making it clear that he regards the rural poor as themselves little more than animals:

> 'Unmanner'd dog! To stop my sport
> Vain were thy cant and beggar whine,
> Though human spirits, of thy sort,
> Were tenants of these carrion kine!' (105–08).

For Bürger, the subject of the hunt carries the weight of social conflict, and it is used to deliver an impassioned indictment of the nobility's privilege and behaviour. The ghastly supernatural apparitions (the demonic huntsman and the dogs of hell) are above all the products of the poem's righteous indignation at the hunter's shocking behaviour towards his pauperized tenants. A violently retributive justice is administered ironically fitting the crime in question: having treated his social inferiors in a brutal way, the Wildgrave has become like a hunted beast. Thus, at the end of 'The Chase', Bürger has an 'awful voice of thunder' address the 'scourge of the poor' from above, telling him that he will 'Be chased for ever through the wood; / For ever roam the affrighted wild' (164, 167, 169–70). His 'fate' will thus serve to 'instruct the proud' that 'God's meanest creature is his child' (171–72). This militant attack on lordly tyranny would have been congenial to the young Wordsworth, the republican opposition poet who wrote (but did not publish) the inflammatory *Salisbury Plain* (1793–94), and ended it with a call for the 'Heroes of Truth' to 'uptear / Th'Oppressor dungeon from its deepest base' and 'rear / Resistless in your might the herculean mace / Of Reason'.[16] Having in the meantime moved from London to Racedown, later to Alfoxden, Germany, and then to his home at Grasmere, however, the Wordsworth of 1800 has renounced his youthful fervour for reform: he no longer sees himself as a writer of polemical prose or verse.[17] It is typical of Wordsworth in this period that he chooses not to pursue the German ballad's element of political protest and anti-aristocratic invective. In 'Hart-Leap Well', the 'knight' is initially shown shouting to his 'vassal', but this theme of class difference is not developed further in the poem, and on the whole Wordsworth rather does his best to mute the German ballad writer's levelling muse. In addition, Bürger loads his poem with dreadful supernatural events and diabolical showmanship, whereas Wordsworth consistently eschews the somewhat macabre sensationalism that dominates his precursor's poem, instead stressing realistic verisimilitude and convincing descriptive detail. There are no preternatural occurrences in 'Hart-Leap Well', and no fiendish horseman appears at the end to punish the irreverent hunter for his actions. Sir Walter, Wordsworth assures us, did not meet with a particularly violent or abrupt end; he lived a full life and 'died in the course of time' (93). The actual physical chase is over by the end of the third stanza, and Wordsworth is even reluctant to relate the violent details of the slaying of the animal: 'I will not stop to tell how far he fled', he says of the stag, 'Nor will I mention what death he died' (31–32). Throughout the poem, on the contrary, Wordsworth underscores the ordinary setting of the action. For example, he gives the dogs individual names (Brach, Swift, and Music), and he also provides a meticulous, almost naturalistic description of the place where the stag finds its last resting-place when Sir Walter finally catches up with it:

> And now, too happy for repose or rest,
> (Was never man in such a joyful case!)
> Sir Walter walked all round, north, south, and west,
> And gazed and gazed upon that darling place.
>
> And climbing up the hill (it was at least
> Nine roods of sheer ascent) Sir Walter found
> Three several hoof-marks which the hunted beast
> Had left imprinted on the verdant ground (45–52).

In a well-known letter to Coleridge written in December 1798, Wordsworth debates the strengths and weaknesses of Bürger's poetry, and in the course of this discussion he contrasts 'incident', which he places 'among the lowest allurements of poetry', with 'character', which he considers 'absolutely necessary' in 'poems descriptive of human nature'.[18] Two years later, in 'Hart-Leap Well', Wordsworth exploits the Bürgeresque motif of the hunt, but in so doing he also passes over the German pulp fiction's fashionable humanitarianism, political radicalism, and extravagant Gothic paraphernalia: he substitutes psychological inquiry ('character') for incensed protest and breathtaking spectacle ('incident'). Wordsworth clearly intends his poem as an educational rather than an incendiary tool; he circumscribes conventional literary topoi in order to ponder on the mysterious nature of the inner life, to extract a hitherto unsuspected core of human truth, and to ask penetrating questions about what makes man act in the way that he does.

The nature and scope of Wordsworth's reorganization of German ballad material become particularly clear in the poem's most central passage, the long apostrophe that the triumphant Sir Walter addresses to the dead hart:

> Sir Walter wiped his face and cried, 'Till now
> Such sight was never seen by living eyes:

Three leaps have borne him from this lofty brow,
Down to the very fountain where he lies.

'I'll build a pleasure-house upon this spot,
And a small arbour, made for rural joy;
'Twill be the traveller's shed, the pilgrim's cot,
A place of love for damsels that are coy.

'A cunning artist will I have to frame
A basin for that fountain in the dell;
And they who do make mention of the same
From this day forth, shall call it HART-LEAP WELL.

'And gallant brute! To make thy praises known,
Another monument shall here be raised;
Three several pillars, each a rough hewn stone,
And planted where thy hoofs the turf have grazed.

'And in the summer-time when days are long,
I will come here with my paramour;
And with the dancers, and the minstrel's song,
We will make merry in that pleasant bower.

'Till the foundations of the mountains fail
My mansion with its arbour shall endure —
The joy of them who till the fields of Swale,
And them who dwell among the woods of Ure!' (53–76).

In his influential study *The Art of the Lyrical Ballads*, Stephen M. Parrish characterizes what he considers Wordsworth's enriching and ennobling dialogue with the German, English and Scottish source-texts which triggered the ballad experiments from 1797 to 1800. In 'The Thorn', according to Parrish, Wordsworth 'made endurable' the theme of the supernatural curse that he had found in 'The Lass of Fair Wone' (1796), William Taylor's translation of Bürger's 'Des Pfarrers Tochter von Taubenhain': '"The Thorn" [...] becomes not a poem about a woman but a poem about a man (and a tree); not a tale of horror but a psychological study; not a ballad but a dramatic monologue' (112, 101). Mary Jacobus, similarly, both reveals and applauds the deepening and ripening of intellect that she locates within Wordsworth's poetry during these formative years: a trajectory which takes his art away from the ephemeral anti-war pamphlet literature of the 1790s; which unlocks his true genius for observing nature and analysing human passions; and which directs his vision 'beyond topical issues to the permanent themes of loss, change, and mortality' (159). The problem with these critical assessments is not that they are invalid, but rather that they are insufficiently historical, that they testify to Romantic criticism's 'uncritical absorption in Romanticism's own self-representations'.[19] Wordsworth, from a certain perspective, does make better poetry out of the German sensation ballads that occupy him during the late 1790s. But in this case, as so often in Romanticism, it is striking that aesthetic finish and trans-historical validity are purchased only at the cost of a thorough political domestication. Wordsworth gives with one hand and takes away with the other; what the poetry gains in dramatic power it simultaneously loses in specific social content. The transformation that occurs in the transition from 'The Chase' to 'Hart-Leap Well', then, is not only the process by which an obscure German ballad is enhanced and refined into visionary English poetry; it is also the process by which continental radicalism is defused and deflected, transmuted into food for virtuous thought.

'Hart-Leap Well' is certainly marked by greater emphasis on mental processes and individual characterization than 'The Chase', or any other Gothic ballad for that matter. Bürger's Wildgrave, finally, remains little more than a generically typecast bad aristocrat, but Wordsworth's Sir Walter is a fully realized character with a name, a voice, and a palpable being. Bürger barely mentions the question of the huntsman's feelings, but Wordsworth brings psychological forces into play and places the human mind in the foreground of his poem. The theme of the English ballad, in a certain sense, is still aristocratic cruelty, but Wordsworth wishes to sympathetically understand, not simply condemn the brutal huntsman for his outrageous actions. Sir Walter, Wordsworth points out, pursues the stag with remarkable energy and determination, even with brutality and more than a hint of sadistic pleasure. Among other things, we are informed that he has wasted three horses and exhausted all his dogs but one in the course of the daredevil 'rout'. At the same time, however, it seems clear that the noble huntsman's passion for the hunt does not proceed from anything like feelings of hatred or contempt for the animal. On the contrary, when the hunt is over Sir Walter refers to the hart as 'gallant brute'. Launching into his long address, the knight in rhetorically ostentatious terms decides to honour the 'glorious act' and memorialize the hunt by erecting a pleasure bower at the site where it took place (38).

Wordsworth, characteristically, is interested not so much in pursuing action *per se*, but rather in plumbing the depths of psychological motivation that underlies action. Sir Walter's claim to love and respect the brute is ironic, of course, given that he has just accomplished the cold-blooded murder of the animal whose memory he now purports to cherish so much. Wordsworth, consequently, throws Sir Walter's lofty speech into striking perspective, by adding the subsequent, brutally realistic lines: 'Then home he went, and left the Hart, stone-dead, / With breathless nostrils stretched above the spring' (77–78). Wordsworth's chase poem concerns primarily the contrast between what Sir Walter says and what he does. In Sir Walter's case, indeed, there seems to be an extremely complex, even a contradictory relationship between words and action, motivation and behaviour: he kills the stag in what he claims is an act of love. The human protagonist confesses that he has no reason to harm the animal, and yet he acts with callousness and aggression. This, however, is exactly the moral and psychological paradox (the conundrum of the human heart) which Wordsworth draws out from the German shock ballad, and which he explores throughout 'Hart-Leap Well'. Why is there, Wordsworth asks, such a disjunction between what people actually feel, what they say that they feel, and what they actually do?

III

No theory of British Romanticism can afford to ignore the creative, innovative, but rarely-acknowledged means by which the emergent Romantic writers salvaged for their own repertoires and interests a broad spectrum of outlandish and heterodox discourses generally deemed licentious, contagious, and fantasy-ridden. For Harold Bloom, 'every poem is a reading of another poem'.[20] According to Mikhail Bakhtin, 'a genre is always the same and yet not the same, always old and new simultaneously. Genre is reborn and renewed at every new stage in the development of literature and in every individual work of a given genre'.[21] Perhaps it is Gary Kelly who comes closest to describing the critical refashioning process which is discussed here. During the 'Romantic revolution in literature', Kelly claims in his essay 'The Limits of Genre and the Institution of Literature: Romanticism Between Fact and Fiction', writers of the young generation sought to elevate eccentric forms of oral and written material through artful mediations that had a specific, two-pronged effect: 'By raising non- or sub-literary discourses and genres, especially speech and prose fiction, to literary status, the new literature could subordinate popular discourses while exploiting them'.[22]

The German ballad Gothicism constitutes a major precursive paradigm for the poetry of *Lyrical Ballads*, one which is simultaneously exploited and exhausted, sublimated and rendered anew. Wordsworth reworks Germany's frenzied fiction into higher and finer products for the imagination, and ushers in the reign of Romantic poetry: 'genuine poetry', Wordsworth calls this supplementary mode of writing, 'in its nature well adapted to interest mankind permanently, and likewise important in the multiplicity and quality of its moral relations' (*Prose*, I, 58). Translated into Wordsworthian terminology, the hackneyed horror story's formulaic narrative is 're-functionalized', to use a Russian formalist term. Pressed into service for British Romanticism's aesthetic and ideological programme, Bürger's potent mixture of Jacobinical sentiment and Gothic sensationalism yields a subtle and searching study of man in his relation to the natural environment: no longer a tale of wonder or polemical broadside, but a 'lyrical ballad' tracing 'the fluxes and refluxes of the mind when agitated' (*Prose*, I, 126). In lieu of a social problem (why do the rich feel at liberty to treat the poor as if they were no better than livestock?) Wordsworth poses a question with psychological or philosophical overtones: how is it that man can have nothing but positive feelings and good intentions, yet can also continue to perform nothing but destructive actions, and even see one as the expression of the other?

It will not do, however, simply to celebrate or corroborate Wordsworth's borrowings from Bürger as the triumph of strong Romantic authorship. Romantic genre experiments, after all, are inherently ambiguous in their methods and effects.[23] In a certain way, the new genre remains always already predicated on, and perhaps even haunted by, the old genre which is simultaneously reconstructed and deconstructed, repeated as well as revised. The British Romantics engage in dialogic and dialectical interchanges with German romance, but critical recasting is not, and cannot be, straightforward denial. The continental ghost can only be laid to rest if it is first brought back to life, and this is both what is powerful and problematic about the antithetical method. Wordsworth's poetry of *Lyrical Ballads*, ultimately, is not without elements or passages which are troublesome because they seem so hauntingly, recalcitrantly Gothic or German. The very title of 'Hart-Leap Well', for example, refers to the poem's perhaps most disturbing detail, the preternaturally high final leap ('it was at least / Nine roods of sheer ascent,' the narrator tells us) that the hart made to get to the well (49–50).

Wordsworth's trans-textuality cuts both ways: 'Hart-Leap Well' could be read not just as a critique of, but also as a compliment to, Bürger — a celebratory borrowing which acknowledges the German writer's pre-eminence and even bestows upon him a kind of eternal life. Wordsworth takes up this problem, and tries to solve it, in the second part of 'Hart-Leap Well'. In this strange appendix to the poem, Wordsworth's narrator appears at the site of the now wasted pleasure bower to debate the meaning of the tale with the original narrator, a garrulous old shepherd. In the shepherd's view, the desolation of the spot where the edifice once stood is caused by the 'curse' of Sir Walter's chase:

> 'A jolly place', said he, 'in times of old!
> But something ails it now; the spot is cursed.
>
> 'You see these lifeless stumps of aspen wood —
> Some say that they are beeches, others elms —

> These were the bower; and here a mansion stood,
> The finest palace of a hundred realms!
>
> 'The arbour does its own condition tell;
> You see the stones, the fountain, and the stream,
> But as to the great lodge! you might as well
> Hunt half a day for a forgotten dream.
>
> 'There's neither dog nor heifer, horse nor sheep,
> Will wet his lips within that cup of stone;
> And oftentimes, when all are fast asleep,
> This water doth send forth a dolorous groan.
>
> 'Some say that here a murder has been done,
> And blood cries out for blood: but, for my part,
> I've guessed, when I've been sitting in the sun,
> That it was all for that unhappy Hart.
>
> 'What thoughts must through the creature's brain have passed!
> From the stone upon the summit of the steep
> Are but three bounds — and look, sir, at this last —
> Master! it has been a cruel leap (123-44).

The Wordsworthian narrator, however, is not prepared to simply let the shepherd have the last word. He proposes an alternative interpretation of the narrative, one which preserves the shepherd's fundamental terms and ideas, but which phrases them in a different way:

> 'Gray-headed shepherd, thou has spoken well;
> Small difference lies between thy creed and mine.
> This beast not unobserved by Nature fell;
> His death was mourned by sympathy divine.
>
> 'The Being, that is in the clouds and air,
> That is in the deep green leaves among the groves,
> Maintains a deep and reverential care
> For them the quiet creatures whom he loves.
>
> 'The pleasure-house is dust — behind, before,
> This is no common waste, no common gloom;

> But Nature, in due course of time, once more
> Shall here put on her beauty and her bloom.
>
> 'She leaves these objects to a slow decay,
> That we are, and have been, may be known;
> But, at the coming of the milder day,
> These monuments shall be overgrown (161–76).

This encounter can be read as Wordsworth's ventriloquistic defence of his own substitutive project: an attempt to distinguish between an immature, politicized supernaturalism and its civilized, humanized surrogate. At the same time, however, the narrator's highly equivocal definition of his own principles ('Small difference lies between thy creed and mine') intimates that *Lyrical Ballads* may be complexly situated *vis-à-vis* the German and Anglo-German magazine poetry which the collection habitually engages. According to the shepherd, the site of Sir Walter's building is 'cursed', haunted by the memory of aristocratic violence. Instead of a permanent curse complete with a groaning well, the poet-figure retorts, nature has imposed upon the landscape a 'slow decay' which will gradually wear itself out and give way to a renewed fruitfulness. Wordsworth's narrator no doubt intends his reading of the landscape as an enlightened and enlightening rejoinder to the shepherd's impatient and blatantly superstitious attitude. He corrects the shepherd much as Wordsworth corrects Bürger: there is no need for violent revolution or spectral punishment, for Sir Walter's life and times are slowly neutralized by the passing of time and the inevitable changes that nature brings in her own due course. Yet a certain scepticism also seems in order here. The poem's conclusion may also leave Wordsworth's reader somewhat mystified about the exact relation between the rustic's primitive Gothicism and the city-bred poet's sophisticated nature-religion. It is by no means entirely clear to what extent the narrator assents to the shepherd's 'well-spoken' words, and to what extent he repudiates them. The narrator gently reproves the shepherd's fondness for childish storytelling, but then he too peddles ghostly representations, and from a certain perspective the spectral agent which he invokes ('the Being, that is in the clouds and air') seems no less mysterious or disconcerting than the one which it replaces. In its own way, indeed, the pantheistic 'lesson' at which Wordsworth's narrator arrives seems as eerily otherworldly as anything contained in the shepherd's, or Bürger's, words (177). The persistence of romantic forms of supernaturalism, it seems, disturbs the poem's otherwise conventional ending. The language in which Wordsworth's speaker announces his new philosophical 'creed' retains its German accent.

Romantic anti-German literature cannot finally overcome the fact that it is belated, that it comes after, and in reaction to, that illicit and nonconformist genre which is both its main antagonist and its principal *raison d'être*. It is a familiar argument that Romantic poetry is crossed by a 'counter-spirit', but only a few critics have ventured to suspect that this presence should be a German spectre, a 'Petermännchen'.[24] The Romantic arch-nemesis Francis Jeffrey, for one, thought so. In his 1802 review of Robert Southey's *Thabala The Destroyer*, Jeffrey provocatively asserted that 'the author who is now before us belongs to a *sect* of poets' whose 'doctrines are of *German* origin, and have been derived from some of the great modern reformers in that country'.[25] William Hazlitt also expressed his view of Wordsworth's aesthetic and political impropriety. 'Mr. Wordsworth', Hazlitt wrote in his *Lectures on the English Poets* (1818),

> is at the head of what has been denominated the "Lake School of poetry" [...] [This school] had its origin in the French Revolution, or rather in those sentiments and opinions which produced that revolution, and which sentiments and opinions were directly imported into this country in translations from the German about that period.[26]

There is ample evidence suggesting that Wordsworth sensed the intrinsic ambivalence of his own genre-reforming endeavour, and that he continued to be nervous about his ballad-coloured poetry's hybrid, compromised, in-between position. Throughout the *Lyrical Ballads* years, Wordsworth was uncomfortably cognizant, as were his reviewers, that his own use of outworn German conventions threatened to destabilize his position as a serious British author, insofar as it placed him on the boundary between literary forms high and low, native and foreign, legitimate and illegitimate. Consequently, Wordsworth surrounds his own publications with critical statements in which he studiously disavows his poetry's cultural roots. At times, Wordsworth's anxious disclaimers of his German inheritance even find their way into the poetry of *Lyrical Ballads*. At the beginning of the second part of 'Hart-Leap Well', for instance, Wordsworth painstakingly divorces himself from those worthless poetasters who are misled by their excessive appetite for narrative accident and economic trade:

> The moving accident is not my trade:
> To freeze the blood I have no ready arts:
> 'Tis my delight, alone in summer shade,
> To pipe a simple song to thinking hearts (97–100).

On some level, Wordsworth clearly continues to feel, and perhaps rightly so, that the German terrible tale, despite his own refurbishing and overhauling manoeuvres, retains too much of a presence and is entirely too close for comfort in the poem. Why else should he labour so hard to outlaw some interpretations and canonize others? If there is no danger that boundaries have become blurred and proper names confused, why the urgency of establishing what is tale and what is a proto-lyric, which is Wordsworth and which is Bürger?

Wordsworth's borrowings from Bürger remain riddled with ambiguity: a source of both strength and weakness, a cause for anxiety as well as confidence. There is no clearer indication of Wordsworth's continuing nervousness about the Teutonic ghosts in the Romantic closet than the way in which he continually hedges his most radically experimental poetry with lengthy prefaces, copious footnotes, and fanciful secondary explanations. Wordsworth, it appears, was the victim, as well as the master, of his own Romantic transactions with German romance.

---

[1] J. M. S. Tompkins, *The Popular Novel in England, 1770–180* (Lincoln: University of Nebraska Press, 1961), p. 289.

[2] 'The Literati and Literature of Germany', *The Anti-Jacobin Review and Magazine*, 5 (1800), 568–80

(p. 568).

[3] Hannah More, *Strictures on the Modern System of Female Education* (London: T. Cadell and W. Davies, 1799), p. 41.

[4] William Preston, 'Reflections on the Peculiarities of Style and Manner in the late German Writers, whose Works have appeared in English; and on the Tendency of their Productions', *Edinburgh Magazine*, 20 (1802), 353–61, 406–08 (pp. 353–54); 21 (1802), 9–18, 89–96 (pp. 9, 18).

[5] David Simpson, *Romanticism, Nationalism, and the Revolt Against Theory* (Chicago: University of Chicago Press, 1993), p. 89.

[6]
> A multitude of causes unknown to former times are now acting with a combined force to blunt the discriminating powers of mind, and unfitting it for all voluntary exertion to reduce it to a state of almost savage torpor. The most effective of these causes are the great national events which are daily taking place, and the encreasing [sic] accumulation of men in cities, where the uniformity of their occupations produces a craving for extraordinary incident which the rapid communication of intelligence hourly gratifies. To this tendency of life and manners the literature and theatrical exhibitions of the country have conformed themselves. The invaluable works of our elder writers, I had almost said the works of Shakespear [sic] and Milton, are driven into neglect by frantic novels, sickly and stupid German Tragedies, and deluges of idle and extravagant stories in verse. When I think upon this degrading thirst after outrageous stimulation I am almost ashamed to have spoken of the feeble attempts with which I have endeavoured to counteract it.

Wordsworth, preface to *Lyrical Ballads* (1800), in *The Prose Works of William Wordsworth*, ed. by W. J. B. Owen and Jane W. Smyser, 3 vols (Oxford: Clarendon Press, 1974), I, 128–30. Coleridge echoes Wordsworth's notorious outburst in the 'Satyrane's Letters' section of *Biographia Literaria*, when he contrasts 'the Shakespearean drama' with 'the pantomimic tragedies and weeping comedies of Kotzebue and his imitators'. Coleridge, *Biographia Literaria*, ed. by W. J. Bate and James Engell, 2 vols (Princeton: Princeton University Press, 1983), II, 184–85.

[7] For critical work that bears on the Romantic writers' German translations, see especially Duncan M. Mennie, 'Sir Walter Scott's Unpublished Translations of German Plays', *Modern Language Review*, 33 (1938), 234–239; Joyce Crick, 'Some Editorial and Stylistic Observations on Coleridge's Translation of Schiller's *Wallenstein*', *Journal of the English Goethe Society*, 54 (1984), 37–75; Timothy Webb, *The Violet in the Crucible: Shelley and Translation* (Oxford: Clarendon Press, 1976); and Frederick Burwick, 'How to Translate a Waverley Novel: Sir Walter Scott, Willibald Alexis, and Thomas De Quincey', *The Wordsworth Circle*, 25 (1994), 93–100.

[8] The German presence in British Romantic literature is explored in F. W. Stokoe, *German Influence in the English Romantic Period, 1788–1818* (Cambridge: Cambridge University Press, 1926); Rosemary

Ashton, *The German Idea: Four English Writers and the Reception of German Thought, 1800–1860* (Cambridge: Cambridge University Press, 1980); Thomas McFarland, 'Field, Constellation, and Aesthetic Object', *New Literary History*, 13 (1982), 421–47; and Julie Carlson, '"Unsettled Territory": The Drama of English and German Romanticisms', *Modern Philology*, 88 (1990), 43–56. In her essay, Carlson trenchantly criticises what she sees as the widespread tendency among Romantic scholars 'to lose sight of the German connection [...] in that dramatic decade of the 1790s', and even to 'dismiss Germany as foreign to English sensibilities'. 'The conventional view', Carlson writes,

> that except for Coleridge, Crabb Robinson, and William Taylor, the British public conceived Germany as a *terra incognita* until the 1830s and 1840s is accurate only if we restrict severely what counts as "knowing" and "German letters". German literature, and particularly German plays, poured into England during the 1790s, and the fact and strength of the deluge [...] cry out for fuller investigation. Twelve years — especially *these* twelve years — should not be dismissed as such a "short time". Rather than viewing the nineties-mania for German drama as, at best, an oddity of the period, we might more profitably consider it another lesson in the oddity of our construction of romantic literary history.

In the face of Romantic criticism's consistent 'effacement of [...] English interest in German plays [...] from our literary histories', Carlson calls for 'some rethinking of Germany's role in England in the early decades of romanticism' (pp. 44–45).

[9] Walter Scott, *Waverley; or, 'Tis Sixty Years Since*, ed. by Andrew Hook (Harmondsworth: Penguin, 1972), p. 130.

[10] This metaphor is borrowed from Jerome Christensen, who interprets Romantic 'tincturing' as 'a change in direction and the conversion of some low impulse, such as the urge to vent one's rage, into a higher, purer emotion, instinct with its own pleasure'. See Christensen, 'The Color of Imagination and the Office of Romantic Criticism', *Coleridge's Theory of Imagination Today*, ed. by Christine Gallant (NY: AMS Press, 1989), p. 229.

[11] Information about the ballad revival in Britain and Germany can be found in Albert B. Friedman, *The Ballad Revival: Studies in the Influence of Popular on Sophisticated Poetry* (Chicago: University of Chicago Press, 1961) and Malcolm Laws, *The British Literary Ballad: A Study in Poetic Imitation* (Carbondale: Southern Illinois University Press, 1972). For specialised studies of 'Lenore', see O. F. Emerson, 'The Earliest English Translations of Bürger's "Lenore": A Study in English and German Romanticism', *Western Reserve University Bulletin*, 18 (1915), 1–120; and Evelyn B. Jolles, *G. A. Bürgers Ballade 'Lenore' in England* (Regensburg: Hans Carl, 1974).

[12] Walter Scott, *'The Chase' and 'William and Helen': Two Ballads from the German of Gottfried Augustus Bürger*, ed. by Jonathan Wordsworth (Oxford: Woodstock Press, 1991), p. 54. All quotations

from Bürger's poetry are taken from this facsimile reprint.

[13] See especially Geoffrey H. Hartman, 'False Themes and Gentle Minds', *Philological Quarterly*, 47 (1966), 55–68; Stephen M. Parrish, *The Art of the Lyrical Ballads* (Cambridge, MA: Harvard University Press, 1973), pp. 86–93; and Mary Jacobus, *Tradition and Experiment in Wordsworth's Lyrical Ballads (1798)* (Oxford: Clarendon Press, 1976), pp. 217–24.

[14] All quotations from Wordsworth's *Lyrical Ballads* are taken from William Wordsworth, *Lyrical Ballads and Other Poems*, ed. by James Butler and Karen Green (Ithaca: Cornell University Press, 1992), ll. 5–8.

[15] *The Letters of John Keats: A Selection*, ed. by Robert Gittings (Cambridge, MA: Harvard University Press, 1970), p. 157.

[16] In *The Salisbury Plain Poems of William Wordsworth*, ed. by Stephen C. Gill (Ithaca: Cornell University Press, 1975), ll. 541–42, 543–45. Wordsworth signed himself 'a Republican' in his 1793 *Letter to the Bishop of Llandaff* (*Prose*, I, 29).

[17] Kenneth R. Johnston provides evidence supporting his thesis that Wordsworth's 1795 move to Racedown was motivated by his disillusionment with an attempted career at radical journalism in London, and also by apprehensions about the Pitt government's recent sanctions against seditious and anti-ministerial activities. See 'Philanthropy or Treason? Wordsworth as "Active Partisan"', *Studies in Romanticism*, 25 (1986), 371–409. This essay's argument about Wordsworth's turn away from an explicitly political rhetoric to a more psychologically oriented discourse is also indebted to Nicholas Roe, *Wordsworth and Coleridge: The Radical Years* (Oxford: Clarendon Press, 1988); Alan Liu, *Wordsworth: The Sense of History* (Stanford: Stanford University Press, 1989); James K. Chandler, *Wordsworth's Second Nature: A Study of the Poetry and Politics* (Chicago: University of Chicago Press, 1984); and Paul D. Sheats, *The Making of Wordsworth's Poetry, 1785–1798* (Cambridge, MA: Harvard University Press, 1973).

[18]
> Bürger is one of those authors whose book I like to have in my hand, but when I have laid the book down I do not think about him. I remember a hurry of pleasure, but I have few distinct forms that people my mind, not any recollection of delicate or minute feelings which he has either communicated to me, or taught me to recognize. I do not perceive the presence of character in his personages [...] Take from Bürger's poems the incidents [...] and still much will remain; there will remain a manner of relating which is almost always spirited and lively, and stamped and peculiarized with genius. Still I do not find those higher beauties which can entitle him to the name of a great poet. I have read "Susan's Dream", and I agree with you that it is the most perfect and Shakesperian of his poems &c., &c. Bürger is the poet of the animal spirits. I love his "Tra ra la" dearly; but less of the horn and more of the lute — and far, far more of the pencil.

The Letters of William and Dorothy Wordsworth: The Early Years, 1787–1805, ed. by Ernest de Selincourt (Oxford: Clarendon Press, 1967), pp. 234–35.

[19] Jerome J. McGann, *The Romantic Ideology: A Critical Investigation* (Chicago: University of Chicago Press, 1983), p. 1.

[20] Harold Bloom, *The Anxiety of Influence: A Theory of Poetry* (NY: Oxford University Press, 1973), p. 93.

[21] Mikhail Bakhtin, *Problems in Dostoyevsky's Poetics*, trans. by Caryl Emerson (Minneapolis: University of Minnesota Press, 1984), p. 106.

[22] Gary Kelly, in 'The Limits of Genre and the Institutions of Literature: Romanticism between Fact and Fiction', in *Romantic Revolutions: Criticism and Theory*, ed. by Kenneth R. Johnston, Gilbert Chaitin, Karen Hanson, and Herbert Marks (Bloomington: Indiana University Press, 1990), p. 161.

[23] This point has been argued persuasively by Karen Swann in 'Public Transport: English Romantic Experiments in Sensation', *American Notes and Queries*, 6 (1993), 137–42.

[24] Wordsworth uses the term 'counter-spirit' in the third of his *Essays on Epitaphs*: 'Language, if it do not uphold, and feed, and leave in quiet, like the power of gravitation or the air we breathe, is a counter-spirit, unremittingly and noiselessly at work to derange, to subvert, to lay waste, to vitiate, and to dissolve' (*Prose*, II, 87).

[25] Francis Jeffrey, review of Robert Southey's *Thabala the Destroyer*, *Edinburgh Review*, 1 (October 1802), 63–83 (p. 63).

[26] William Hazlitt, *Lectures on the English Poets*, in *The Complete Works of William Hazlitt*, ed. by P. P. Howe, 6 vols (London: J. M. Dent, 1931), V, 161.

'A new species of humorous writing': Thomas Love Peacock and the Renegotiation of Genre

Jerome de Groot

The second of Thomas Love Peacock's novels, *Melincourt*, was published in 1817. An anonymous review in the *Literary Gazette* commented warmly on what it perceived to be Peacock's innovative style:

> Though with the most inveterate Novel-name that we have latterly found in a title-page, this work cannot well be denominated a novel. It contains little love, less incident, and, if we remember right, not even the common etiquette of a single swoon ... All the rest is conversation and character ... we should not ... be surprised if it led the way to a new species of humorous writing; which, taking the novel for its foundation, and the drama for its superstructure, should superadd to both the learning and inquiry of the essay ... the author of *Melincourt* can fairly be said to have advanced [the novel] another degree higher in the moral and intellectual scale of literature.[1]

In linking the novel to the generically destructive writings of the late 1790s the reviewer tacitly identifies *Melincourt*'s semi-radical heritage.[2] However, by simultaneously emphasizing the conscious literariness and intellectuality that comprise much of the tone of the novel the review situates *Melincourt* in something of a political middle ground: radicalized in form, but distinctly educated and bourgeois in aspiration. Such a reading draws the sting of any overtly politicized genre manipulation in *Melincourt*, suggesting that the novel confines the practices of its forebears by establishing them as standardized literary practice. The review concludes that through writing across genre the novelist has evolved a new genus of humour, grafting together different modes and forms, reanimating tropes by bringing them into interplay. As Frankenstein ruptures the established progenitive structure by reanimating dead limbs and organs, so Peacock's novels steal elements from literature's charnel houses to create anew, appropriating texts and tradition to a new and specific purpose. Peacock deconstructs to reconstruct: generic codes and literary expressions become part of an extensive intergeneric conversation. A literary magpie, he uses misquotation, allusion, footnote and generic manipulation to create polyvocal texts that highlight the fragmentation of social discourse and disrupt traditional notions of literary and social hegemony. As the *Literary Gazette* hints, the political nature of this generic manipulation is resolutely bourgeois and well-educated: his learned allusions (in French, Latin and Greek) are rarely translated; his footnotes assume a high level of classical and literary knowledge; and his lower class or peasant characters tend to be crudely drawn, speaking the dialect of Peacock's Dorset birthplace even when purportedly Welsh or Scottish.

Recent developments in genre theory have emphasized the 'necessity of seeing literary form as part of cultural and political context.'[3] New theories have been seen in contrast, and sometimes in conflict, with earlier concepts of generic transmission and inheritance, notably the arguments of Harold Bloom and Stuart Curran.[4] Contemporary critical thinking has rehistoricized genre, defining 'the site of a constant renegotiation between fixed canons and historical pressures, systems and individuals [...] [genre is] the privileged locus for a revaluation of cultural values.'(Rajan and Wright, 1). In a period in which inheritance as a concept was being assailed, engaging with literary inheritance had myriad implications, many of which have still not been fully considered.[5] Peacock addresses issues of inheritance throughout his works, from those of a practically financial nature, to ideas of family and genealogy considered through the orphaned and single-parented that are scattered throughout his novels. The majority of his Shakespearean references are to three plays themselves dominated by notions of inheritance: both parts of *Henry IV* and *Hamlet*. The novels themselves are literally literary orphans. Peacock wrote in the 1837 preface to volume LVII of Bentley's *Standard Novels* that 'I left them to speak for themselves; and I thought I might fitly preserve my own impersonality', signing himself 'the author of *Headlong Hall*'.[6] The novels have to work to create themselves: having no allegiance to paternalistic or legitimating authorship, they are dislocated creations of intertextuality.[7] Peacock uses his literary inheritance to subtle purpose, reconstructing and recreating. His novels make wide and varied reference to individual genres: Romance, Gothic fiction, drama, conversation novel, symposium, opera buffa, the burlesque novel, fashionable literature, comic romance, academic treatise, dictionaries and etymologies.[8] He quotes and paraphrases generic rules extensively. The majority of writing about Peacock has ignored the implications of this extensive use of genre; even Marilyn Butler, his best modern critic, has tended to underplay the importance of the intergeneric compound that creates the fabric of his texts. Generic codes are reordered and reused to produce anew. By disrupting the traditional hegemonies of literary and social discourses Peacock's politically motivated destratification of genre facilitates the 'emergence of a more democratized discursive field' (Rajan and Wright, 12).

The generic disruptions of the early nineteenth century disturbed traditionally conservative notions of a coherent progressive literary history in favour of a chaotic, revolutionary extension of the literary franchise. The expansion of the generic canon with the recovery of the ballad and the romance had led to a politicization of literary form. Peacock, however, is defiantly of his class. He satirizes and attacks the burgeoning educated middle class but it is also his frame of reference and audience. His works can be read in tandem with the writers of the new journals.[9] Jon Klancher has posited a link between the rise of an educated and politicized middle-class audience and the increase in periodical and journal writing: he contends that the 'protean collocation of styles' which characterized the journals meant that 'the readers gathered by this discourse [formed] not only an empirical audience, but a collective interpreter mapping out the cultural physiognomy of England.'[10] The emphasis on the readership's own construction of the text imposed by the essentially authorless nature of the journal is also an element of Peacock's purpose.[11] His novels empower the middle-classes, interjecting notes of subversion into the cant of power and authority; like the journal writers he understood that 'the middle-class audience must be redirected to become fully conscious of its hegemonic cultural power' (Klancher, 48). However, whilst sharing a similar purpose, Peacock was not well inclined towards the politics of the press: 'There is a common influence to which the periodical press is subservient: it has many ultras on the side of power, but none on the side of liberty.'[12] In 'An Essay on Fashionable Literature', an unpublished treatise prepared shortly after the first appearance of *Nightmare Abbey*, Peacock emphasized the important historicity of literature:

> As every age has its own character, manners, and amusements, which are influenced even in their lightest forms by the fundamental features of the time, the moral and political character of the age of nation may be read by an attentive observer even in its lightest literature, how remote soever *prima facie* from morals and politics (VIII, 265).

Peacock stresses that literary form and expression is inextricably embedded in the political and social moment. He follows this introductory comment by detailing at length the political bias of the new journals and attacking the imposed mindlessness of modern literary culture. The essay has a two-pronged argument: that journals and reviews are politically biased, and that their excessive influence creates a print culture that supports the inert structures of authority, both literary and political. He asserts that 'The success of a new work is made to depend, in a great measure, not on the degree of its intrinsic merit, but on the degree of interest the publisher may have with the periodical press', concluding that 'the best recommendation a work of fancy can have is that it should inculcate no opinions at all, but implicitly acquiesce in all the assumptions of wordly wisdom' (VIII, 272, 274).

In Peacock's first novel, *Headlong Hall* (1815), questioning and debate provide the novel's impetus and dynamic, establishing the Platonic Symposium structure that underpinned all his major works. He takes the conventions and forms of this classical paradigm and uses it to highlight the absurdities of modern life and opinion. As Plato parodies the styles and personal philosophies of his speakers, Peacock mocks and paraphrases contemporary opinion and thinking. The guests come together to meet a convivial host, to eat, drink, and philosophize. Socrates' questioning of received ideas and traditions was imitated in several treatises of the eighteenth century, including some that Peacock owned and was influenced by, notably John Horne Tooke's *Diversions of Purley*.[13] This text, purporting to be a Grammar, defined language in political terms: 'So CHURCH, for example, (*Dominicum*, aliquid) is an Adjective; and formerly a most wicked one; whose misinterpretation caused more slaughter and pillage of mankind than all the other cheats together.'[14] By considering the sources of language, Horne Tooke highlights the ideological mediation of expression, and considers the latent political nature of words.[15] His purpose and formal strategy is close to Peacock's: he uses Socratic dialogue to question and disrupt received ideas, utilizing classical allusion, pun, and extensive quotation. Horne Tooke derides Johnson as the defender of intellectual and lexicographical orthodoxy.[16] In *Headlong Hall*, Panscope, 'one of those who value an *authority* rather than a reason', uses Johnson as an authority by quoting a famous rebuttal which itself alludes to a classical sententiae:

SQUIRE HEADLONG. Bravo! Pass the bottle. The very best speech that ever was made.

MR. ESCOT. It has only the slight disadvantage of being unintelligible.

> MR. PANSCOPE. I am not obliged, sir, as Dr. Johnson observed on a similar occasion, to furnish you with an understanding.[17]

Here, as ever, Panscope's view of the world is created by others and he has no thought in his head other than those of his precious authorities. This excessive and unthinking reliance on past authority to mould one's world view is ridiculed as ludicrous. Such authority is weakened by the mischievous disruption of traditionally unquestioned structures; Johnson, symbolic of establishment piety, is cited to defend unintelligible cant. The malleability of literary or intellectual authority is satirized through this ability to be made to defend anything. Sceptical Socratic questioning and comment cut through the verbiage to discern the emptiness of such thought.[18]

The Diversions of Purley assumes an educated readership, yet an audience that needs to be disabused of some of their erroneous assumptions about discourse:

> **F.**
> Must we always be seeking after the meaning of words?
>
> **H.**
> Of important words we must, if we wish to avoid important error. The meaning of these words especially is of the greatest consequence to mankind; and seems to have been strangely neglected by those who have the most use of them (II, 3).

Peacock demonstrates this ambiguity of language; for him the building blocks of fiction were politicized because words themselves had an innately ideological function. His false etymologies and sharp puns remind the reader of the ambiguity inherent in language, of the need to correlate word and object. In his reclamation of classical paradigms and language he asserts the power of such texts to 'shake the dominion of venerable mystery and hoary imposture'(VIII, 272). His puns seem to be a paradigm for his use of language: the reinvigoration of a word, a double meaning, an ambiguous exactitude. Puns work by echoing and referring to manifold extraneous texts and contexts; these rough, untamed words are much like the primitive landscape of Headlong Hall that Mr Milestone wishes to force into conformity with his allegedly correct taste, to make 'perfectly *en règle*' (35).[19]

In the summer of 1820 Shelley wrote an epistolary poem to his friend Maria Gisborne, including in his musings on friendship short thumbnail sketches of those of his companions and acquaintances that she might meet in London. The lines on Peacock, 'an enemy to every shape of tyranny and superstitious imposture', are typically generous and perceptive, and have been earnestly quoted by critics of the novelist eager for biographical information.[20] Few have thought to emphasize quite how well they describe and reflect Peacock's qualities as a comic writer:

> — his fine wit
> Makes such a wound, the knife is lost in it;
> A strain too learned for a shallow age,
> Too wise for selfish bigots.[21]

Shelley pinpoints, with remarkable brevity, the soul of Peacock's wit. The multitude of meanings in the single word 'fine' suggest that Peacock and his writings are, among other things, 'consummate', 'finished', 'pure', 'highly accomplished', 'delicate', 'subtle' and 'refined' (*OED*). The fleeting echo of *Twelfth Night* ('strain', I. 1. 4), is as brilliant as it is brief: encompassing Peacock's sense of literary ancestry and the music so important to their friendship, it also highlights the awkward precision of Peacock's own allusive punning. Shakespearean quotation pervades Peacock's versions of modern discourse. The simplistic use of quotation in these polite societies, usually as a verbal flourish or to illustrate a point, highlights the bourgeois confining of what Peacock termed 'opinion'; such diluted use of a writer and his work smoothes any potentially disruptive element in the words. Shelley further recognizes that the mainspring of Peacock's style is the distinct combination of the 'fine' stiletto of Horatian precision and the robust Juvenalian broadsword. He goes so far as to replicate such a technique here, with the subtle aphoristic observations above following a burlesque caricature of Peacock as a 'cameleopard' (ll. 234–40). There is also a certain amount of playful needle in 'fine', with its sense of 'affectedly ornate or elegant', that combines with the pun on 'learned' to poke fun at Peacock's self-taught and often pedantic classicism. Shelley elucidates the importance to Peacock of classical or scholarly literature: he finds in it the ability to elevate one's thought above the 'shallow age' of Castlereagh and Pitt, the age of fashionable works that 'command attention without the labour of application, and amuse the idleness of fancy without disturbing the sleep of understanding' (VIII, 263). Peacock combined allusion and pun, as Shelley does in these lines, to create a sense of displacement, an implicit contrast between an idealized world of classical humanism and the corruption of early nineteenth-century England.[22] Peacock's punning is to a practical satirical and humorous purpose whether subtle, learned, or absurd. In *Nightmare Abbey* Mr Glowry's wife accepts his hand 'from interest' then discovers that 'she had mistaken the means for the end — that riches, rightly used, are instruments of happiness, but are not in themselves happiness.'[23] Scythrop's mother proves as fallible as her son in choosing her match. There are at least two pointed puns in this description of her motives: a quibble on 'interest', and the obvious 'mis/taken'. The final sententious comment reflects Peacock's thoughts on the true value of words; in themselves of no intrinsic value if not backed up by action or physical consequence. Mr Flosky reads a novel entitled *Devilman*, a punning inversion of the title to Godwin's 'Gothic' work *Mandeville*, of which the opening of *Nightmare Abbey* is also a physical parody or humorous inversion. Punning or humour-descriptive names are a common method of Peacocks, inferring as they do much about the abstract sociological background of a character. Scythrop's name is both a pun, in the echo of misan*throp*e, and a neologism, from the Greek 'of sad or gloomy countenance'. It is also a reference to his genes, taken, as it is, 'from the name of a maternal ancestor, who had hanged himself one rainy day in a fit of *tædium vitæ*' (5). These descriptive names connect with Peacock's delight in false etymologies and genealogies in emphasizing the inherited nature of language and signification: 'which names, by the way, appear to be female diminutives of the Italian words *danaro contante*, signifying *ready money*, and genteely hinting to all fashionable Strephons, the only terms on which the *commodity* so denominated would be disposed of'.[24]

Peacock differs from his eighteenth-century forebears such as Horne-Tooke because *Headlong Hall* is not only a Socratic dialogue, but part of a semi-dramatized text, complete with stage directions and breaks for song. For instance, Panscope only gets involved in the above debate after '(*suddenly emerging from a deep reverie*)' (35).[25] The fabric of the novel itself is a stylistic montage of different genres and modes of expression: drama melds with philosophical treatise, allusion interrupts paraphrase, and conversational novel interrogates romantic subplot. The novels make both explicit and tacit acknowledgement of a wide and varied range of sources. They subscribe to an innovatory, interventionist, European comic tradition, taking elements of their form from Aristophanic drama, Petronian satire, Rabelaisian narrative, Cervantes's novels, and Voltaire's prose satires. They have components of burlesque and farce: consider the destructive consequences of Scythrop's precipitous pursuit of Marionetta (*Nightmare Abbey*, 36–37), or of Mr Escot attending breakfast with Cadwaller's skull under his arm.[26] The novels owe much to the new Italian operas of Mozart and Rossini.[27] Indeed, when *Maid Marian* was adapted as an opera in 1822, critics quickly pointed out how apt such a transaction was: 'The book is rich in the requirements for a drama: plot, incident, strongly marked characters, and good language, with poetry of considerable merit.'[28] Peacock takes generic components and adds several unpredictable elements. There is a Tacitean compression of description which can be identified in the technique of tagging figures by characteristic movements: Mr Asterias slowly perlustrates, and Scythrop habitually stalks. Peacock imposes Sternian authorial interruption and ironized distance: '*Mr Flosky suddenly stopped: he found himself unintentionally trespassing within the limits of common sense*' (*Nightmare Abbey*,

102). His immediate source was the generic conversation novel, primary models of which were to be found in the works of Robert Bage and Thomas Amory.[29] Peacock adds Voltairean satire and dialogue, mock-symposium, romance, narrative, parody and allusion. Part of the structural layering of Peacock's texts is the number of intertwining narratives or narrative structures. *Melincourt*, for example, utilizes a straightforward third person descriptive voice, dramaturgic stage directions, lengthy footnotes, and inserted narratives such as Fax's retelling of Desmond's story. Peacock's self-reflexive and distanced narrative style, which only occasionally gives the reader a minor ironized handhold, emphasizes the conscious literariness of his novels and the purposeful stylized manipulation of genre.

As Marilyn Butler has shown, figures in Peacock's novel are not specific targets, but compounds of various positions and arguments.[30] In *Headlong Hall*, the central figures of Escot and Foster, as well as the supporting characters, echo and paraphrase several different contemporary philosophers. They take subtly complex positions, and satirize modern intellectual life in general rather than attacking any particular figure. Peacock uses paraphrase throughout his work to different effects. It is a method of appropriating words and ideas and reusing them, ultimately reconstructing their significance and refocusing their meaning. Often sources are footnoted, which emphasizes the false nature of their reappraisal and the insecurity of the text. In *Nightmare Abbey* sections of *Childe Harold's Pilgrimage* are integrated into the text of Mr Cypress's speeches and then identified in detailed footnotes. The words are not consciously or typographically quoted, and the tension between their status as speech and the footnote giving their source is used to highlight the absurdity and pompous impracticality of the poetry: 'There is no worth nor beauty but in the mind's idea. Love sows the wind and reaps the whirlwind' (160).[31] The character of Cypress is not specifically Byron but one who has learnt from Byron his dissipated and uncommitted way of life; once again, the subtext confirms that writers should attempt to change society.[32] The ambiguous status of the words themselves throws the text into confusion. Elsewhere allusion and quotation is supported by typographic or spoken protocols; here the words are appropriated by the speaker and then reappropriated by the narrator/author. The imposition of such a spectral metanarrative or refracting of context confuses the already fragmentary text. Peacock's appropriation of others' words questions the ownership of text, highlighting a fragmentation of discourse. He attacks traditional notions of authorship and textual creation by introducing unresolved ambiguities and multiple levels of narration.

This textual misquotation pervades Peacock's novels. The majority of his allusive quotations are misquotations or neologistic conjunctions, echoes and reverberations. The epigram to *Nightmare Abbey*, for instance, is a conjunction of two pieces of Butler.[33] Elsewhere in the novel Scythrop melodramatically announces, "'the world is a stage, and my direction is *exit*'", pompously misquoting to dramatic and unintentionally comic effect (207). "'Feelings and poetical images are equally out of place in a calm philosophical view of human society'" argues the realist Fax in *Melincourt*, deciding "'Some must marry, that the world may be peopled'" (141). This echoes, maybe wittingly, Benedick's decision to woo Beatrice in *Much Ado About Nothing* (II. 3. 229–30). Fax is not strictly citing a poetical image but a practical aphorism used by a dramatic poet, an action that itself comments on Fax's literary status within a dialogue. Society is unwittingly mapped by a polyvocal model, utilizing literary inheritance to create new ideals and positions. This specific use of Shakesperean reference also illustrates the nature of the text as a tessellation of fragmented voices, an intergenetic creation of generic and literary inheritance. Fax only uses a short sentiment from Shakespeare, and wrenches it out of context to serve his own purpose. Peacock's recontextualization and reclamation of others' words is not simply linguistic but conceptually generic and philosophical. Often quotation is not erroneous but something that could be called constructive requotation, a reanimation of others' words. Peacock highlights that all quotation is misquotation by virtue of the change in context undergone by appropriated text. He recreates texts to present a collage of conflicting voices. He appropriates others' words by quotation, misquotation, recreation, allusion and echo. In general, established earlier patterns of allusive literary reference had presupposed a dynastic and hierarchical order; Peacock transposes such concerns.[34] The allusions that characterize his novels emphasize communality. The allusions highlight the monomania of the characters and the isolation of the settings by reaching outwards, refracting and relocating the text. Misquotation or requotation is in itself a creative recreation.[35]

Peacock defined the ideal style of satiric and comic writing as 'an exquisite and fastidious selection of words', emphasizing the didactic function of such work with examples from Juvenal, Horace, and Aristophanes (VIII, 6). This is a denotation that informs all of his own comic writing, a calculated precision and deft management of climax which he took from Gibbon and Menippean satire. His works display a fascination with verbosity and tightly controlled absurdity. Furthermore, for the more destructive purposes of the satire, 'the jokes are instinct (as working jokes have to be) with the manner of what they contemn.'[36] Peacock's texts are delicately self-conscious: his ironized style and sharp technique mean that his manipulations of genre must be seen to be intentional and therefore political in nature. The stance of the narrator distances the author from the text. Peacock was well aware of the political investments of novel writing and genre experiment. It has been generally argued that his *Four Ages of Poetry* berates Shelley's notion that change could be achieved through poetry.[37] In this anonymously published treatise, Peacock complained about the inertia of modern literature, especially poetry. He argued that Coleridge's 'new principle' and theory of poetics ended up creating

> a modern-antique compound of frippery and barbarism, in which the puling sentimentality of the present time is grafted on the misrepresented

ruggedness of the past into a heterogeneous congeries of unamalgamating manners, sufficient to impose on the common readers of poetry (VIII, 20).

This passive marriage of tradition and everyday normality incensed Peacock: to his mind, contemporary poetry failed in its duty to society by seeking to simply add a modern flavour to standard tropes and genres. He considered that a true thinker and innovative artist 'from the materials of useful knowledge thus collected, appreciated, and arranged, forms new combinations that impress the stamp of their power and utility on the real business of life' (VIII, 21). The only way that society and literature can progress is by this politicized recreation and regeneration; in contrast, what Peacock sees happening is simply conjunction, tacit compliance with literary tradition rather than innovative dialogue and questioning.[38] He was generally frustrated by the naive idealism of his intellectual set; he notes in his *Memoirs of Shelley*: 'I was sometimes irreverent enough to laugh at the fervour with which opinions utterly unconducive to any practical result were battled for as matters of the highest importance to the well-being of mankind' (VIII, 265).

In Peacock's three major novels of the 1810s, middle-class intellectuals make the majority of the discursive running. Squire Headlong was originally 'seized with a violent passion to be thought a philosopher and a man of taste' (*Headlong Hall*, 10). He goes about this by surrounding himself with figures that can think for him (Escot, Foster and Jenkinson, with an extensive supporting cast). The aristocratic elements in the novels, the Squires, Lords, and Knights, exhibit a fascination with intellectual discourse that does not imply their own involvement or decision either way; they often play the role of amused chairman, passing around the bottle when things get too heated. Peacock's novels attack the complacency of the middle classes: he sketches the bourgeois Mr Dross as 'a tun of a man, with the soul of a hazel nut [...] Mrs Dross aspired to be *somebody*, aped the nobility' (*Melincourt*, 173). Peacock emphasizes the need for the political self-determination of the middle classes, rather than their present subservience to the values and institutions of the corrupted aristocracy. In his review of Moore's

Letters and Journals of Byron, Peacock outlines the specious literary culture that supports this imposed servility:

> we have given very fair specimens of the matter and manner of the volume before us, and an outline of its contents, with such remarks as were imperiously demanded from us by our sense of the moral duty of exhibiting to our readers the real scope and purpose of a series of shallow sophisms and false assumptions, wrapped up in a bundle of metaphors, put forth with a specious semblance of reason and liberality, and directed to the single end of upholding all abuses and delusions by which the aristocracy profit (IX, 139).

The aristocracy, by inviting, flattering, and seducing the bourgeois intellectuals with food and wine, ghettoize their thought. These philosophers are brought to alienated and isolated castles in which to discuss and talk but ultimately to shift their thinking and talking further away from having any practical effect. Another *bon viveur* and collector of intellectuals, Squire Crotchet, opines,

> The sentimental against the rational, the intuitive against the inductive, the ornamental against the useful, the intense against the tranquil, the romantic against the classical; these are great and interesting controversies, which I should like, before I die, to see satisfactorily settled.[39]

Crotchet's words expose the rigid falsity of his approach to philosophical and intellectual discussion. Peacock's conception of debate is that it is a means toward understanding the truth of the world in its complex variety, and as such this satisfactory closure is not an option. The novels are set in far off places and halls: Nightmare Abbey is connected to 'the civilized world' by causeways raised above the fens that are sometimes treacherous (63); Melincourt Castle is built on 'a rock, of which three sides were perpendicular, and which was only accessible on the fourth by a narrow ledge, forming a natural bridge over a tremendous chasm' (103). They are safe, cosy places: Anthelia Melincourt is only harassed when she leaves the castle and enters the outside world. Mr Glowry's Abbey is 'a venerable family mansion, in a highly picturesque state of semi-dilapidation', the perfect pathetic fallacy for Scythrop's melancholic dark romantic musings; whilst the pun on 'state' widens the focus and suggests that the excessive self-obsession of the characters is somehow symptomatic of a national malaise (*Nightmare Abbey*, 1). In *Melincourt*, taking the characters out of the protective arena of their fragile experience exposes them to the cruel realities of the mundane world, in which their charity and intellectualizing can do little to help. Sir Oran-Hauton provides the most germane comment on the proceedings by refusing the chair offered him at the election and causing a huge fight; once again the ape's natural inclinations provide an honourable reaction to the corruption endemic in civilized society. As the protagonists wander around Gullgudgeon, Forester considers,

> '*We ought now to be convinced, if not before,*' said Mr Forester, '*that what Plato has said is strictly true, that there will be no end of human misery till governors*; and that all the evils which this country suffers, and, I fear, will suffer, to a much greater extent, [...] *are owing to the want of philosophy and true political wisdom in our rulers*' (271–72).[40]

Forester does try to do things, but his little community is a mockery of a pastoral utopia, and is a legacy or inheritance from his father anyway. Peacock glancingly criticizes the idealistic community-building of his literary contemporaries. Forester's lapse into explanatory quotation is a reflex protection from the naked misery created by human greed, and highlights the exclusion of these privileged thinkers from the experiences of the poor. Forester's more practical henchman Fax watches the proceedings with a faintly amused air, as for him they are 'an illustration [...] of the old maxim *experience teaching wisdom*' (272). He gives out a little fairly meaningless charity, the form of which highlights the inherent worthlessness of mere paper: 'get gold and silver for it as soon as you can' he advises (272). Even Forester's wandering is part of a proscribed progress imposed upon him by the imperious aristocrat Anthelia Melincourt, 'mistress of herself and of ten thousand a year' (103).

By 1831 Peacock could happily mock what he portrayed as the increasingly desperate attempts of the established classes to defend their physical and cultural space. At the close of *Crotchet Castle* the drinkers are besieged by rural rioters demanding arms and food. The party in Chainmail Hall fights off the 'rabble rout' with 'the old iron' whilst discussing in a civilized manner the cause and nature of their grievances (252). This confrontation with the reality they had been debating ends in 'an inglorious victory: but it deserves a devil and a bowl of punch', and the scene culminates with the guests dropping 'one by one into sweet forgetfulness' (253, 258). The battle at Chainmail Hall is a more profound version of the protagonists in *Melincourt* visiting Gullgudgeon: the outside world is now not visited and seen at arm's length, but has begun to infringe without warning, necessitating violent purgation. Peacock highlights the literal novelty of this experience by coining a new expression: Reverend Dr Folliot warns that the enemy 'may still be excubant' (254).[41] The conflict is then followed with an ironic quasi-pastoral finale including the singing of sentimental lyrics, drinking, dancing, and wedding bells. The actors in a pastoral drama are normally the kind of farm workers the introverted dinner guests have just dispatched into the darkness. The party defending the Hall comprises of the Church, the landed gentry, and the army; the peasants are fought off by the old established elite using archaic medieval weapons thus demonstrating arcane privilege desperately attempting to wield its power. The publication of *Crotchet Castle* occasioned reviews which attacked Peacock as

> one of the people marked with the indelible d----d cockney blot; [...] an ignorant, stupid, poor devil, who has no fun, little learning, no facility, no *easiness* — a fellow whose style of thought is in the very contrary vein of the Rabelaisian — a dolt who thinks that the daily nonsense vomited up by all sorts of asses is something of moment.[42]

It is illustrative that Peacock is indicted somewhat archaically with the others of the Cockney School, an implication that he is involved in what was perceived as a politically motivated popularization of art.[43] By enfranchising 'daily nonsense' he evinces his ignorance and betrays what little learning he has. The reviewer reacts to Peacock's style and artistic purpose rather than his actual political stance, sensing the innate political inferences that may be drawn from such a consideration. Peacock gives everyone their voice, pejoratively or not, and this is part of his political engagement: a review of *Melincourt* judged that 'the writer errs [...] in giving his own powerful diction to the female characters', in itself a vindication of the polyvocal nature of Peacock's text.[44] In his own novels Peacock strove to provide an alternative to the entrenched values of the literary establishment. His novels work to a purpose, their technical sharpness and heavily ironized style indicating a creative self-consciousness: Peacock emphasizes the role of the author in creating socially and politically aware work.[45] The relationship between literature and society is dialectical, and Peacock passionately argues that literature can change society, that novels or fictions should 'embody opinion in a very cogent and powerful form' (IX, 251). He self-consciously uses the historicity of literature to attempt to change the thinking of his readership. By referring to contemporary thought, genre, and event, yet manipulating and changing their contexts, he establishes the uncertainty of discourse and understanding, the innate ambiguity of expression. He emphasizes the need to refract generical inheritance through contemporary political thinking, to progress by using the old to make the new.

---

[1] *Literary Gazette*, 22 March 1817, quoted in Bill Read, *The Critical Reputation of Thomas Love Peacock with an Annotated Enumerative Bibliography* (unpublished D.Phil., University of Boston, 1959), p. 150. Ellipses and square brackets are editorial additions by Read.

[2] For which see Judith Thompson, '"A Voice in the Representation": John Thelwall and the Enfranchisement of Literature', in *Romanticism, History, and the Possibilities of Genre: Reforming Literature 1789–1837*, ed. by Tillotama Rajan and Julia M. Wright (Cambridge: Cambridge University Press, 1998), pp. 122–49.

[3] Anne Janowitz, 'Women, hacks, and rebels', *Times Literary Supplement*, 18 Sept 1998, p. 14.

[4] In particular Bloom's *The Anxiety of Influence: A Theory of Poetry*, 2nd edn. (NY and Oxford: Oxford University Press, 1997) and Curran's *Poetic Form and British Romanticism* (NY and Oxford: Oxford University Press, 1986).

[5] 'The complex and highly political process of negotiation, appropriation, and subversion by which Romantic writers engaged with their generic inheritance in an age which faced widespread challenges to all inherited institutions remains to be fully explored,' Thompson, p. 123.

[6] Preface reprinted in *The Novels of Thomas Love Peacock*, ed. by David Garnett, 2 vols (London: Rupert Hart-Davis, 1963), I, xxi.

[7] Speculation in contemporary literary Reviews as to whom the anonymous novelist might be ranged from the outlandish (*The British Critic*, October 1817, identified Sir William Drummond) to the flattering (*The Monthly Review*, February 1819, suggested Walter Scott). Quoted in Read, pp. 153, 154.

[8] It is not my purpose to add to the considerable scholarship that has amassed identifying Peacock's sources and borrowings, for which see especially Marilyn Butler, *Peacock Displayed: A Satirist in his Context* (London: Routledge and Kegan Paul, 1979) and Jean-Jacques Mayoux, *Un Epicurien Anglais: Thomas Love Peacock* (Paris: Libraire Nizet et Bastard, 1933).

[9] Peacock was generally well reviewed in the Journals although his irreverent clerical figures caused some worry, and his formal innovations were often disregarded: 'This little work has not a high character as a novel' considered the *North American Review* in September 1817. Quoted in Read, p. 152.

[10] Jon Klancher, *The Making of English Reading Audiences, 1790–1852* (Wisconsin and London: University of Wisconsin Press, 1987), p. 51.

[11] For a discussion of discarnate meanings in Romantic texts and their relationship to an audience, see Tilottama Rajan, *The Supplement of Reading: Figures of Understanding in Romantic Theory and Practice* (Ithaca, NY and London: Cornell University Press, 1990).

[12] All references to Peacock's non-fictional works are from the *Halliford Edition of the Works of Thomas Love Peacock*, ed. by H. F. B. Brett-Smith and C. E. Jones, 10 vols (London and NY: Constable and Gabriel Wells, 1924-34). 'An Essay on Fashionable Literature', *Halliford*, VIII, 273. Consider also the self-absorbed characters of the Journal writers Gall, Treacle, Nightshade and Mac Laurel in *Headlong Hall*.

[13] *Sale Catalogues of Libraries of Eminent Persons*, ed. by A. N. L. Munby (London: Mansell with Sotheby Parke-Bernet Publications, 1971), p. 189. For a discussion of the influence of Horne Tooke on Peacock see Butler, pp. 38–39; or James Mulvihill, 'A Tookean Presence in Peacock's *Melincourt*', *English Studies*, 67.3 (1986), 216–20.

[14] John Horne-Tooke, *ΕΠΕΑ ΠΤΕΡΟΕΝΤΑ, Or the Diversions of Purley*, ed. by Richard Taylor, 2 vols (London: Thomas Tegg; Dublin: John Cumming; Glasgow: R. Griffin, 1829), II, 21.

[15] For a discussion of Horne Tooke's ideas in relation to eighteenth-century theories of language and Romantic responses to his work, see William Keach, 'Romanticism and Language', in *The Cambridge Companion to British Romanticism*, ed. by Stuart Curran (Cambridge: Cambridge University Press, 1993), pp. 95-120.

[16] 'But seek no further for intelligence in that quarter, where nothing but fraud, and cant, and folly is to be found — misleading, mischievous folly; because it has a sham appearance of labour, learning, and piety', *Diversions of Purley*, II, 5-6. Peacock also owned Johnson's *Dictionary* (Munby, p. 175).

[17] *Headlong Hall and Gryll Grange* ed. by Michael Baron and Michael Slater (Oxford: Oxford University Press, 1987), p. 33. All references to *Headlong Hall* are from this edition.

[18] For other political uses of Plato in this period, particularly concerning Shelley and Peacock's use of Socratic dialogue, see Jennifer Wallace, 'Shelley, Plato, and the Political Imagination', in *Platonism and the English Imagination*, ed. by Anna Baldwin and Sarah Hutton (Cambridge: Cambridge University Press, 1994), pp. 229-42.

[19] Raymond Williams considers the political nature of such arranged landscapes as 'the expression of control and of command', in *The Country and the City* (London: Chatto and Windus, 1973), pp. 153-55.

[20] Shelley on Peacock, quoted from Ian Jack, *English Literature 1815-1832* (Oxford: Clarendon Press, 1963), p. 215.

[21] Percy Bysshe Shelley, 'Letter to Maria Gisborne', ll. 240-43, in *Shelley's Poetry and Prose*, ed. by Donald H. Reiman and Sharon B. Powers (London: W. W. Norton, 1977).

[22] A technique intended 'to recall his readers to a lucid, judicious perspective on the activities of the modern world', Bryan Burns, 'The Classicism of Peacock's *Gryll Grange*', *Keats-Shelley Memorial Bulletin*, 36 (1985), 89-102 (p. 90).

[23] *Nightmare Abbey* (1818), quoted from the unedited facsimile edition (Oxford: Woodstock Books, 1992), p. 2. All references to the novel are from this edition.

[24] *Melincourt* (1817) quoted from *The Novels of Thomas Love Peacock*, I, 108. All references to the novel are from this edition.

[25] Conversely, Peacock's plays have very minimal stage-directions; the directions in the novels are more in the vein of dramatic commentaries, but they still serve a theatrical function.

[26] 'Several of the ladies shrieked at the sight of the skull; and Miss Tenorina, starting up in great hast and terror, caused the subversion of a cup of chocolate, [...] [Markmaduke Milestone],

catching for support at the first thing that came in his way, which happened unluckily to be the corner of the table-cloth, drew it instantaneously with him to the floor, involving plates, cups and saucers, in one promiscuous ruin', *Headlong Hall*, p. 60.

[27] For the influence of the opera on Peacock's work and political thinking see Howard Mills, 'The Dirty Boots of the Bourgeoisie: Peacock on Music', *Keats-Shelley Memorial Bulletin*, 36 (1985), 77–88.

[28] *Literary Chronicle*, December 1822, quoted in Read, p. 156.

[29] Bage's *Mount Henreth* (1781), Amory's *Life and Adventures of John Buncle* (1755) and Graves's *Columella* (1776) are all examples of novels constructed by dialogue for the most part. Peacock followed these novelists in using such a technique to social or political ends; see Carl Dawson, *His Fine Wit: A Study of Thomas Love Peacock* (London: Routledge and Kegan Paul, 1970), p. 169.

[30] For instance, see the discussion of *Headlong Hall* in Butler, pp. 40–42.

[31] This is an echoing misquotation of *Childe Harold's Pilgrimage*, Canto IV.

[32] Cypress's actions ape those of Byron: 'Sir, I have quarreled with my wife; and a man who has quarreled with his wife is absolved from all duty to his country. I have written an ode to tell the people as much, and they may take it as they list' p. 154.

[33] Constructed and erroneously quoted from *Hudibras* (Part I, Canto 1, ll. 505–06 and Part III, Canto 3, ll. 19–20) and *Upon the Weakness and Misery of Man* (ll. 70–71 and ll. 229–31). The epigram to *Headlong Hall* follows a similar pattern by misquoting Swift's 'Cadenus and Vanessa' ll. 730–33 (substituting 'All Philosophers' for 'Or, as philosophers').

[34] See, for example, Christopher Ricks, 'Dryden: Poet as Heir', *Studies in the Eighteenth-Century*, 3 (1976), 229–40.

[35] See, for example, M. J. C. Hodgart, 'Misquotation as Re-creation', *Essays in Criticism*, 3 (1953), 28–38.

[36] Eric Griffiths, 'Wittgenstein and the Comedy of Errors', in *English Comedy*, ed. by Michael Cordner, John Kerrigan and Peter Holland (Cambridge: Cambridge University Press, 1994), pp. 288–316 (p. 289).

[37] 'In Thomas Love Peacock's critique of Shelley, Peacock senses this contradiction between Shelley's political hopes and his attempt to use poetry to accomplish them', William G. Rowland Jnr, *Literature and the Marketplace: Romantic Writers and their Audiences in Great Britain and the United States* (Lincoln and London: University of Nebraska Press, 1996), p. 99. See also Jean Hall, 'The Divine and the Dispassionate Selves: Shelley's *Defence* and Peacock's *The Four Ages of Poetry*', *Keats-Shelley Journal*, 91 (1992), 139–63.

[38] 'But he did not want to think that the pressure of historical necessity entirely deprived the individual artist of free will, or absolved him from responsibility for his productions, or made the question of value in art meaningless', Butler, p. 49.

[39] *Crotchet Castle* (1831) quoted from *Nightmare Abbey and Crotchet Castle*, ed. by Raymond Wright (Harmondsworth: Penguin, 1986), p. 139.

[40] The italics are in the original text, quoting Lord Monboddo.

[41] This is the first recorded usage (*OED*).

[42] *Fraser's Magazine*, August 1831, quoted in Read, p. 164.

[43] For a discussion of this group see Nicholas Roe, *John Keats and the Culture of Dissent* (NY and Oxford: Clarendon Press, 1997).

[44] *Monthly Review*, July 1817, quoted in Read, p. 151.

[45] '[A]mong the most illustrious authors of comic fiction are some of the most illustrious specimens of political honesty and heroic self-devotion. We are here speaking, however, solely of the authors of the highest order of comic fiction — that which limits itself, in the exposure of abuses, to turning up into full daylight their intrinsic absurdities' (IX, 261).

Shelley's 'The Triumph of Life':
A Resistance to History and the Art of Forgetting

Rieko Suzuki

Shelley's last major poetic work, 'The Triumph of Life', has been praised by many critics, from T. S. Eliot to Harold Bloom, for its poetic excellence and philosophical integrity.[1] The poem has attracted much critical attention, and the diverse interpretations it has invited demonstrate that the meaning of the poem is open to debate. This, however, has as much to do with the highly precarious status of the text as it does with the richness of the poem. The holograph of the 'Triumph', which is marked by extensive cancellations and gaps, reveals that it was still a work in progress. Shelley left numerous uncancelled passages and incoherent lines, and it is left to editors to make of the manuscript a readable text.[2] Mary Shelley was the first to undertake this mammoth task; her efforts materialized in the text published in the 1824, and the revised text of the 1839 edition of Shelley's poetry.[3] Although her pioneering edition did much to pave the way for the succeeding editors, it also played a manipulative role in shaping the way in which the poem should be read. Lisa Vargo argues that while Mary Shelley's contribution to the 'editing' of the text has been well acknowledged, her 'versioning' has never been brought to critical attention.[4] Donald H. Reiman, who coined the term 'versioning', explains:

> In the case where the basic problem facing the scholar or reader involves two or more radically differing versions that exhibit quite distinct ideologies, aesthetic perspectives, or rhetorical strategies, the alternative to 'editing', as conventionally understood, maybe what I call 'versioning'.[5]

Even with the efforts of recent editors such as Reiman and G. M. Matthews, the text continues to have a plural status, and 'versioning' is an essential feature of the textual history of the 'Triumph'.

Vargo argues that Mary Shelley's version carries out, as it were, a mission inspired by both private and public motives. Editing Shelley's works functioned as a personal communication with her dead husband, and chacteristic of her editions in terms of the 'Triumph' is her keenness to obliterate the role Jane Williams played in her husband's creative activity during and prior to his composition of the 'Triumph'.[6] None of the three lyrics embedded in the manuscript of the 'Triumph' were published in the 1824 edition, only one in the 1839 edition, and the other lyrics concerning Jane Williams were either excluded likewise, or included without any mention of her name in the title.[7] Her public motives, on the other hand, are detectable in her 'Note on Poems Written in 1822' (1839): her text is meant to serve as a commemoration of the poet, for his aspiration and spiritual struggle, which was not duly recognized in his own time.[8]

If we consider Mary Shelley's text and the holograph manuscript as two contesting texts, her 'versioning' begins to take on a clear shape. The dialectical struggle dramatized in the poem, which is visually presented in the manuscript, is undermined in Mary Shelley's text. This is partly due to the solidification of the body text, but not wholly unrelated to the mission, as Vargo puts it, which characterizes her version. Mary Shelley, for example, ignores the embedded lyrics in the 'Triumph' by simply stating that there is a 'chasm [...] in the MS. which is impossible to fill up' (1824, 85). The gaps in the manuscript which are occupied by lyrics to or about Jane Williams deserve particular attention. Reiman argues that 'To Jane: The Keen Stars Were Twinkling' was probably composed 'during the time that Shelley found himself struggling to continue with the 'Triumph'', which means before Shelley attempted to fill the chasm after line 280 (*BSM*, I, 341). There is an intriguing connection between what the manuscript visually tells us (that Shelley's inability to continue the "Triumph" led him to compose the lyric) and the two opposing impulses, the historical imperative and the resistance to it, that govern the poem. The obstructive role the lyrics play in the manuscript is easily transferable to the obstruction that is dramatized in the poem, and the intertextuality of the lyrics and the 'Triumph' seems closely related to the thematic preoccupation of the poem.

The poem opens with a sunrise which is dramatized as a brusque movement replacing darkness and giving life to all forms of nature:

> Swift as a spirit hastening to his task
>   Of glory and of good, the Sun sprang forth
> Rejoicing in his splendour, and the mask
>
> Of darkness fell from the awakened Earth (1–4).[9]

It is not, however, a simple transition from night to day, but involves a further act of unmasking which complicates what night and day represent. While all other forms of nature are in awe of the sun and act accordingly, we are told that the speaker alone is unable to participate in this worship:

> But I, whom thoughts which must remain untold
>
>   Had kept as wakeful as the stars that gem
>   The cone of night (21–23).

The narrator's resistance to the sun's narcissistic indulgence in its own glory and the speaker's implied masking require further context to make sense of what the opening symbolizes. For this, the four discarded openings in the manuscript (designated as 'A' to 'D' by G. M. Matthews, according to the generally accepted order in which they were composed) prove instructive: they are less allegorical and more descriptive in their depiction of the sunrise scene.[10] The fact that they were not cancelled by Shelley signifies their worth as sources of the final version. For example, the discarded openings 'B' and 'C' suggest that Shelley associated darkness with 'The gloom / Of daily life' and 'the death of daily life', and attempted to depict the sun and earth in terms of father and daughter, or male and female, relationships (2–3, 20). The speaker's inability to sympathize with the sun denotes that he is faced with an obstacle which prevents him from engaging in basic human activities, and his unwillingness to conform invites him to experience the trance which is the body text of the 'Triumph'. The first ten lines of 'To Jane: The Keen Stars Were Twinkling' sit together with discarded opening 'B', and although this is probably accidental, the physical state of the manuscript illustrates the contrast which Shelley brings to the fore in the opening.[11] The silenced speaker, who is unwilling to embrace day in the 'Triumph', finds a correlative voice in 'To Jane' which is actively engaged in the opposite of day: the speaker in the lyric is preoccupied with Jane's singing which is in harmony with the twinkling stars and the moonlight, 'revealing / A tone / Of some world far from ours' (20–22).[12] The narrator's detachment from the acting sun in the opening can be complemented by the speaker of the lyric who is embracing the inaction associated with night:

> The stars will awaken,
> Though the moon sleep a full hour later,
> Tonight;
> No leaf will be shaken
> While the dews of your melody scatter
> Delight (13–18).

The pageant that the narrator witnesses in his trance, unlike the sun 'Of glory and of good', is problematic for various reasons. It includes the ignorant mass whose actions are characterized by their blindness:

> none seemed to know
> Whither he went, or whence he came, or why
> He made one of the multitude (47–49).

They are nonetheless compelled to move onwards by a force which eventually drives over them. With the ignorant crowd are the historical figures who, despite their power, 'neglected to know themselves' (212). Their actions, motivated by self-interest, perpetuate power devoid of good, which consequently chains them to the Car of Life. It was precisely when Shelley was working on this grim view of history that he left the 'Triumph' to compose the lyric 'To Jane'. The disheartened narrator in the 'Triumph' neither acts to respond to the 'good' sun nor to the mischievous pageant, but remains inert. The lyric dramatizes this state of inaction in which the speaker is temporarily exempted from the burden of the real world. But as Rousseau, who acting as the narrator's guide in the 'Triumph', urges him to 'follow thou, and from spectator turn / Actor or victim in this wretchedness' (305–06), the pressure for the narrator to act intensifies.

The manuscript visually portrays the dynamics of the textual interplay between the 'Triumph' and the lyrics. One vector is the linear development of time which forcefully runs through the 'Triumph' in the form of a list of historical precursors whom the narrator is expected to learn from and eventually exceed. The other vector is the vertical axis, as it were, which explores the momentary space in which physicality is exploited. Although this is most apparent in Rousseau's encounter with the 'shape all light', the embedded lyrics, 'To Jane' and 'Lines Written in the Bay of Lerici', also testify to Shelley's preoccupation with temporality and physicality (352). These two contesting forces make the manuscript an engaging text and aid the structural integrity of the poem. In Mary

Shelley's version, on the other hand, the dialectical struggle which the poem poses is weakened by her complete exclusion of the lyrics. In short, Mary Shelley's text diverges from the manuscript, which engages in the negotiation of the historical and the temporal, by confining the dynamics of the 'Triumph' to a historical narrative of the past and its linear continuation.

Forgetfulness features as an essential act in the 'Triumph'; it is a means to fill the lacuna between past and present.[13] The narrator, in the opening of the poem, is overcome by a sensation which enables him to regain the past:

> I knew
>
> That I had felt the freshness of that dawn,
> Bathed in the same cold dew my brow and hair
> And sate as thus upon that slope of lawn (33–36).

The narrator is able to restore his past experience because he has forgotten the rest. In other words, securing what belongs at once to the past and present depends on the fine balance of remembering and forgetting. The trance, which initiates the narrator's vision of the pageant, is described as an indeterminate state between being awake and asleep; in a similar way, the narrator's knowledge plays on the border of remembering and forgetting. This act of forgetting, which allows one's authentic personal experience to come to the fore, is further reiterated by Rousseau in his autobiographical account. Rousseau first finds himself under an 'oblivious spell' which has the universal effect of curing pain (331):

> A sleeping mother then would dream not of
>
> The only child who died upon her breast
> At eventide, a king would mourn no more
> The crown of which his brow was dispossest (321–24).

This pain, resulting from experience, pervades the 'Triumph': both the narrator and Rousseau are weary of their historical past. They are unable to embrace history wholeheartedly because, unlike the sun of 'glory and good' which gives life, it does the exact opposite: it leads men to erroneous actions and eventually seizes their lives. The only agent which is capable of restoring the life of creativity from the devastating effects of historical impetus is forgetfulness. By obliterating the past, one is able to exercise full creativity, just as the sun of the poem's opening does.

Forgetfulness in Rousseau's account also proves to be a highly erotic state. His harmonious relationship with nature culminates in his encounter with the 'shape' who epitomizes sensuality:

> the fierce splendour
> Fell from her as she moved under the mass
>
> Of the deep cavern, and with palms so tender
>   Their tread broke not the mirror of its billow,
>   Glided along the river, and did bend her
>
> Head under the dark boughs, till like a willow
> Her fair hair swept the bosom of the stream
> That whispered with delight to be their pillow (359–66).

Rousseau's height of oblivion is accompanied by eroticism of a kind that will only exert its power as long as one can avert self-awareness. The 'shape', therefore, becomes destroyed when Rousseau is overcome by his own historical impetus: 'Shew whence I came, and where I am, and why' (398). The impossibility of sustaining oblivion in history is the crux of the poem.

Shelley's repeated deviation from the historical narrative of the 'Triumph' in order to pursue the lyrics anticipates Rousseau's delineation of the historical burden and of forgetfulness. 'To Jane' dramatizes the speaker's indulgence in temporality relieved from the historical past; what is more, Jane's singing is given utmost importance for its ability to 'reveal' what otherwise would remain unknown. That 'singing' and not 'thinking' is given prior significance is instructive: it suggests that forgetting is not an intellectual activity. Rousseau *found* himself asleep under the 'oblivious spell' because one cannot *will* to forget. For Shelley then, Jane Williams figures as a means of forgetting and of sustaining the momentary space outside historical continuity.

Reiman argues that 'Lines Written in the Bay of Lerici' was composed before the end of Rousseau's autobiographical account, and his speculation suggests that its composition took place either before, or coincidentally with, the description of the 'shape all light'.[14] While 'To Jane' anticipates the scene of the 'shape', in 'Lines', the motifs become almost identical. Since we do not know the exact creative process of the 'Triumph' and the lyrics, it is perhaps dangerous to over-estimate the intertextuality of these texts; however, it is worth noting that they resonate in particular places where the 'Triumph' requires reinforcement. The resistance to history governing 'To Jane' recurs with an intensity both in 'Lines' and in the scene with the 'shape'. This development, furthermore, seems to be caused by the pressure which Rousseau puts on the narrator to act.

The 'Lines Written in the Bay of Lerici' begins by dramatizing the present as a momentary space outside historical continuity: 'The past and future were forgot / As they had been, and would be, not' (31–32). The image of the albatross provides a powerful moment of inaction:

> an albatross asleep,
> Balanced on her wings of light,
> Hovered in the purple light (10–12).[15]

It is again the physical 'tone' and 'touch' which make the speaker indulge in the present (16, 22). But as such moment of inaction cannot be sustained for long, the hovering motion of the albatross becomes replaced by the gliding movement of the vessels (37). As the progression of time is introduced, the speaker's momentary state of oblivion gives way to reflection:

> Too happy, they whose pleasure sought

> Extinguishes all sense and thought
> Of the regret that pleasure [ ]
> Destroying life alone not peace (55–58).

The speaker is unable to act because his action must be accompanied by forgetfulness, which can only be prolonged for a short time before it becomes consumed by his reflectiveness.

Nietzsche argues in 'On the Uses and Disadvantages of History for Life' that forgetting and remembering 'are necessary in equal measure for the health of an individual, of a people and of a culture'.[16] He particularly stresses the significance of *forgetting*, by which one is able to 'draw a horizon around itself' so that the past will not overshadow the present potential. This 'untimely meditation' turns out to be timely in Shelley's age of gloom: in the 'Triumph', the focal point in history is post-Napoleonic Europe, and the despair from which liberals, such as Shelley, suffered due to the failure of the French Revolution, sets the tone of the poem. The 'Triumph' is perfectly in accordance with Nietzsche's use of history in that it seeks the right balance between forgetting and remembering.

If we substitute 'forgetting' and 'remembering' with the 'unhistorical' and 'historical', as Nietzsche does, the 'Triumph' can be related to a wider social issue initiated by Rousseau's *Essay on the Origin of Languages*.[17] Rousseau's contention is that language makes us social animals: the development of language has enabled our lives, which were initially immediate and therefore fully contained in the present, to become reflective and thus governed by historical consciousness. It is a curious fact that Rousseau's text has never received the consideration it deserves in relation to the 'Triumph' while critical attention has focused on his more autobiographical works, such as *Julie*, *Confessions* and *Reveries*. This is also telling of the way in which the 'Triumph' has been read in the past as a biographical poem.[18] Even Paul de Man's celebrated essay, 'Shelley Disfigured' which reads the 'Triumph' as concerned with language, passes over Rousseau's *Essay*.

The *Essay's* preoccupation with origins, immediacy, and reflectiveness is equally detectable in the 'Triumph'. Rousseau goes to great lengths to describe how language emerged from passion, and how the first language of passion eventually developed into the language of reason (245–46). Rousseau wants us to believe that, in the beginning, language was fully contained in the present: it was poetic, expressive, and above all, immediate (246–47). The transition from speech to writing is seen as a tragic event by Rousseau; his myth centres around the loss of authenticity which first characterized speech (253–54). In this seemingly continuous development from speech to writing is the unaccountability of the origin of the latter: if writing emerged from speech, then it must mean that speech already possessed the seeds of writing. Faced with this dilemma, Rousseau is compelled to admit that writing already existed at the birth of language. In order to preserve the authentic origin of passion, Rousseau then devises a secondary origin of need, by introducing a geographical polarization of south and north: the people of the south, who came first, spoke out of passion, whereas the people of the north spoke out of need (259–76). But one polarization only leads to another, and Rousseau's inability to map out a single origin becomes the target of Derrida's deconstructive reading.[19]

Rousseau's myth is effectively subverted in the 'Triumph'. Despite the poem's obsession with origins, it is at the same time devoid of them. The historical narrative of the 'Triumph' does not begin with the dawn of civilization, but with what I have called the brusque sunrise, and the only human voice within the scene is already burdened with history. The narrator, for example, asks Rousseau 'Whence camest thou and whither goes thou? / How did thy course begin', but he is not able to get a satisfactory answer from him (296–97). Rousseau's origin is described as an awakening to slumber; this is not an origin as such, but a transitory state in which he remembers his forgetfulness. In his narrative, Rousseau, likewise asks the 'shape' in vain about his own origin. Rousseau's wish, as purported in the *Essay*, to see the historical development of language as originating in passion and eventually being taken over by reason is not sustained in the 'Triumph': rather, the poem suggests that passion and reason are coexistent and that it is the proportion in which they come to interact that determines history.

Shelley's repeated deviation from the historical narrative of the 'Triumph' to pursue the lyrics provide a good example of the negotiation between passion and reason, the unhistorical and the historical. The lyrics begin when he breaks away from the 'Triumph' in order to indulge in the immediate present, and ends by anticipating the historical burden of the 'Triumph'. 'To Jane', for all her power of singing which, like *nepenthe*, enables the speaker to remain oblivious, ends by prefiguring the real world of language, sun and reason:

> Sing again, with your dear voice revealing
>   A tone
>   Of some world far from ours,
> Where music and moonlight and feeling
>   Are one (20–24).

By imagining a holistic harmony, the speaker wishes to transcend the real world of positing powers: the sun, in the opening lines of the 'Triumph', imposes itself on night, and language stamps out the 'fire' of thoughts as we shall see later. But its very construct proves that such an attempt is a temporary displacement from the real world. In 'Lines', the unhistorical moment in which 'The past and future were forgot' becomes overwhelmed by the historical burden which prevents the speaker from acting. This dialectical struggle between passion and reason reaches a pivotal point in the 'Triumph' with the entrance of the 'shape all light' (31).

The story of Rousseau's origin and his encounter with the 'shape' is one of the most enigmatic instances in the 'Triumph', and has been the subject of various interpretations. It is possible to read this scene as an account of Rousseau's life as it is delineated in his semi-autobiographical works. It moves from either his birth or awakening to self-consciousness, to the culmination of his imagination in *Julie*, to his disillusionment with the real world as described in the *Confessions*, followed by the solitude of the *Reveries*.[20] Convincing as this may be on a literal level, it limits the scope for a more symbolic account of the issues which the poem raises: the narrator's obsession with origins and his forgetfulness are repeated in Rousseau's experience so that we read the scene as a repeated cycle rather than a separate linear progression. Rousseau's *Essay* is instrumental in interpreting this scene because it engages with origins and the development from passion to reason in his argument on language. Although de Man confirms the presence of Rousseau's *Essay* when he reads this scene as a thematization of language, his argument excludes the *Essay* possibly because de Man does not focus on the historicity of texts. It is Rousseau's rebuttal, of the belief advocated by the *philosophes* that language originated in reason, which Shelley takes on board. However, in the 'Triumph' Shelley expounds the myth put forward by Rousseau and subverts it.

In Rousseau's autobiographical account, he finds himself in a pre-linguistic world of forgetfulness. One of the first things he notices is that:

>   all the place
> Was filled with many sounds woven into one
> Oblivious melody, confusing sense (339–41).

From this auditory background emerges the 'shape all light'. The 'shape' is an optical illusion created by the sun's reflection on the water and on Rousseau's eyes. Rousseau is as much responsible for this 'shape' as the sun is; the 'shape' symbolizes the work of both ideal and human creativity, and this is why 'imagination' finds its fullest expression in this scene. Rousseau explains that imagination is another human attribute which was awakened by the birth of language. Although imagination is innate to man, Rousseau argues, it can only be exercised with the aid of language, for without it, the common humanity that exists amongst men would be unknown (260–61). The sensuous description of the 'shape' denotes the passion of her beholder; however, Rousseau's passion is not for a real woman but for his imaginary creation. As Rousseau tells us in the *Confessions*, he withdrew to the world of imagination because reality could not supply him with objects worth his passion.[21] It is this passion, evoked by his own imagination, that invites critics like Reiman to identify the 'shape' with Julie.[22] The 'oblivious melody' of nature becomes language, because without it, imagination would not have had a role to play (341). Rousseau elaborates on how song and speech were both products of passion and on how their first expression was an imitation of natural sounds (276, 280–81). The 'oblivious melody' of nature finds its expression in the language of passion, and its birth awakens imagination.

If language, even in its germinal stage as the expression of passion, already contains the seed of the language of reason, it is because language operates under the economy of time. Its regulative development, based on logic, coincides with the progress of history. In the 'Triumph', the 'shape' acts out the inevitable: what first appears as the expression of passion gives way to that of reason, by means of which passion is destroyed. The 'shape' invites Rousseau not to indulge in the present, but to ask her about his historical past.

The movement of the 'shape' at first seems congenial with the natural surroundings: she 'Glided along the river' 'with palms so tender / Their tread broke not the mirror of its billow' (363, 361–62). The pivotal point occurs when 'her feet ever to the ceaseless song / [...] moved in a measure new' (375, 377). De Man reads the scene as both the birth of language and the divorce between the semantic aspect of language and its material and literal aspects (113–14). 'Measure', not only accentuates the regulative movement of the 'shape', but also denotes language as articulated sound distinct from 'the ceaseless song / Of leaves and winds and waves and birds and bees' (375–76). De Man takes this further by saying that measure is 'any principle of linguistic organization, not only as rhyme and metre but as any syntactical or grammatical scansion', and therefore, the feet of the 'shape' can be interpreted, not just as the poetic metre of the 'Triumph', but as 'any principle of signification' (113). It is, therefore, the feet of the 'shape' as well as the 'feet' of language which destroys Rousseau's thoughts:

> All that was seemed as if it had been not,
>   As if the gazer's mind was strewn beneath
> Her feet like embers, and she, thought by thought,

Trampled its fires into the dust of death (385–88).

The thought loses its 'fire' by becoming subservient to the linguistic structure. To pose the problem differently, the regulative development of language destroys the passion which initially evoked it. Language, which has become rational and controlled, assumes time, which has become regulated and retrospective. Thus the unhistorical moment, which passion governed, gives way to a heightened sense of history: 'Shew whence I came, and where I am, and why' (398).

The historical process which Rousseau delineates in the *Essay*, from the immediacy of language to its reflectiveness, repeatedly occurs in the 'Triumph'. This process is not historical in the way that Rousseau understood it, but historical in the sense that history *is* process. Permanent state in oblivion would make us similar to animals and children, and pure reflectiveness of the past would prevent us from acting at all. As Nietzsche argues, forgetting is essential to action, and the proportion in which one forgets and remembers is the determining factor of history. In this sense, Edward Duffy's contention that the 'Triumph' 'is an effort to represent life as most fundamentally a kinetic energy' succinctly summarizes the view that the poem is about a struggle of two opposing impulses.[23]

Interpreting Rousseau's fragmented answer of 'Happy those for whom the fold / Of' which terminates the poem, Reiman suggests that Shelley may have had the 'folding-star' in mind, on the basis that, in his later poetic career, Shelley 'more and more frequently drew upon the Christian metaphor of the sheepfold as a symbol of Christian salvation, usually using in conjunction the symbol of Venus as

Hesperus, the evening star' (1965, 83). Whether Rousseau's answer would have initiated a more positive development as Reiman argues, or tailed off due to Shelley's inability to continue the poem as Duffy conjectures, we will never know (Reiman 1965, 84; Duffy, 151). What we can say, however, is that Rousseau's involvement with 'Life' ends with the bitter self-awareness that he cannot be one of those whom he characterizes as being 'happy'. Happiness is an oblivious state, and Rousseau, who could neither escape the 'car' as the 'sacred few' did, nor completely 'tame' his spirit to it, is left with the realization that he had enough self-awareness to detach himself from the 'car' in the beginning, but not enough to avoid its devastating effects. Rousseau's double perspective, that he is at once able to overlook history but is also implicated in it, is the cause of the weariness which eventually compels him to drop out of the pageant.

That both the 'Lines' and the 'Triumph' end truncated in indeterminacy is indicative of the process which is crucial to the poem. The narrator of the 'Triumph' is in a double limbo: because of his ambivalent status, it is not clear to the reader whether he can reassume his initial vantage point as a seer, or whether he is already implicated in the pageant through his associations with Rousseau. In the latter case, he is compelled by Rousseau to 'turn / Actor or victim in this wretchedness'. Rousseau drops out of the pageant in despair at the knowledge that one is either 'actor' or 'victim' in the pageant. He is a fallen hero who had the potential to join the 'sacred few', but instead, 'plunged' and 'bared' himself to the devastating effects of the car (467):

> if the spark with which Heaven lit my spirit
> Earth had with purer nutriment supplied
>
> Corruption would not now thus much inherit
> Of what was once Rousseau (201–04).

Despite his fall, Rousseau is still able to free himself from the car because he 'was overcome / By my own heart alone' (240–41). Rousseau's comprehensive account of his past signifies that it is now the narrator's turn to find out what his involvement with life entails.

It is intriguing that Mary Shelley's version ends with the narrator's question, 'Then what is Life?' Her intention may have been to leave it unanswered rather than to end with Rousseau's anguished reply that suggests a return to where the poem begins: in the same way that Rousseau cannot be one of 'those' whom he describes as being 'happy', the narrator is unable to partake in the solar-worship and thereby be unmasked. The 'Triumph' repeats the process by which the inability to act defeats the will to act. The embedded lyrics function as a way of forgetting which makes action possible, but the oblivious state soon gives way to reflection, preventing action from taking place. This process is what the 'Triumph' is about under the guise of a historical narrative. Mary Shelley's version, however, is keen to emphasize the linear development of the poem by transforming this process into Shelley's growing aspiration. But this is greatly misleading: the poem is not about aspirations, it is about confronting reality and making a way through it. It is also a most persuasive account of how we, as participators in both unhistorical and historical existence, engage in history. The poem is a work in progress, not just because it was left that way, but because it dramatizes the process of becoming. Mary Shelley's version recasts that into a record of what the poet stood for, and his continuing aspiration by careful obliteration of the future potential present in the holograph. Her version may be convincing as testament to what the poem is partly about, but it does not tell the whole truth.

---

[1] Eliot hailed it as 'Shelley's greatest tribute to Dante', and 'also the greatest' of his poems, 'Talk on Dante', *Adelphi*, 27 (1951), 110–12 (p. 110); Harold Bloom similarly praised its achievement of perfection: 'The full implications latent in all of Shelley's mythmaking are finally visualized in this account of the triumph of life over almost all human integrity and aspiration', see *Shelley's Mythmaking* (Ithaca, NY: Cornell University Press, 1969), p. 221.

² There are four extant discarded openings, and four passages that were later either cancelled or superseded. See Appendix B and C, *Bodleian Shelley Manuscripts*, 22 vols (NY: Garland, 1986–97), I. All future references will be referred to as *BSM*.

A good example of incoherent lines occurs at ll. 281–82, for which Reiman and G. M. Matthews provide different readings: see *Shelley's Poetry and Prose*, ed. by Donald H. Reiman and Sharon B. Powers, 3rd edn (NY: Norton, 1982), p. 463; '"The Triumph of Life": A New Text', *Studia Neophilologica*, 32 (1960), 271–309 (p. 294).

For the textual history of the 'Triumph', see Donald H. Reiman, *Shelley's 'The Triumph of Life': A Critical Study Based on a Text Newly Edited from the Bodleian Manuscript* (Urbana: University of Illinois Press, 1965; repr. NY: Octagon Books, 1979), pp. 119–28.

³ *Posthumous Poems of Percy Bysshe Shelley* (London: John and Henry L. Hunt, 1824) and *The Poetical Works of Percy Bysshe Shelley* (London: Edward Moxon, 1839).

⁴ 'Close your Eyes and Think of Shelley: Versioning Mary Shelley's *Triumph of Life*', in *Evaluating Shelley*, ed. by Timothy Clark and Jerold E. Hogle (Edinburgh: Edinburgh University Press, 1996), pp. 215–24.

⁵ *Romantic Texts and Contexts* (Columbia: University of Missouri Press, 1987), p. 169.

⁶ Reiman suggests that Shelley began the 'Triumph' in late May, working intermittently until his death on 1 July 1822 (*BSM*, I, 343). While the embedded lyrics were composed simultaneously with the 'Triumph', the other lyrics concerning Jane Williams were composed during the period between January 1822 and Shelley's composition of the 'Triumph'.

⁷ 'Lines Written in the Bay of Lerici' was first published by Richard Garnett in *Macmillan's Magazine*, 6 (June 1862), 122–23. 'To Jane: The Keen Stars Were Twinkling' was first published in part (ll. 7–24) by Thomas Medwin, entitled 'An Ariette for Music. To a Lady Singing to her Accompaniment on the Guitar' in *The Athenæum* (17 November 1832); this was reprinted by Mary Shelley in *Poetical Works*, 1st edn (1839) and republished in full under the title 'To —' in the 2nd edn. The lines beginning 'The hours are flying' or 'Time is flying' were first published in part by Neville Rogers in *Shelley at Work: A Critical Inquiry* (Oxford: Clarendon Press, 1956), p. 288, and were printed in a different version by Sir John Shelley-Rolls and Roger Ingpen in *Verse and Prose from the Manuscripts of Percy Bysshe Shelley* (London: privately printed, 1934). I have followed Reiman's classification and designation which he adopts in *BSM*, I, for these embedded lyrics.

'The Magnetic Lady to her Patient' was first published by Medwin in *The Athenæum* (11 August 1832), and was included in *The Poetical Works* (1839). 'To Jane: the Invitation' and 'To

Jane: the Recollection' were published together in their original single form as 'The Pine Forest of the Cascine near Pisa' by Mary Shelley in *Posthumous Poems*. 'With a Guitar. To Jane' was published by Medwin in *The Athenæum* (20 October 1832), and was included in *The Poetical Works* as 'With a Guitar'.

[8] Mary Shelley's 'Note' gives a fatalistic account of Shelley's untimely death which is bound up with his composition of the 'Triumph': 'much of the *Triumph of Life* was written as he sailed or weltered on that sea which was soon to engulf him', 'He has, as it now seems, almost anticipated his own destiny', *Shelley: Poetical Works*, ed. by Thomas Hutchinson, corrected by G. M. Matthews, (Oxford and NY: Oxford University Press, 1971), pp. 677, 679.

[9] All citations from the 'Triumph', unless stated otherwise, are from *Shelley's Poetry and Prose*.

[10] G. M. Matthews, 'The "Triumph of Life" Apocrypha', *TLS*, (5 August 1960), 503.

[11] 'Because Shelley had long since rejected *TLDO* [Triumph of Life Discarded Opening] 'B' [. . .] we must assume that he had the entire sheaf of loose papers before him as he wrote, including both blank sheets and rejected passages' (*BSM*, I, 341).

[12] All citations from 'To Jane', unless stated otherwise, are from *Shelley's Poetry and Prose*.

[13] See Paul de Man's 'Shelley Disfigured', in *The Rhetoric of Romanticism* (NY: Columbia University Press, 1984), pp. 93–123 (pp. 104–05). J. Hillis Miller, likewise, argues for the significance of forgetting in 'Shelley's "The Triumph of Life"', included in *Shelley*, ed. by Michael O'Neill, Longman Critical Reader (London: Longman, 1993), pp. 218–40.

[14] Reiman argues: '*LBL* [Lines Written in the Bay of Lerici] seems to have been composed before *TL* 406–37 (ff. 44–45) and, I would guess, also before *TL* 373–391 (ff. 42–43)', Appendix D, *BSM*, I, 340.

[15] All citations from 'Lines Written in the Bay of Lerici' are, unless stated otherwise, from *Shelley's Poetry and Prose*.

[16] Friedrich Nietzsche, 'On the Uses and Disadvantages of History for Life', *Untimely Meditations*, trans. by R. J. Hollingdale (Cambridge: Cambridge University Press, 1983), pp. 59–123 (p. 63).

[17] Jean-Jacques Rousseau, *The First and Second Discourses Together with the Replies to Critics and Essay on the Origin of Languages*, ed. and trans. by Victor Gourevitch (NY: Harper and Row, 1989), pp. 240–95.

[18] Reiman raises this issue in 'Shelley's "The Triumph of Life": the Biographical Problem', *PMLA*, 78 (December 1963), 536–50. His reading, however, which depends heavily on Rousseau's *Julie*, is not entirely different from Matthews's biographical reading of the poem which Reiman

criticizes: whereas Matthews focuses on the relationship between Shelley and Jane Williams, Reiman stresses the significance of Saint-Preux's love for Julie.

[19] *Of Grammatology*, trans. by Gayatri Chakravorty Spivak (Baltimore: Johns Hopkins University Press, 1976), p. 229.

[20] Carlos Baker interprets Rousseau's state when Rousseau 'found' himself 'asleep' as signifying his birth; Harold Bloom claims that it is the process of 'growing up'; and Reiman partly agrees with Bloom in his view that it is about 'Rousseau's awakening to self-consciousness': see *Shelley's Major Poetry: the Fabric of a Vision* (Princeton: Princeton University Press, 1948), p. 265; Bloom, 1969, pp. 263–64; Reiman, 1965, p. 60.

Reiman argues that 'The Triumph of Life' echoes *Julie* in thought and expression often enough and coherently enough to remove all doubt as to Shelley's model for Rousseau's spiritual pilgrimage' and that '[i]n "The Triumph" Julie becomes Rousseau's vision of the 'shape all light' and Saint-Preux's love of Julie is transformed into Rousseau's pursuit of that mortal vision of the Ideal' (1965, 60).

[21] *The Confessions of Jean-Jacques Rousseau*, trans. by J. M. Cohen (London: Penguin, 1954), pp. 396, 398.

[22] See Reiman, 1963, p. 546.

[23] *Rousseau in England: the Context for Shelley's Critique of the Enlightenment* (Berkeley: University of California Press, 1979), p. 145.

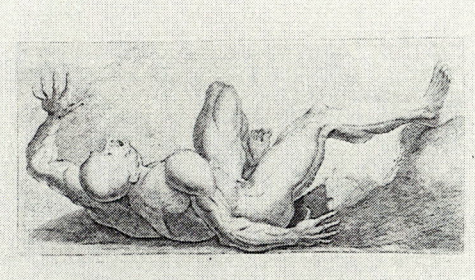

Chap. III.
Of the MUSCLES of the Penis.

Anatomists generally describe two Pair of Muscles belonging to the *Penis*, viz. *Acceleratores* and *Erectores*. Besides these, we sometimes meet with a third Pair mentioned and figured by *Stephen* * *Riverius*.

VII.
Accelerator Urinæ.

SO called from its Action, in promoting the Ejection of the Urine and Seed. Authors have been mistaken in assigning the Origination of this Muscle in Men, either to the *Sphincter Ani*, or the Tubercles of the *Ossa Pubis*, it arising fleshy from the superiour Part of the *Urethra*, as it passes under the *Ossa Pubis*, and incompassing the external Part of the Bulb of its cavernous Body, on which its two Sides meet and join each other in the *Perinaeum*, the whole being one Muscle, and not two. But on that Part of the *Urethra*, from which the *Scrotum* is pendulous, its Sides part again from each other, with two fleshy Elongations, which become thin Tendons at their Insertions on each side into the *Corpora Cavernosa Penis*, nor do they terminate on the Sides of the *Urethra*, as some Anatomists pretend. But the Variety we meet with of Nature's Sportings in these Muscles, more than in those of other Parts, may perhaps be the occasion, that Authors differ so much in their Accounts of them.

* *Lib.* 2. *P.* 196.

Besides

Plate 1. William Cowper, *Myotomia Reformata*, p. 8. Reproduced by permission of the Syndics of Cambridge University Library.

Plate 2. William Blake, *Jerusalem*, plate 47. Reproduced by permission of the William Blake Trust.

Plate 3. William Cowper, *Anatomy of Humane Bodies*, Table 45. Reproduced by permission of the Syndics of Cambridge University Library.

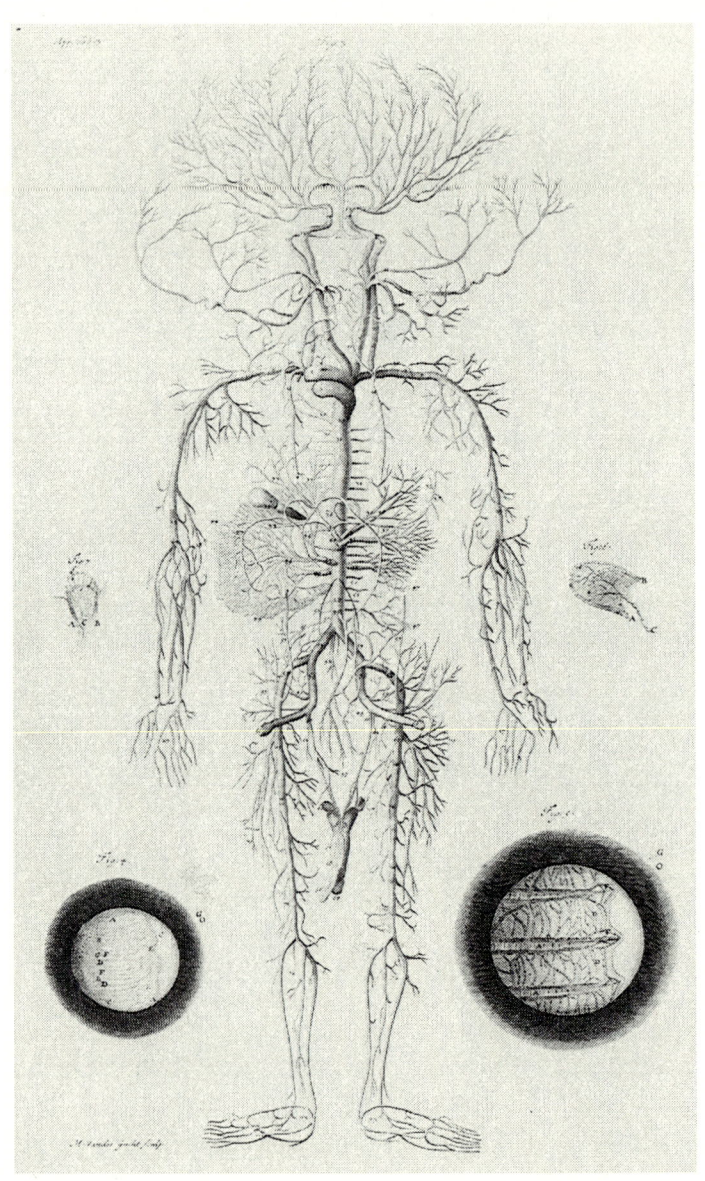

Plate 4. William Cowper, *Anatomy of Humane Bodies*, Appendix 3. Reproduced by permission of the Syndics of Cambridge University Library.

Plate 5. William Blake, *Jerusalem*, plate 25. Reproduced by permission of the William Blake Trust.

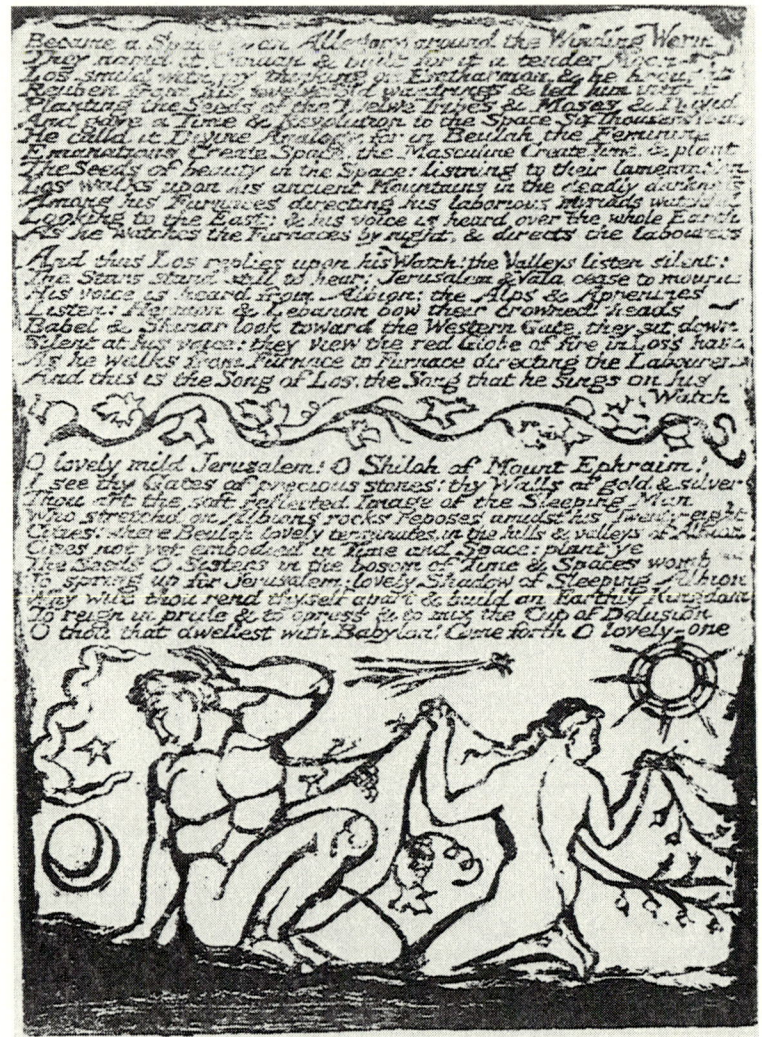

Plate 6. William Blake, *Jerusalem*, plate 85. Reproduced by permission of the William Blake Trust.

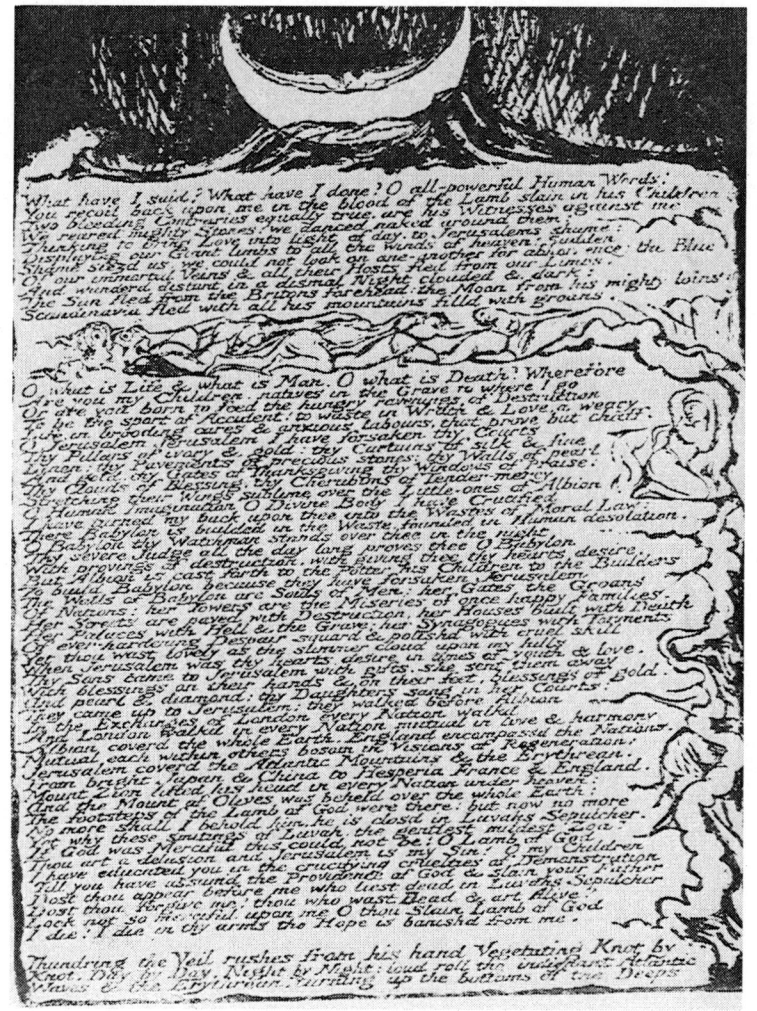

Plate 7. William Blake, *Jerusalem*, plate 24. Reproduced by permission of the William Blake Trust.

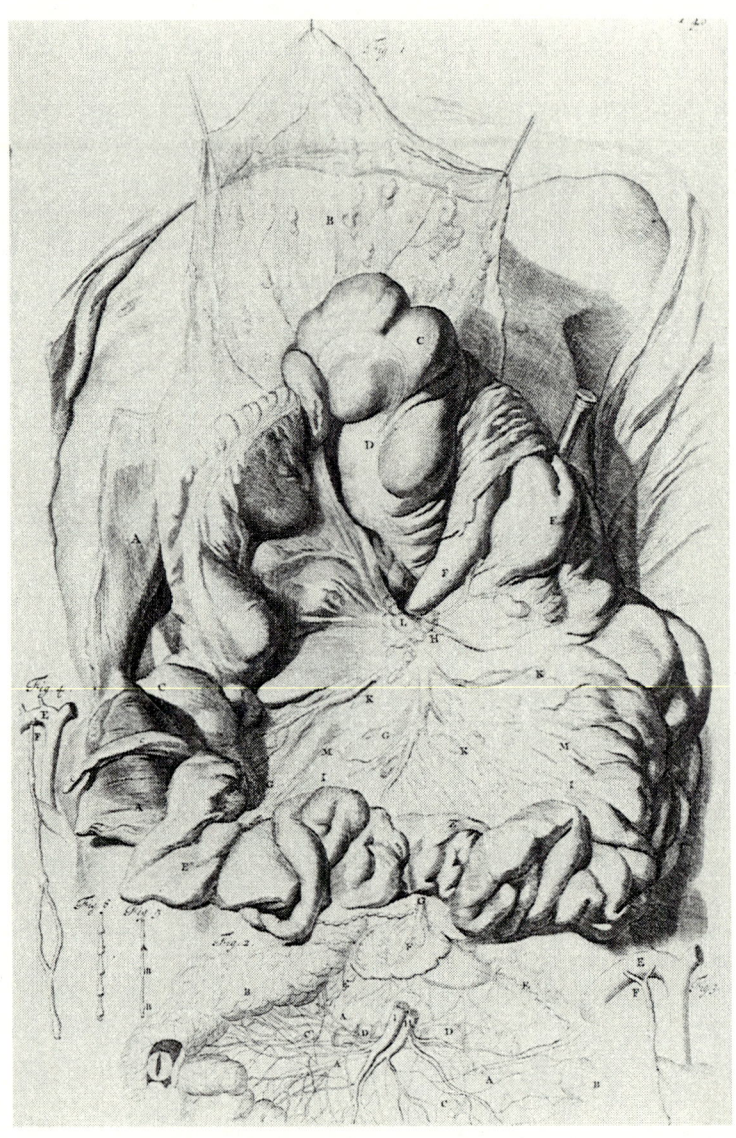

Plate 8. William Cowper, *Anatomy of Humane Bodies*, Table 40. Reproduced by permission of the Syndics of Cambridge University Library.

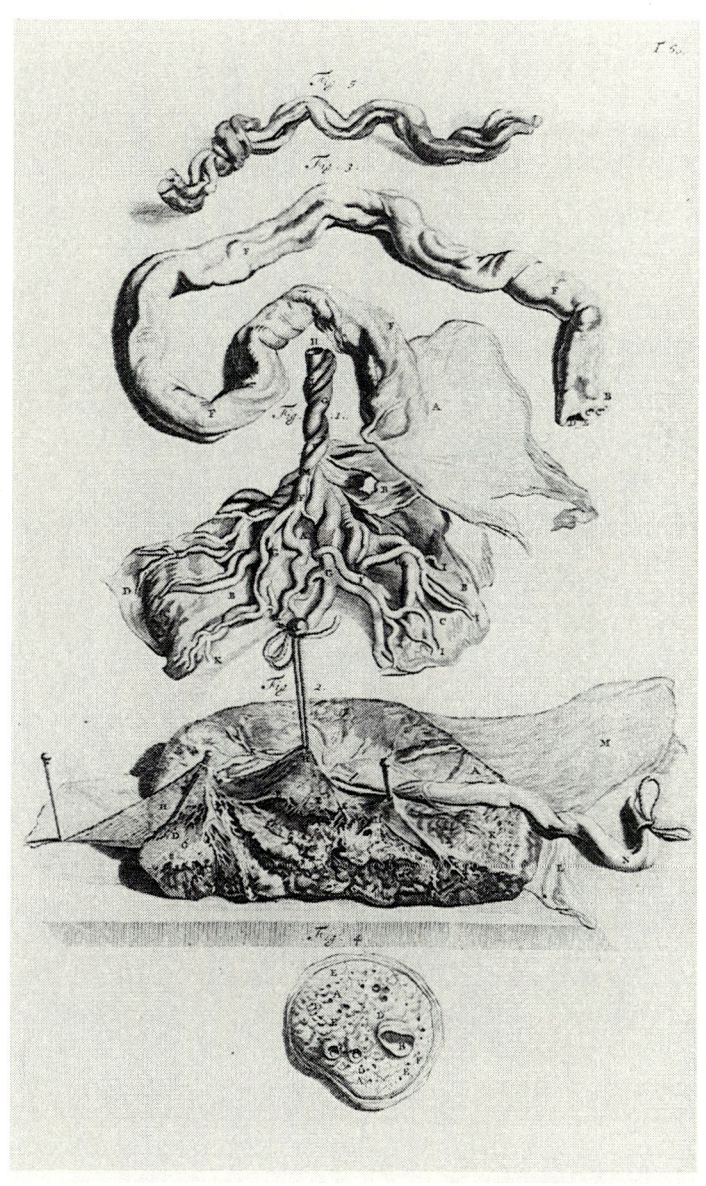

Plate 9. William Cowper, *Anatomy of Humane Bodies*, Table 60. Reproduced by permission of the Syndics of Cambridge University Library.

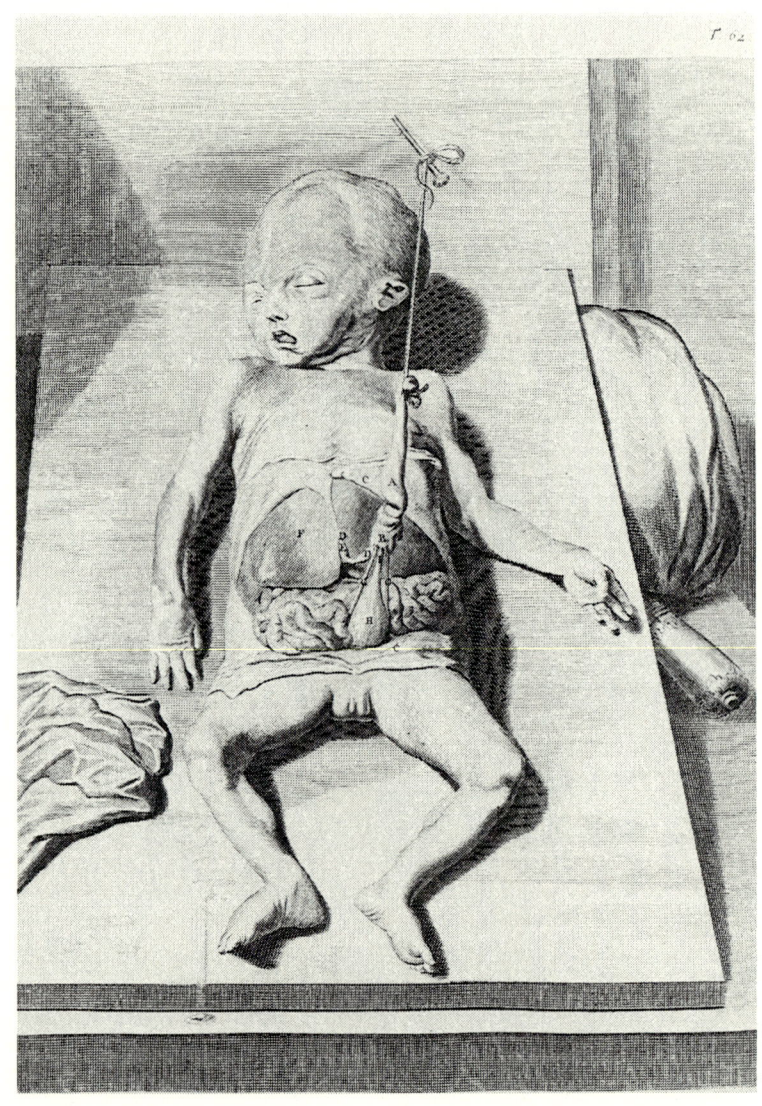

Plate 10. William Cowper, *Anatomy of Humane Bodies*, Table 62. Reproduced by permission of the Syndics of Cambridge University Library.

Plate 11. Dante Gabriel Rossetti, 'Mnemosyne'. 1881. Delaware Art Museum

Plate 12. Dante Gabriel Rossetti, 'La Belle Dame Sans Merci'. Circa 1855. © the British Museum

Plate 13
John William Waterhouse, La Belle Dame Sans Merci, 1893.

Hessisches Landesmuseum Darmstadt

Plate 14
BAG13619 La Belle Dame Sans Merci, Exh. 1902 (oil on canvas) by Sir Frank Dicksee (1853-1928)
City of Bristol Museum and Art Gallery/Bridgeman Art Library, London/New York

Plate 15
RA15156 La Belle Dame Sans Merci, 1926 by Frank Cadogan Cowper (1877-1958)
Private Collection/Bridgeman Art Library, London/New York

Plate 16. William Russell Flint, 'La Belle Dame Sans Merci'. 1908. Board of Trustees of the National Museums and Galleries on Merseyside (Walker Art Gallery, Liverpool)

'You'll pardon me for being jocular':
La Belle Dame sans Merci and Keats's Light Verse

James Kidd

Two received ideas about Keats still limit both the specialist's and the common reader's understanding of his character. First, that he was a sensitive man, easily wounded, deficient perhaps in the comic sense that can delight in smart repartees or revenges; and second, that he was skeptical about the intellect, and believed an 'irritable reaching after fact & reason' was typical of the analytical mind: the part of him that laughed, and read books of philosophy, did not write his poetry, and to prove it he gave us *Lamia*, with the philosopher Apollonius who laughs into oblivion the thing of beauty that poetry has been vouchsafed by myth.[1]

Keats once bought a small pub in London and one day was visited by Dr Watson, confrère of the famous Baker Street sleuth. Watson came late in the evening accompanied by a friend and the pair of them took to hard drinking in the back snug. When closing time came, Keats shouted out the usual slogans of urgent valediction such as 'Time now please!', 'Time gents!', 'The License gents!' 'Fresh air now gents!' and 'Come on now altogether!' But Dr Watson and his friend took no notice. Eventually Keats put his head into the snug and roared 'Come on now gents, have yez no Holmes to go to!'

The two topers then left in that lofty vehicle, high dudgeon.[2]

On 4 December 1941, the young Philip Larkin wrote a letter to his friend Jim Sutton detailing his most recent reading habits. He was currently 'getting his nose' into

> the latest work of the brilliant new Post-Masturbationist Poet, Shaggerybox McPhallus [whose] latest book of verse, 'The escaped Cock', deals almost exclusively with problems of intense spiritual value, which are yet so universal in their application as to be ensured of a wide public.[3]

He quoted a couple of stanzas from the McPhallus canon to illustrate what all the fuss was about:

> And this is why I shag alone
> Ere half my creeping days are done.
> The wind coughs sharply in the stove,
>   There is no sun
>
> To light my way to bed: the leaves
> Are brown upon the icy tree;
> The swallows all have left the eaves
>   Silently, silently (Motion, 1993, 58–59).

The crudeness of Larkin's parody of Keats's *La Belle Dame sans Merci* is typical of his social style while at university. Under the diverse influences of Auden's poetry, the novels of Lawrence and Isherwood, and the sarcastic, drunken charm of fellow undergraduates like Kingsley Amis, he set about ruthlessly and scornfully dismantling the majority of texts whose path he was compelled to cross by Oxford's English syllabus. Auden, Isherwood, Lawrence 'and the rest amounted,' Andrew Motion states, 'to a new kind of secret' that was shared by undergraduates and ignored by the majority of tutors. Together, these authors encapsulated an intellectual 'spirit of revolt' against what Larkin described as the 'smothering embrace of literature'. They inspired him to 'write without losing touch with ordinary, exhilarating reality' (Motion, 1993, 44).[4]

Motion writes that any thoughts Larkin might have had of approaching his studies with a show of earnestness evaporated the moment he entered Amis's social orbit:

> Once Amis had arrived [seriousness] was out of the question — [Larkin] had to settle instead for a world in which serious enthusiasms were coated with mollifying ironies, or buried altogether under layers of jokes (Motion, 1993, 58).

The same impulse to challenge pomposity that drove his desire to be thought a disaffected wit in Oxford's social circles filtered through to inform his literary outbursts:

> First I thought *Troilus and Criseyde* the most *boring* poem in English. Then I thought *Beowulf* was. Then I thought *Paradise Lost* was. Now I know that *The Faerie Queene* is the *dullest thing out. Blast* it (Motion, 1993, 59).[5]

Nowhere was 'the smothering embrace of literature' more in evidence for Larkin than in what Christopher Ricks has termed 'Romanticism's pathos of self-attention'.[6] The 'Days of "To a Skylark" are gone', he announced to Jim Sutton, before deciding that 'Auden's *Poems* is his best'.[7] Reading Auden unaffectedly 'describing things so near every day life' in 'language thrilling and beautiful' was 'like being allowed half an hour's phone conversation with God' for a mind reared on 'Westminster Bridge' and 'Ode to a Nightingale'.[8] Kingsley Amis confirmed this: 'We paid special attention to the Romantic poets'.[9] This 'attention', more specifically, was comic, lewd and mediated through sarcastic jokes and literary pranks. Amis later described such critical bravado as the 'sheer childishness' of first-year students antagonized by a degree course that did not reflect their own devotion to contemporary art.[10]

Keats proved a favourite target for Larkin's wit that checks 'lyricism with mockery, and [spurns] any kind of pretension' (Motion, 1993, 54). Larkin singled him out as a lover of Shakespeare: 'To me, Lawrence is what Shakespeare was to

Keats and all the other buggers'.[11] Later, co-opting Amis's copy of the collected works, he annotated the lines: 'Ethereal, flushed, and like a throbbing star [...] Into her dream he melted' from *The Eve of St. Agnes* with the studied critical comment, 'YOU MEAN HE FUCKED HER'.[12] No doubt the graffiti mocking Keats gained irritation at the regularity with which they and those of 'all the other buggers' cropped up in the lectures, seminars and tutorials that Larkin tried to avoid.

Larkin's sardonic scepticism about Keats's poetry was not without precedent. In *Keats and Embarrassment*, for example, Christopher Ricks recalls Byron's infamous stricture on 'Johnny Keats's p--- a bed poetry'.[13] Ricks writes that while such a response is 'astonishing', it is not 'surprising'.[14] Indeed, he proposes that 'an important element of Keats's writing is that it should permit of the possibility of such a reaction':

> it would be wrong to laugh at the scene in *King Lear* when Gloucester imagines himself to be jumping from the cliff, but less wrong than a denial that the possibility of laughter (the comedy of the grotesque) is importantly active within our response.[15]

Keats's poetry, Ricks suggests, can withstand any jokes or mocking comments made at its expense, as can the scene from *King Lear*, because it is alive to its own comic potential. Ricks's insight into the darkly comic possibilities of Keats's writing might encourage subsequent criticism to consider confronting the relations between his comic light verse and his serious artistic productions. *La Belle Dame sans Merci*, the poem which Larkin chose to parody, is a case in point. The poem can be read within the context provided by a number of lighter poems which predict and echo its central concerns. Biographers and critics, however, have consigned Keats's comic muse to footnotes in the poet's creative life, while anthologies of light or humorous verse have rarely included him.

In the first of the two light verse anthologies produced by Oxford University Press, W. H. Auden wrote that this decision to omit Keats could be explained by broader problems inherent in Romanticism.[16] The Romantics, he believes, with the obvious exception of Byron, 'turned away from the life of their time to the contemplation of their own emotions and the creation of imaginary worlds: Wordsworth to nature, Keats and Mallarmé to a world of pure poetry, Shelley to a future Golden Age' (x). The turn inwards, away from the social, excludes them from Auden's definition of light verse. Auden's own comments, however, seem to contradict themselves: his conclusion that the Romantic poets rejected 'entertainment' in favour of adopting the role of the 'unacknowledged legislators' of the world suggests the very social intention that he had previously denied (xvi).[17]

Auden's aversion to Keats's light verse was not unprecedented. T. S. Eliot, writing seventeen years earlier about Andrew Marvell, was also dubious about its value. Eliot pays Keats's lighter poems a backhanded compliment by noticing them at all: '[Marvell's wit] is the structural decoration of a serious idea. In this it is superior to the fancy of *L'Allegro, Il Penseroso*, or the lighter and less successful poems of Keats'.[18] While Eliot does not believe that Keats's light verse is utterly unsuccessful, he articulates his scepticism about its artistic value by comparing it unfavourably with Marvell's wit. The critique is twofold: Keats's lightness is inferior to Marvell's wit because it is not the 'structural decoration of a serious idea'. The contrast essentially proposes that Keats's 'lighter' poems were incongruous with the exposition of a 'serious idea'.

In *Life of Allegory: The Origins of a Style* Marjorie Levinson suggests that notions of seriousness, such as those espoused by Eliot, have been crucial to the formation of a canonical and critically respectable Keats:

> Further, by the providential tale of intellectual, moral and artisanal development we find coded in Keats's letters, we put the vulgarity which cannot be so easily sublimed in the early verse and show its gradual sea-change into the rich, inclusive seriousness that distinguishes the great poetry.[19]

Levinson challenges this traditional conception of the poet and his work. Her approach questions the assumptions that have perceived a correlation between 'seriousness' and Keats's 'great poetry'. His brief poetic career, she suggests, did not culminate simply with 'the rich, inclusive seriousness' of the narrative poems, odes and unfinished epics. His late art also included squibs and satires, light verse and nonsense rhymes. Her re-appraisal of the Keats *oeuvre* recognizes this variety. She suggests, for example, that Keats did not find his true poetic voice until *Lamia* and that the 'satiric-comic expression' of 'The Cap and Bells' which followed truly articulated his newly acquired and assured 'critical subjectivity'.[20]

Levinson contests the prevailing view that the grievous circumstances of Keats's life resulted only in a corresponding seriousness in his art. While she accepts that suffering, pain and disappointment increasingly dominated his existence, she stresses that levity, comedy and his sense of humour were crucial responses to them. By contrast, from Shelley's *Adonais*, Leigh Hunt's *Lord Byron and Some of his Contemporaries* and Richard Monckton Milnes's *Life, Letters and Remains of John Keats* onwards, biographical accounts have maintained the tragic role he seemed to play and found that his sense of humour and capacity for levity were incompatible with it, especially as he neared his death in Rome. John Bayley has argued that this critical effort attempts to 'bestow a gloss of unity and respectability' on Keats's verse and to make it suitable for public consumption.[21] This pursuit of respectability is, Kingsley Amis suggests, necessarily at odds with light verse:

> The obvious opposite of 'high' is 'low,' and light verse is low both in the Augustan and the Victorian senses; it is [...] offensive to decorum. It can only be dignified as a preparation for bathos. Unless engaged in parody, it prefers forms incompatible with decent seriousness: jogging rhythms, elaborate rhymes, stanzas that erect trip-wires for the unwary reader. It deals with low matters, with subjects, scenes and concerns that are either poetically or morally unsuitable for high consideration. It uses low terms, whether rustic, technical, facetiously anachronistic, or vulgar, ill-bred, obscene.
> Its chief weapon is impropriety.[22]

Amis's description of light verse as an affront to 'decent seriousness' suggests its potential to disrupt the conventional portrait of Keats which Levinson has identified. The similarity in their language is striking. The 'low' tone, form and subject matter of Amis's vision of light verse, which can be 'vulgar, ill-bred, obscene', is congruous with the problematic 'vulgarity' which Levinson notices in Keats's early poems.

Light verse's 'impropriety' proposes a crucial reason why biographers, seeking to present a unified and respectable profile of Keats, have been nervous about confronting the subject. The most recent biography of the poet by Andrew Motion is no exception.[23] Motion introduces his study by declaring that he wants to challenge widely held conceptions of Keats. He mentions T. S. Eliot as one such predecessor: for Motion, however, it is not Eliot's commentary on Keats's light verse that is debatable, but the belief that he 'did not appear to have taken any absorbing interest in public affairs' (Motion, 1997a, xxi). Motion's work represents the summation of research that has striven to establish Keats's poetry, not as the escapist outpourings of Shelley's *Adonais*, but the product of a liberal and socially engaged artist:

> Embedding his life in his times, I have tried to re-create him in a way which is more rounded than his readers are used to seeing [...] My intention is not to transform Keats into a narrowly political poet. It is to show that his efforts to crystallize moments of 'Truth' combine a political purpose with a poetic ambition.[24]

The act of re-creation places new emphasis on Keats's training at Guy's Hospital, the Dissenting atmosphere of his school, his early reading of *The Examiner* and his friendships with Charles Cowden Clarke and other liberal radicals, such as Leigh Hunt, William Hazlitt and Charles Lamb.

Motion's introduction is anxious to justify the addition of another *Life* of Keats to those that already exist (Motion, 1997a, xxv). His more rounded portrayal is, however, limited by this central desire for the poet to be seen as politically active. In reference to Keats's light verse there is little to differentiate Motion's approach from his biographical antecedents. He concentrates his critical focus almost exclusively on the major poems, all but neglecting Keats's sense of humour and occasional, light and comic verse. His introduction had sounded more promising on this point. He had suggested that it was commonplace to 'follow Aileen Ward in connecting the sonnet "Nebuchadnezzar's Dream" with the Tory government's trial of the radical William Hone' (Motion, 1997a, xxii–xxiii). Yet, Motion does not seem to take his own advice and assigns only thirteen lines, less than the poem itself, to discussing its political ramifications. The poem's parodic and satiric homage to Hone's attacks on the government would seem to illustrate the same image of Keats as Motion's more extensive exposition of the radical references to Peterloo in *To Autumn*.[25]

His Keats succeeds in appearing politically informed and socially engaged. However, the portrait is reverential, respectable, grave and somewhat strait-laced. Motion has reinforced the divide that Levinson wished to close between the rich, inclusive seriousness of his great poetry and the vulgarity of his early and occasional verse. This partiality is also apparent in Motion's recent collection of poems, *Salt Water*, which includes a lengthy prose section detailing his recreation of Keats's final sea voyage to Italy.[26] The poet that haunts Motion is doomed; 'emaciated and wretched', he is heading inexorably towards his painful and protracted death in Rome (Motion, 1997b, 110). The narrative of Motion's journey is compared at intervals to that of Keats's own:

> *21 October*. The Maria Crowther *reaches Naples but is detained in quarantine for ten days. Keats is exhausted and ill; he writes to Charles Brown telling him that during this time 'My health suffered more from bad air and a stifled cabin than it had done the whole voyage'* (Motion, 1997b, 110).[27]

Keats's own account of his confinement, however, balances this heartache and despair with the energy of Ricks's 'comedy of the grotesque':

> I am so weak (in mind) that I cannot bear the sight of any hand writing of a friend I love so much as I do you. Yet I ride the little horse, — and, at my worst, even in Quarantine, summoned up more puns, in a sort of desperation, in one week than in any year of my life.[28]

'Yet I ride the little horse' refers both to the horse rides which Keats took to ease his bodily suffering and to the act of writing poetry.[29] Humour provides solace from misery and emotional pain, as does poetry. Keats combines the two to joke about the squalor of his confinement, poking fun at his debilitated physical state, by deftly squeezing the irony and pathos out of the slang term. While he does not have physical freedom, his imagination and punning sensibility liberate him.

Anthony Burgess's portrait of the artist as a dying young man in *Abba Abba* challenges the conventional conception of Keats and evokes the poet that writes this kind of letter.[30] The fictional representation in the novella is anything but respectable. Keats's constant joking is alternately tender and savage, vulgar and intellectual. He pokes gentle, blasphemous fun at Severn's kindly attempts to convert him to Christ before his lungs give up the ghost. When his friend denies him the laudanum he wants to end his agony once and for all, and replaces suicide with the consolations of doctrine the lightness of his objections vanishes: 'Fuck and shit to your lying gentle Jesus and your false hopes. If you will not buy me laudanum I will buy it myself' (58). The viciousness of the outburst, and the fear of his friend, is offset by the black, farcical action of the scene, as the pair debate and fight over Keats's right to kill himself. Crucially, his irreverent evocation acknowledges Keats's facility as a writer of light verse. To exemplify this, Burgess introduces Giovanni Gulielmi, an Italian translator of Keats's poems, who has recently been working on both *Ode to a Nightingale* and the light verse sonnet *To Mrs. Reynolds's Cat*. Gulielmi, Burgess shows, pays each poem, low and high, equal respect as a work of art.

Burgess's Keats successfully unites levity and seriousness. This is highlighted in his encounters with Gulielmi's friend Giuseppe Belli, who combines his career in the Church with writing lewd sonnets about dogs, genitalia, sex and drinking. Belli's spiritual calling clashes with his poetic one: although he would end his days as the official censor for the Roman Catholic church, he felt continually compelled to produce his vulgar and comic poems. When lightness strikes him, he berates himself with not being 'serious enough':

Gulielmi said:
'For God's sake, what do you mean by *serious*?'
'Eternal truths,' Belli said too promptly, 'impressive spiritual essences. God and country and the roaring giants of history. Not, by Bacchus, cats.'
'Cats are the eternal truths, and the taste of the noonday soup, and farting, and snot, and the itch on your back you can't quite reach to scratch. Rome, as those lying and cheating bastards down there, not Rome as the imperial or the papal *essence*. Think of all those odes to Bonaparte, where are they now? The reality, and you can read it in the *Gazette de Francfort*, is a swollen body on St Helena and the cancers working away in it.'
Belli bunched his fine face, shrugged, belched out a Roman *beeeeeeh*, became upright and handsome and serious. 'A balance should be possible. Between the claims of the physically transient and the spiritually permanent. But finally it is the spirit that counts, since, as you say, there is a dying body on St Helena. Poetry should hymn the spirit and not talk of asthmatic cats.'
'We've had too much spirit, I think. I think the time *is* coming when sonnets must be written about the pains of constipation' (22–23).

While levity for Belli is synonymous with 'shameful triviality', high art exemplified 'eternal truths' (23). Burgess suggests, as Auden had done, a political, even revolutionary dimension to light verse: by embracing the material world with vulgar language, it poses a potential threat to the conventional values of the establishment.

Belli's internal conflict with these two sides of his personality seeks the resolution of a balancing middle way. Burgess proposes that Keats could have achieved this balance. While T. S. Eliot wonders whether Keats would ever have got to grip with the epic, *Abba Abba* offers an alternative vision. It suggests that the sensual, vulgar, and comic poems that Belli wrote, mixing elevated diction with the low vernacular, provide a dissenting vision of the kind of poetry Keats might have written and dared to publish had he lived. Having translated Belli's sonnet on the penis Burgess's Keats feels none of the Italian poet's shame about the poem. By contrast, he is animated by the experience. He meditates excitedly on the verbal connection between his name, *cazzo*, the Italian slang word for the male member and his own sonnet on a 'cat'.

While Burgess indulges his own enjoyment of Joycean word play in *Abba Abba*, he also recognizes Keats's capacity for punning. Burgess's punning sentence

"'By the waters of babble on there we shat down and flung our arses on the pillows'" is a parody of Keats's own bad joke on a room's furnishings: 'N.B. I beg leaf to withdraw all my Puns — they are all wash, an base uns' (17; 24 January 1819, 280). When writing about Keats's pun, Ricks has suggested that

> Keats's mind, so alertly prefigurative, was especially liable to puns and to portmanteaux, often of course quite premeditatedly; his letters are full of conscious effects of which Lewis Carroll or James Joyce would have been proud (Ricks, 1974, 69).

Keats's sense of humour is manifested in *Abba Abba* through word play and punning and represents a sensibility continually alert both to its creative impulses and the world around. Burgess's Keats toys with language as a means to expose and connect ideas and sensations.

Abba Abba imitates the narrative of *La Belle Dame sans Merci* to evoke Keats's experience of life in Rome. He exists in an all-male world, free from any meaningful encounters with women, but is continually haunted by them. While he is cared for by Severn, visited by his doctor, converses with the Italian translator Gulielmi and disputes with Belli, the ghost of Fanny Brawne invades his imagination, as in reality she did his letters home, taunting and infuriating him with her memory. Burgess's depiction of Keats's relationship with Isaac Marmaduke Elton, a fellow consumptive, draws explicitly on that between the narrator and the 'knight at arms' in the poem. Elton, a Lieutenant in the Royal Engineers, represents the pale and ailing 'knight at arms', with Keats, his patient confidant and gentle mocker, the first narrator. The pair play the roles laid down for them: Elton's obsessive self-centredness contrasts with Keats's initial sympathy and concern. They are bonded by insecurity, by fear of death and fear of betrayal by their lovers. The males bond through misogynistic jokes. Elton rails bitterly about the betrayal of his intended fiancée while Keats, trying not to empathize too closely, soothes his companion by reciting Burton's comic warnings against the attractions of love from the *Anatomy of Melancholy*.[31] While Elton's aggressive enjoyment of Keats's performance makes for uncomfortable reading,

Burgess suggests that their collusion is a source of light relief from the desperation of their mutual plight.

Burgess detects such black humour and tragic hilarity (Ricks's 'comedy of the grotesque') as pervading Keats's final days:

> John awoke to the bright December morning coldnosed and well, and he knew why. He had strapped on to a soldierly back the burden of dying for love. This was not war, this was not epidemic. Death did not like to be laughed at. Its multiplication was not funny, but its duplication was sidesplitting. For himself and Elton to be spitting arterial blood together would be the most comical thing in the world. One deals a red ace, the other trumps it. Elton could attend to his own death first; his, John Keats's, could follow at an uncomic interval. Death would endeavour, in its glum way, to keep things serious (35).

Burgess's gallow's comedy recognizes that the gravest situations possess the potential for levity, albeit of the darkest kind. Keats's sense of humour, Burgess suggests, allows room for broader perspectives and true consolation. When his Keats loses that detachment and capacity for empathy, he is left with only introspective bitterness. It is a complex, unflattering, but moving depiction that it is mediated through humour.

With these rare exceptions, timidity about Keats's comic muse is universal. Even Flann O'Brien, whose 'Cruiskeen Lawn' column for *The Irish Times* is remembered for the surreal bad jokes and shaggy-dog stories that comprised his 'Keats and Chapman' anecdotes. He listed 'among his happiest moments the hypothetical occasion of being assured "that I will never meet Keats in the hereafter"'(O'Brien, 1993, 9). While O'Brien's comment suggests that he imagined the poet would be displeased with the depiction, his affection for his pair of punning poets suggests that he did not wish to avoid Keats in the after-life because he had satirized him. The column's first instalment related the story of Keats dissecting a pigeon owned by Chapman and then writing 'On first looking into Chapman's Homer'.[32] The good-humoured tone of such tales displays none of the scepticism of Larkin's parody: it recognizes that Keats's levity does not always fit with critical conceptions of a respectable poet. O'Brien's depiction appreciates a facet of Keats's life that is rarely mentioned. The continual trials Keats faced during his short existence have encouraged critics and biographers alike to concentrate their attention on seriousness over comedy when reading both his life and work. His facility for producing light and comic verse has been all but ignored. Although his playful and sometimes lewd sense of humour is acknowledged as being crucial to the enjoyment of reading his letters, it rarely impinges upon considerations of his poetry. His light verse, numerous satires, comic songs and squibs are rarely taken into consideration within the scope of critical discussions of the poet; they are relegated, instead, to passing comments or brief mentions in biographies.

Keats's own attitude to his light and comic writing was contradictory and changeable. He published only a fraction of the light verse he wrote during his lifetime. However, the sheer amount and variety of it that he produced shows his enjoyment of the exercise. Most was included in his correspondence to close friends. He complemented the songs and ballads, the comic and nonsense verse of his letters by scribbling doggerel on scraps of paper or beside major work in progress; even when he was occupied with the business of writing serious poetry, his creative mind, it seems, was alive to its comic motivations. If this reticence implies Keats's modesty about his humorous muse, then the self-deprecating comments and apologies with which he often footnoted these 'rhyming fit[s]' might reinforce it (14 March 1818, 117). A more pressing reason for restricting the readership, however, was the personal and risqué subject matter of the light verse itself. After being roundly derided by critics for *Endymion*, he was understandably cautious about these unpolished compositions. The reader is encouraged to take them with a pinch of salt.

Keats jotted the following lines to alleviate the boredom of an especially dull lecture while studying medicine at Guy's hospital in 1815:

> Give me women, wine, and snuff
> Untill I cry out 'hold, enough!'
> You may do so sans objection

> Till the day of resurrection:
> For, bless my beard, they aye shall be
> My beloved Trinity (18–19).

At first glance, the poem does seem to be no deeper than it is long. The occasion of its conception, however, suggests a graver possibility. Keats puns darkly on 'resurrection' to carry the slang term for corpses stolen from cemeteries for the purpose of anatomical research. Pleasure is not merely extolled for pleasure's sake: Keats believes that it provides a necessary and exhilarating escape from the suffering that, as a medical student, he witnessed at close quarters. Grasping pleasure while one still can is defiantly celebrated by the blasphemous displacement of the Holy Trinity in the final lines. The distinctly beardless twenty-year-old anticipates his disgraceful dotage, where he will cheer himself, not with future happiness in heaven, but with the memory of delight in times gone by. The disposable, humorous impromptu rejoices in the brief but immediate relieving of the pains of existence. Although it knows that sensual delight, like laughter, does not last long, it revels in the joy of its quick, animating fix. The composition of the poem itself had vivified, if only for a few seconds, the deadly boredom of a lecture. Larkin the student would doubtless have approved. Keeping a sense of humour, especially while those around are losing theirs, concludes Keats, is a vital quality.

A similarly uneasy undercurrent runs beneath the jovial surface of his sexual light verse. Keats wrote 'Where be ye going, you Devon Maid' and 'Over the hill, and over the dale' in 1818; both ballads draw on the influence of Chatterton. In her edition of Keats's poems, Miriam Allott suggests that the opening stanza of 'Where be ye going, you Devon maid' cites Chatterton's Minstrel's song 'As Elynour bie the greene lesselle was syttnge' in *Aella* (1777).[33] Benjamin Bailey recalls Keats's enjoyment of Chatterton's ballads: 'Methinks I now hear him recite, or chant, in his peculiar manner, the following stanza of the "Roundelay sung by the minstrels of Ella" [*sic*]'.[34] Bailey notes that 'Come with acorn cup and thorn', the first line of the 'Roundelay', 'possessed the great charm' to Keats's ear:

'Indeed,' he continues, 'his sense of melody was quite exquisite, as is apparent in his own verses'.[35] The melody and rhythm of light verse are, both Auden and Amis agree, crucial to its effect. Keats's own comments about Chatterton add to the impression that he was a suitable inspiration for such writing:

> I always somehow associate Chatterton with autumn. He is the purest writer in the English Language. He has no French idiom, or particles like Chaucer — 'tis genuine English Idiom in English Words. I have given up Hyperion — there were too many Miltonic inversions in it — Miltonic verse can not be written but in an artful or artist's humour. I wish to give myself up to other sensations. English ought to be kept up (21 September 1819, 384).

Amis had written that the opposite of 'low is high' and Keats here makes a similar distinction: the final sentence contrasts Chatterton's 'English Idiom' with Milton's 'artful or artist's humour.' Chatterton's pure diction, Keats suggests, allows the possibility of lightness that Milton's elevated style could not.

'Where be ye going, you Devon maid' is a wooing song that imagines mutual attraction, flirtation, foreplay and satisfaction:

> 1
> Where be ye going, you Devon maid,
>   And what have ye there i' the basket?
> Ye tight little fairy, just fresh from the dairy,
>   Will ye give me some cream if I ask it?
>
> 2
> I love your meads and I love your flowers,
>   And I love your junkets mainly;
> But 'hind the door, I love kissing more —
>   O look not so disdainly!
>
> 3
> I love your hills and I love your dales,
>   And I love your flocks a bleating —
> But O on the hether to lie together
>   With both our hearts a beating.

> 4
> I'll put your basket all safe in a nook
> And your shawl I hang up on this willow,
> And we will sigh in the daisy's eye
> And kiss on the grass green pillow.

The pulse of the opening stanzas quickens to catch the excited anticipation of pleasure in the offing. However, the wistful close knows that even as the lovers exult in their fulfillment, their joy is at an end. Their shared 'sigh' is erotically charged but also disappointed; the problem with seizing the day is that it is over much too quickly. Keats tailored the tenor of each poem to suit the personality of a particular male friend. While 'Over the hill', written for James Rice (24 March 1818, 123), is lively and sexually charged, this poem, for Benjamin Haydon (14 March 1818, 117), is less explicit and more idealized.[36] It relies heavily on the punning innuendo that was a feature of their social circle. 'Junkets', for example, in line six, is an in-joke between them, alluding to Leigh Hunt's wisecracking nickname for John Keats.

The conclusions of these poems are of especial interest. They strike an unexpectedly different note from the bawdy comedy of their opening. 'Where be ye going, you Devon maid' ends with a lyrically described fantasy, far removed from the low, punning diction of the first stanza. The comic nature of the verse form is altered by this impulse, the language and rhythm modulated to convey the moment of creative inspiration. The union of the lovers is intensely conceived: 'But O on the hether to lie together / With both our hearts a beating' (11–12). The internal rhyme suggests their intimacy, while nature itself bends to embrace their desire. Keats's lightness of touch conveys the unconfined bliss of heated passion, while remaining sceptical enough to be anxious about the speed of its passing. The flexibility of his comic tone accentuates the pleasure in the positive, but does not lose sight of the negative.

This awareness enables him both to embrace and confront the worrying aspects suggested by his chosen light verse genre. While Keats's diction, form and rhythmical structure are informed by Chatterton, his subject matter alludes to a number of sources: most notably the seduction songs of the Cavalier poets. Bruce King, writing specifically about Thomas Carew's witty 'Ingratefull beauty threatned', summarizes a central theme of the Cavalier's erotic verse: 'Behind the gallantry of the poem lies a struggle for dominance'.[37] In such poems as 'To my inconstant Mistris', 'A deposition from Love' and 'To a Lady that desired I would love her', Carew, King proposes, inverts traditional poetic compliments 'to threaten, or pretend to threaten' women (541). Keats suggests the potential misogyny of his re-writing of the genre in his prefatory comments to Haydon: 'Here's some doggrel for you Perhaps you would like a bit of Bitchrell' (14 March 1818, 117). Keats here toes a fine line between being misogynistic and exposing misogyny. Haydon, as intended reader, haunts the poem with his presence. Is Keats truthfully confronting the offensive aspects of the male psyche? Or are the pair of young men colluding in an unfunny and sexist literary joke about seducing a woman heedless of her feelings?[38] Keats's final word on the poem is inconclusive: 'I know not if this rhyming fit has done anything — it will be safe with you if worthy to be put among my lyrics' (14 March 1818, 117).

The Devon maid is certainly anonymous in Keats's version; she is explicitly idealized as passive sustenance to feed the male's dominant appetite. However, the knowingness of the pastiche recognizes the limitations of the genre; the narrator's gratification is not related with the enjoyably naughty puns of the poem's opening, but with the reflective mood of the final stanza. Celebration is weighed against scepticism. His desire for meaningless sex, free from responsibility, ends as much in disillusion as delight. The reality of the encounter, devoid of mutual sympathy, has left him satiated physically, but emotionally unfulfilled. The very passivity he wanted in the Devon maid has quietly come back to mock him. This is the price masculinity pays for believing in *carpe diem* as a way of life: the brief stab of pleasure is followed by empty despondency. Keats's sense of humour exposes the ominous absurdity of this drive even as it enjoys it.

'Over the hill and over the dale' faces up to similarly awkward questions and concludes in an appropriately complex fashion:

> Over the hill and over the dale,
>   And over the bourn to Dawlish —
> Where gingerbread Wives have a scanty sale
>   And gingerbread nuts are smallish.
>
> Rantipole Betty she ran down a hill
>   And kick'd up her petticoats fairly.
> Says I, I'll be Jack if you will be Gill —
>   So she sat on the grass debonnairly.
>
> Here's somebody coming, here's somebody coming!
>   Says I, 'tis the wind at a parley.
> So without any fuss, any hawing and humming,
>   She lay on the grass debonnairly.
>
> Here's somebody here and here's somebody there!
>   Says I, hold your tongue, you young gipsey.
> So she held her tongue and lay plump and fair
>   And dead as a venus tipsy.
>
> O who wouldn't hie to Dawlish fair,
>   O who wouldn't stop in a meadow?
> O who would not rumple the daisies there,
>   And make the wild ferns for a bed do?

The female object of desire disappears entirely from view. Her final sighting in the penultimate stanza hints at a sinister reason why this might be: 'So she held her tongue and lay plump and fair / And dead as a venus tipsy' (15–16). 'Dead', following 'plump and fair', is startling. Neither the poem as a whole nor the line itself would support any other reading of it than her sexual gratification. 'Tipsy', which carries few tragic connotations, does suggest an ominous parallel with the hoodwinking of Madeleine in *The Eve of St. Agnes*. Has the male taken advantage of Rantipole Betty whilst she is under the influence of alcohol, as Porphyro exploited Madeleine in her hallucinatory dream state?[39]

The poem fantasizes the woman into the perfect partner for a one-night stand: 'Says I, I'll be Jack if you will be Gill — / So she sat on the grass debonnairly' (7–8). Although the male's decision to cast Betty in the role of his mate in a nursery rhyme of his making suggests his naivety, her flirtatious, responsive and unembarrassed reaction to the speaker's advances overrides any concerns he might have. However, unlike the Devon maid, Betty is not only granted a name, but a personality, with desires and a sense of humour of her own. The epithet 'Rantipole' hints at her boisterous energy, while the series of active verbs by which she defines herself exhibits a vigorous and confident independence. Despite her co-operation, if the narrator thinks she is going to come quietly, he is in for a shock.

The disparity between the narrator's idealized construction of the woman and Betty herself produces the enjoyable comic *frisson* of the opening stanzas. Betty, it seems, cannot stop laughing at his earnest attempts to concentrate on his sexual performance. Her amused shriek, 'Here's somebody coming, here's somebody coming', puts him completely off his stride. His ludicrously weak excuse that it was just the wind sounds as though it is said through clenched teeth. Has she undermined his confidence in his prowess by accusing him of premature ejaculation? She is pacified by his explanation, again capitulating 'debonnairly', but not for long. Her second cry, 'Here's somebody here and here's somebody there', suggests that she has turned her amused attention to his genitals. Deixis in erotic poetry has phallic implications; her excited call highlights his excitement. The tentative balance between mutual flirtation and the male narrator's selfish desire is destabilized by her mockery. He no longer aspires to achieve the shared communion he had idealized in his nursery rhyme, but vents his frustration with a thinly veiled threat. He hopes to stop her opposition and deny her independence by preventing her from speaking: he objectifies her as the means to his end. He does not perceive her as 'Gill' any longer, but as an anonymous 'young gipsey'. If he cannot resolve the power struggle in sympathy with her, he will do it alone.

By addressing the final stanza to the reader, the narrator seeks confirmation of his version of events, seeking the approval of laughter. Keats recognizes that a shared sense of humour is one way of defining friendship, as the in-joke with Haydon suggests. Comedy can be cruel: a negative assertion of like-mindedness achieved by mocking those not in on your joke. However, the narrator of the poem frames his gloating with a series of questions that reveals the uncertainty which underlies his boastfulness. Although he has the last word, constructing the narrative to bolster his ego, his insecurity gives itself away. A friend who shares his appetites may join in celebration of the conquest, but another reader is free to detect the gaps in his story.

Is this what Keats expected from James Rice here: applause for the lively but misogynistic adventures of his lotharios? His comic sense refuses such narrow-mindedness. The bad taste shock of 'dead as a venus tipsy' is a test that demands to know which side of the fence you are on, asking which sense of humour you find funny. The extreme nature of the joke leaves little grey area: to laugh at it is to endorse the male's behaviour. If, on the other hand, one finds it tasteless, the jovial surface of the male's narrative cracks to reveal the sinister possibilities of his desire. Keats's comic muse is undeniably attracted to his rakish characters in spite of their flaws. In 'Over the hill and over the dale', Keats pours some cold water on this admiration by embracing Betty's jokes and revelling in the absurdity of the male narrator's response. She takes the men on at their own game, asserting herself by ridiculing the narrator's machismo. It is noticeable how the male's own sense of humour vanishes when exposed to the alienating force of her laughter.

The light verse offers a critique of comedy as an ideological weapon. While the characters Keats creates employ wit and jokes to assert their selfish desires, his own comic sense is based on sympathy. He seeks to identify and explore the differing comic motivations of his protagonists, but retains enough scepticism in his identification not to blind himself to their aggressive and selfish potential. By mixing praise with distrust, his light verse is both generous and questioning, empowered to confront the uncertainties, mysteries and doubts inherent in the conflicts of everyday experience. Keats prefaced his definition of *negative capability* by writing of the superiority of humour to wit: it is superior because it makes one *feel*.[40] The self-obsessed knight at arms in *La Belle Dame sans Merci*, by contrast, is unable to feel anything not connected with himself and displays a fundamental lack of humour from the first word of the poem to the last. Unlike the males in the light verse, he is the same at the end of his story as he was at its beginning, fixed by his past emotional experience. He takes his masculine pride so seriously that he would rather perpetuate an idealistic misconception than admit the possibility of a mistake, even when it is staring him in his wasted face.

Keats himself suggests that the pathos inherent in love sickness, as experienced by the knight, is a suitable subject for light verse:

> Nothing strikes me so forcibly with a sense of the rediculous [*sic*] as a man in love I do think [he] cuts the sorryest figure in the world — Even when I know the poor fool to be really in pain about it, I could burst out laughing in his face — His pathetic visage becomes irrisistable (17–27 September 1819, 401).

He recognizes that emotional pain can elicit both laughter and sympathy. He is not describing *La Belle Dame sans Merci*, but his comic poem, 'Pensive they sit and roll their languid eyes', where a collection of self-absorbed lovers attend a tea-party and spend a great deal of time staring off into space:

> Pensive they sit and roll their languid eyes
> Nibble their toasts, and cool their tea with sighs,
> Or else forget the purpose of the night
> Forget their tea — forget their appetite (1–4).

Keats introduces the poem with the comment, 'The[re] would be no fighting as among Knights of old', which, although prefacing comedy, serves equally to summarize *La Belle Dame sans Merci* itself. The irony of this poem and of *La Belle Dame sans Merci* is that the male protagonists are so immersed in their individual desire that they forget the originating impulse for it: the 'sighs' at the end of line two suggest despair and not sexual rapture.[41]

The relation of *La Belle* to light verse is suggested by its echoing the scenery and language of 'Where be ye going, you Devon maid' and 'Over the hill and over the dale.' In order to emphasize the crucial difference in the temperaments of the respective ballads, Keats's *La Belle Dame sans Merci* draws on a different, darker tradition of ballad writing: for example, as Miriam Allott notes, the 'various traditional ballads expressing the destructiveness of love' collected in Thomas Percy's *Reliques of Ancient English Poetry* (1765) (500n.). While these ancient ballads provide Keats with the model for the diction and metrical style, he adds an innovation of his own; curtailing the final line of each stanza and punctuating it with severe monosyllabic words. The lighthearted punchline of the lighter ballads's rhythmic momentum is sabotaged as its movement slows towards stasis.

Whereas the light verse had investigated darker subtexts through its comedy of errors, *La Belle Dame sans Merci* reverses the equation. The knight's condition is clearly desperate, but Keats, as he had suggested with 'Pensive they sit and roll their languid eyes', was alive to its comic potential. Although the narrative is driven by a different diction and mood, Keats's linguistic manipulation remains. His somber wit conveys the dangerous instability of the relationship, conveying it in stanza seven:

> She found me roots of relish sweet,
>   And honey wild, and manna dew,
>   And sure in language strange she said —
>   I love thee true (25–28).

The relationship had been equal up to this point. In the preceding stanzas, the knight and the lady had shared a similar amount of poetic space. This particular stanza, in which the lady apparently confesses her love and feeds the appetite of the male, is dominated by her alone. As the balance of power swings her way, Keats destabilizes her declaration with a pun: it is the word 'sure', ironically, that is uncertain. Does the line read 'She definitely said in language strange that she loved me'? Or is the doubting knight trying to convince himself in hindsight: 'Surely she said that she loved me'? The very word that he believes provides confirmation of the lady's love only challenges his confidence.

Keats's verbal playfulness enjoys misleading the knight and highlighting his utter inability to translate the duality of what is happening. Take this moment from stanza five: 'She look'd at me as she did love, / And made sweet moan' (19–20). 'As' is haunted by an 'if' that does not come. Is she looking whilst she was loving? Or does it rather suggest: 'She look'd at me as if she might be in love with me?' The sweetness of her moan does not resound as sweetly in this uncertain context. The knight, Keats proposes, does not merely lack a sense of humour, but a sense about humour and its capacity to enjoy the uncertain with healthy scepticism. His desperation to be convinced by his own version of events, that he is right and she is bad, is conveyed by a refusal to detect the melancholy doubts of his own melancholy puns. Like his comic counterparts, he by-passes them by prioritizing his ideal and not accommodating her reality. Unlike them, however, he could not tell a joke to save his life.

With this context in mind, the elements of the 'comedy of the grotesque' in *La Belle Dame sans Merci* sound less unlikely. The poem suggests that tragic distress prompts a peculiar combination of compassion and ridicule, in much the same way as bawdy farce did in the light verse. This unsettling admission about an individual's capacity to laugh at the wrong moment acknowledges the different attitudes that readers bring to an act of interpretation. In *La Belle Dame sans Merci*, this is exemplified by the voice that narrates the opening stanzas. The knight wants to inspire the sympathy of the narrator to reinforce his demonization of the lady. The prospect of the males conspiring against the woman within the poem echoes the uneasy suggestions of misogynistic collusion in the light verse.

While the unnamed narrator displays concern for the knight, his opening words suggests another reading: 'O what can ail thee, knight at arms / Alone and palely loitering?' (1–2). His acknowledgment of the unnatural passivity of the knight with his first question echoes Keats's own introduction to 'Pensive they sit and roll their languid eyes': 'The[re] would be no fighting as among Knights of old.' This knight is certainly not fighting as he should, but lurking forlornly about the place, complaining over and over that he has been rejected by the evil woman. The narrator's reaction to the knight's tale of woe is not voiced within the poem. His silence is uncertain and suggestive. Is the similarity between the final stanza, spoken by the knight, and the first, uttered by the narrator, a sign that a dangerous, collusive sympathy has developed between the pair? Or, will the narrator follow Keats's belief that there is nothing so ridiculous as a man in love and 'burst out laughing in his face'. The open-ended conclusion does not deny the possibility of potential laughter.

Keats's own amused close reading of *La Belle Dame sans Merci* seems to be reacting with, rather than against the poem. Having included the poem in a letter to George and Georgiana Keats, he offers an explanation of the lines: 'And there I shut her wild wild eyes / With kisses four' (31–32):

> why four because I wish to restrain the headlong impetuosity of my Muse — she would have fain said 'score' without hurting the rhyme — but we must temper the Imagination as the Critics say with Judgment. I was obliged to choose an even number that both eyes might have fair play: and to speak truly I think two apiece quite sufficient — Suppose I had said seven; there would have been three and a half a piece — a very awkward affair — and well got out of on my side (14 February–3 May 1819, 330).

Robert Gittings believes that Keats is dismissing 'the poem with a joke which suggests he never valued it highly [...] To him it was a piece of occasional light verse' (447). This conclusion is founded on a misreading: Keats begins by satirizing, not the poem itself, but the attitude of 'Critics' who might review it, continuing with a joke that pokes fun at the constraints of his rhyme scheme.

The logic of Gittings's verdict is significant. Keats did not value *La Belle Dame sans Merci* highly because he believed it was just a piece of light verse. It sounds as though it is Gittings, not Keats, who is dismissive. He showed his distaste for Keats's comic poetry in his editorial policy for the selection of Keats's letters he produced for Oxford University Press.[42] One letter was excluded completely, and another abridged, on the grounds that they contained, what Gittings termed, 'undistinguished' comic poems, of which 'Where be ye going, you Devon maid' was one. Gittings is not squeamish about Keats's enjoyment of levity in general: he was happy enough to allow his lewd sense of humour have free rein within the scope of a letter. He is unabashed, for example, when he includes the relation of drunken banter about the derivation of the word 'cunt' in the selection.[43] However, he refuses to allow this temperament to make its way into a poem.

It is equally interesting to speculate whether Motion intended his conception of Keats to redress the unsavoury aspects of his previous subject, Philip Larkin. Perhaps they have more in common than he believes. While Larkin's parody was no doubt inspired by 'sheer childishness', it refuses to treat Keats with the traditional reverence and respect that John Bayley argues against. Although the parody expresses Larkin's scepticism about Keats's artistic worth, it manages to sound at least 'half in love' with the Keats's original. Larkin's parody swiftly achieves a lyrical tone. Seeking to avoid the curt awkwardness of the original verse-form's concluding line, Larkin runs the final sentence over the first stanza's end which Keats never does. By the second stanza *To Autumn* appears to have replaced *La Belle Dame sans Merci* in Larkin's thoughts; when he reaches 'Silently, silently', he ignores Keats's scansion completely. Larkin seems to be thinking not just of a different poem, but of a different poet, Blake not Keats. The crude shock of the opening couplet, mocking Keatsian self-absorption and sexual inadequacy, echoes the central theme of the poem. Nor does Larkin keep it up. Unlike Byron, Larkin, the shy, virginal student, was compelled to concede the irony of laughing at Keats's sexual self-reliance. He admitted as much in a letter, albeit one written more than fifteen years later: 'Hope love in a cottage goes better than Keats supposed', he writes to Patsy Murphy in 1955, misquoting *Lamia*, 'better than wanking in digs, anyway.'[44]

However, he says nothing, no matter how crude, that Keats's poem has not suggested already. As Ricks has written with reference to Byron, Larkin's inability to carry the parody out acknowledges the capacity of Keats's poetry to accommodate mockery and laughter through a continual awareness of its own absurdity and comic potential. In this case, Levinson's theoretical approach in *The Life of Allegory* is suggestive. She finds parody an apt term to describe Keats's poetic style. *La Belle Dame sans Merci*, for instance, asserts its own authority by deconstructively reconstructing its source materials. Keats's re-writing of the poem is, she asserts, itself an act of self-parody that makes this tactic explicit. Humour, she argues, is an act of self-expression, whereby Keats defines himself and his writing as a product of, and reaction against, the traditions that produced him. Her thesis brings Keats far closer to the spirit of Larkin's parodic burlesque: 'By the stylistic contradictions of his verse, Keats produces a writing which is aggressively literary and therefore not just 'not literature' but, in effect, anti-Literature: a parody (5)'. Aptly perhaps, it is creative writers, and not critics and biographers, who have revealed Keats the humorist. The comic tactics of Byron's, Larkin's, Burgess's and O'Brien's responses to him identify a much ignored part of his personal and creative character. Whether it is as Larkin's parody of a masturbating lyricist, the terrible punster and practical joker of O'Brien's surreal newspaper column, or the sardonic dying poet of Burgess's *Abba Abba*, who relieves the suffering of his final days by translating a lewd and low Italian sonnet about the male member, Keats's sceptical but generous humour of human sympathy is rescued from its footnote in his life.

---

[1] David Bromwich, *Hazlitt: The Mind of a Critic* (Oxford: Oxford University Press, 1983), p. 364.

[2] Flann O'Brien, from 'Keats and Chapman', in *The Best of Myles: A Selection from 'Cruiskeen Lawn'*, ed. by Kevin O'Nolan (London: Flamingo Modern Classics, 1993), p. 188.

[3] Andrew Motion, *Philip Larkin: A Writer's Life* (London: Faber and Faber, 1993), p. 58. The letter that Motion quotes was not included in the *Selected Letters of Philip Larkin: 1940–1985*, ed. by Anthony Thwaite (London: Faber and Faber, 1992).

[4] Motion adds Larkin's judgment, 'Art is awfully *wrong*, you know', which he included in a letter to Jim Sutton, 12 August 1943 (Motion, 1993, p. 44).

[5] The judgment doubled as an act of vandalism, being scrawled in the St. John's library copy of *The Faerie Queene*.

[6] *The Force of Poetry* (Oxford: Oxford University Press, 1984), p. 276.

[7] Letter from Philip Larkin to Jim Sutton, 1 April 1942, in Motion, 1993, p. 75.

[8] From an unpublished 1943 'autobiographical essay' in the Philip Larkin Archive held by the Brynmor Jones Library at the University of Hull, quoted in Motion, 1993, p. 44.

[9] Quoted in Motion, 1993, p. 58.

[10] Letter from Kingsley Amis to Andrew Motion, 24 November 1986; quoted in Motion, 1993, p. 59.

[11] Letter from Philip Larkin to Jim Sutton, 6 July 1942; quoted from *Selected Letters*, pp. 34–35.

[12] John Keats, *Complete Poems*, ed. by Jack Stillinger (Cambridge, MA and London: Harvard University Press, 1978), ll. 318, 320. All further references to Keats's verse will be taken from this edition. Letter from Kingsley Amis to Andrew Motion, 24 November 1986; quoted in Motion, 1993, p. 59.

[13] Christopher Ricks, *Keats and Embarrassment* (Oxford: Oxford University Press, 1974).

[14] However, Ricks's assertion that Byron's comments do not surprise because his 'achievements, as a man and as a poet, owe their strength and their insights to quite opposite impulses from Keats's' could apply to Larkin as well (Ricks, 1974, p. 78).

[15] '[To] react so is wrong (in underrating Keats's sense of responsibility and delicacy)', Ricks continues, 'but not as wrong as it would be to experience the poetry as altogether precluding any such response' (Ricks, 1974, p. 78).

[16] W. H. Auden's *Oxford Book of Light Verse* (Oxford: Oxford University Press, 1938).

[17] Auden surmises that this lack of lightness placed an alarming strain on a number of the Romantic poets: 'It is significant', he writes, 'that so many of these poets died young like Keats, or went mad like Hölderlin, or ceased producing good work like Wordsworth, or gave up writing altogether like Rimbaud', p. xvi.

[18] From the essay on 'Andrew Marvell', first published in the *TLS*, 31 March 1921; quoted here from *Selected Prose of T. S. Eliot*, ed. by Frank Kermode (London: Faber and Faber, 1975), p. 164.

[19] Marjorie Levinson, *Keats's Life of Allegory: The Origins of a Style* (Oxford: Blackwells, 1988), p. 2.

[20] She concludes, however, that 'We see that there is nothing "bad" in the poem and, sad to say, nothing very good either', Levinson, p. 253.

[21] John Bayley, *The Uses of Division: Unity and Disharmony in Literature* (London: Chatto and Windus, 1976), p. 155.

[22] Kingsley Amis, *The New Oxford Book of Light Verse* (Oxford: Oxford University Press, 1978), p. viii.

[23] Andrew Motion, *Keats* (London: Faber and Faber, 1997). All future references to this text will be made to Motion, 1997a.

[24] Motion, 1997a, p. xxv. See also Nicholas Roe's study *John Keats and the Culture of Dissent* (Oxford: Oxford University Press, 1997), in which Keats's life and writing are placed within the context of a radical political tradition. Roe has reassessed, for instance, Keats's education in Enfield under John Clarke by showing its similarities to the Dissenting academies that were established in and around the major cities of England.

[25] Motion dedicates twenty-one lines to considering the contemporary political importance of Keats's reference to 'gleaners' and 'bees' in *To Autumn* (1997a, p. 462).

[26] Andrew Motion, *Salt Water* (London: Faber and Faber, 1997); this text will be referred to as Motion, 1997b hereafter.

[27] Motion's italics distinguish between the two journeys.

[28] John Keats, *The Letters of John Keats*, ed. by Maurice Buxton Forman (Oxford: Oxford University Press, 1952), 30 November 1820, p. 529. All future references to Keats's letters will be taken from this edition unless otherwise indicated.

[29] Robert Gittings writes that the words '" I ride the little horse" do not refer to his rides in Rome [...] but to the "little Pegasus" of stanza 71 in his own *Cap and Bells*, an allusion Brown would recognize. They meant that Keats was once more letting his mind play with the idea of a poem', Robert Gittings, *John Keats* (London: Penguin, 1968), pp. 612–13.

[30] Anthony Burgess, *Abba Abba* (London: Minerva, 1977).

[31] For this Burgess uses the same passage Keats had copied out to George and Georgiana Keats (17–27 December 1819, pp. 404–05). Keats concluded the passage by writing 'This I think will amuse you more than so much Poetry' (p. 405).

[32] Flann O'Brien, *The Various Lives of Keats and Chapman and The Brother*, ed. by Benedict Kiely (London: Grafton Books, 1988), p. 9.

[33] Allott quotes the stanza in *Keats: The Complete Poems*, ed. by Miriam Allott (London: Longman, 1970), p. 318n.

[34] Walter Jackson Bate, *John Keats* (1st edn 1963; London: The Hogarth Press, 1992), p. 216.

[35] Bailey goes on to say that one of Keats's 'favourite topics [...] was the principal of melody in Verse, upon which he had his own notions, particularly in the management of open & close vowels' (Bate, p. 216).

[36] It is notable that Motion does not mention the former at all in his biography.

[37] From the essay 'The Strategy of Carew's Wit', in *Ben Jonson and the Cavalier Poets*, ed. by Hugh Maclean (NY: W. W. Norton, 1974), pp. 540–548 (p. 541).

[38] In his essay, 'The Cavalier Ideal of the Good Life', Earl Miner suggests that such male collusion was central to the Cavaliers: 'Most important is the premise of the good life, which involves social intercourse with like-minded people. Very frequently that relation turns on the band of friends, male equals joined in fraternal affection and esteem', Maclean, pp. 465–479 (p. 469).

[39] 'Tipsy', in conjunction with 'dead', may also be a dark reference to Keats's medical training; as 'resurrection' was in 'Give me women, wine and snuff'. In describing the agonies of the patients at Guy's, Motion notes that 'their bones were broken for resetting, their bodies opened, and their limbs amputated, all without any anaesthetic except alcohol' (1997a, p. 78).

[40] Letter to George and Thomas Keats, 21 December 1817:

> I dined too (for I have been out too much lately) with Horace Smith & met his two brothers with Hill and Kingston & one Du Bois, they only served to convince me, how superior humour is to wit in respect to enjoyment — These men say things which make one start, without making one feel, they are all alike; their manners are alike; they all know fashionables; they have a mannerism in their very eating & drinking, in their mere handling — They talked of Kean & his low company — Would I were with that company instead of yours said I to myself! I know such like acquaintance will never do for me & yet I am going to Reynolds, on Wednesday (pp. 70–71).

[41] The repetition of 'forget' echoes those in *Ode to a Nightingale*, where the visionary state of the narrator achieved through the nightingale's song separates him from the material mode of existence, see ll. 21–30.

[42] John Keats, *Letters of John Keats: A Selection*, ed. by Robert Gittings (Oxford: Oxford University Press, 1970).

[43] Letter to George and Thomas Keats, 5 January 1818, p.76.

[44] Letter from Philip Larkin to Patsy Murphy (neé Avis), *Selected Letters*, 18 October 1955, p. 253.

Resurrecting Thomas Lovell Beddoes

Michael Bradshaw

Like the red outline of beginning Adam

Thomas Lovell Beddoes's works are generally macabre in character; and the macabre supernatural has long provided a ready language for his critics. But the rise from the grave as a trope for the use of a literary past and inheritance has sometimes had a strangling effect on responses to Beddoes, and popularized a view of him as primarily a (doomed) reviver of the past, a view which does little justice to his subtle and troubled dialogues with precursors of various ages. Lytton Strachey calling him 'The Last Elizabethan', and Ezra Pound calling him the 'prince of morticians' are two influential examples of the simplifying view that Beddoes, lacking his own voice, crudely took on the voices of others.[1]

Beddoes himself developed over a number of years his own language of grave-robbing and galvanism, in order to anatomize and satirize a belated generation and its uncertain relation to the past. His ghostly idiom expresses the dislocation experienced in between an age of revolutionary purpose and a succeeding age as yet unknown. Beddoes's darkling generation has responsibilities both towards the

Romantics and towards their successors. In Matthew Arnold's phrase, he is 'Wandering between two worlds / One dead, the other powerless to be born'.[2] The ghostly in Beddoes, expressing the shifting, elusive and indeterminate, is the site of anxious dialectic between various competing impulses in his works — between his Shelleyan idealism and his Hebraic monism, between the immortality of the soul and the resurrection of the body (the two rival versions of human immortality which obsessed him), between the thrust towards organic literary wholeness and the stubborn habit of fragmentation. The ghostly negotiates between a powerful dead generation of literary innovators and a stranded generation of imitators. For Beddoes's editors and readers in the later nineteenth century, the ghostly is the expression of uncertain inheritance, in which past voices linger on, and control shifts between living and dead authors. The present reading of Beddoes aims to illustrate, with the aid of three close-textual examples, the flux of influence and control between the living and the dead. In this intertextual drama Beddoes will play both the living and the dead poet; he will be both the sickening receiver of overpowering influence from Shakespeare and intoxicating influence from Shelley, and also (more briefly) the transmitter of sapping, life-denying sensations to his successors in the Victorian world. Although the theoretical model lurking in the background here is the Bloomian formula *apophrades* (the return of the dead), Beddoes enters no power-struggle for mastery with his mentor strong poets; on the contrary, it is part of his richness, and his power to fascinate, that he uses these allegiances for abject self-display and for the textual excoriation of his own weakness, urging his own extinction as the necessary lifeblood of lost generations past and to come.

Periodical writing of the 1820s on the subject of ghosts provided some ready metaphorical applications, and strongly indicated the usefulness of the ghost as expression of the lingering, imperfect connection of the present generation with its more impassioned predecessors. An anonymous article called 'A Chapter on Goblins', for instance, was certainly known to Beddoes, as it appeared in the same 1823 number of *Blackwood's* which carried the review of his own *The Brides'*

Tragedy. This article concludes with a lament that the advance of rationalism has been driving phantoms out of the landscape: 'the child of romance looks back with regret to those wild beliefs and superstitions of which the progress of science and education has deprived him'.[3] Advances in the rational sciences are driving romantic spectres out of their old haunts. The child of romance, like the hunter, desires an open field. The population of ghosts in the landscape is associated with certain narrative freedoms which s/he will not willingly forego. It is the *absence* of the ghosts, rather than their presence, which occasions the feeling of nostalgic dislocation; ghosts are simultaneously present and absent, most poignantly apparent to those who miss them.

An anonymous article by Mary Shelley, 'On Ghosts', published in *The London Magazine* the following year, similarly portrays ghosts as fleeing, driven from their moonlit haunts by scientific explanation.[4] This article concludes by repeating a story told by M. G. Lewis, the tale of 'The King of the Cats'. In this traditional folk-tale, typically transplanted to Germany by Lewis from its usual Scottish setting, an appalled passer-by witnesses a feline funeral; a procession of grief-stricken cats lowers a tiny coffin bearing a crown into the grave. When the witness later tells the tale, an old black cat slumbering by the fireside starts up and declares himself the new king, before shooting up the chimney and never being seen again. The story clearly concerns succession, inheritance and continuity. A domestic character is transformed by a supernatural event; he is roused to fulfil his duty in succeeding a waning generation and becomes something wild, monstrous and unfamiliar in meeting this destiny. The emptying of the landscape of its native ghosts provokes in us feelings of rootlessness and lack of belonging. Where have all the ghosts gone? Where have we come from; where are we going? In both these anecdotal and exploratory articles, old Hamlet is mentioned as an important model of a ghost, just as *Macbeth* is mentioned repeatedly in reviews of Beddoes's and others' macabre writing from the 1820s, as a standard of gruesomeness, a frequent phrase being that of 'supping full of horrors'.⁵ Both of these Shakespearean models can be seen to haunt the revising literature of Beddoes.

The literary present for Beddoes is more deeply in shadow due to the brilliance of the light which has just departed:

> The disappearance of Shelley from the world seems, like the tropical setting of that luminary [...] to which his poetical genius can alone be compared with reference to the companions of his day, to have been followed by instant darkness and owl-season [...] if I were the literary weather-guesser for 1825 I would safely prognosticate fog, rain, blight in due succession for it's dullard months (August 1824, 589).

There follows a section naming possible successors to the sun, described respectively as a comet and a moon; the allegory draws self-consciously on *Epipsychidion*, so that Shelley remains as a ghostly presence in the text which laments his absence. The letter continues, referring to Shelley's *Posthumous Poems*, whose publication Beddoes had assisted with a subscription: 'P.S. Shelley's book! This is a ghost indeed, and one who will answer to our demand for hidden treasure' (590). Two years later, he wrote to Thomas Forbes Kelsall, his friend and, later, literary executor, from Göttingen:

> Here is a Dr. Raupach who lays a tragedy or two in the year — mostly windeggs — but he's the best of the folks about Melpomene's sepulcre in Germany. Schiller, you know, took her out of the critical pickle she lies in & made a few lucky galvanic experiments with her, so that people thought she was alive when she was only kicking (October 1826, 621).

The muse of tragedy is currently suffering the indignity of having her limbs electrified in the modern age's crude attempts to reproduce her art. Beddoes previously alluded to the illness of Melpomene in a letter to Procter, criticizing George Darley's poor credentials to be her 'physician' (3 March 1824, 581). The tomb of tragedy is not a shrine or resting-place, but a laboratory. Under the artificial, Frankenstein-like attentions of her newest followers, Melpomene has become a gruesome and rather risible monstrosity.

In a letter to Kelsall in January 1825, Beddoes made what has become his best remembered statement on tragedy. Here too the issue is the desired revival of the genre, and the shocking results of failure:

> Say what you will — I am convinced the man who is to awaken the drama must be a bold trampling fellow — no creeper into worm-holes — no reviser even — however good. These reanimations are vampire-cold. Such ghosts as Marloe, Webster &c are better dramatists, better poets I dare say, than any contemporary of ours — but they are ghosts — the worm is in their pages — & we want to see something our great-grandsires did not know (595).

And even as he protests too much against the habit of literary grave-robbing, Beddoes here surrenders to the language of *Hamlet*, wryly showing himself to be reliant on a received historical canon. While arguing for the creation of the new in literature, Beddoes's attention is most strongly focused on the perversities of reanimation, and in so deprecating the attempt to write in an Elizabethan or Jacobean style, he is putting the case against himself with something like definitive eloquence. Each of Beddoes's images of literary revival holds in dual perspective a bringing back to life and an unreachable lifelessness, an ineluctable process of decay.

In Beddoes's only successful publication, *The Brides' Tragedy* (1822), one of the shaping influences on the speeches of the protagonist Hesperus is his problematic relationship with his forbears in Elizabethan and Jacobean tragedy. Although *The Brides' Tragedy* is written in the spirit of literate genre-revival, allusion and echo fluctuate in explicitness and force. Particularly in soliloquies, Beddoes occasionally makes an obtrusive reference to the theatre of another time, which exerts the influence of a dead hand on the developments of his own *Tragedy*. Hesperus, named after the evening star, harbinger of death and immortality, has married secretly below his station. Compelled to marry again to secure his father's release from imprisonment, he plots the murder of his first bride, all the while becoming increasingly fixated on the enticing rhythms of death and decay. When

Hesperus speaks a soliloquy in a tapestried chamber, steeling himself for the murder, an earlier play is conjured from the latent substratum of influence, and intrudes directly onto the surface of the text:

> Yon stout dagger
> Is fairly fashioned for a blade of stitches,
> And shines, methinks, most grimly; well, thou art
> An useful tool sometimes, thy tooth works quickly,
> And if thou gnawest a secret from the heart,
> Thou tellest it not again: ha! the feigned steel
> Doth blush and steam. There is a snuff of blood.
> *[Grasps his dagger convulsively.*
> Who placed this iron aspic in my hand? (II. 4. 47–54)

Having Hesperus play the ghost of Macbeth in such a signalled manner is exactly the sort of writing Beddoes alludes to in his letter of January 1825, when he complains of the raising of ghosts by playwrights: 'just now the drama is a haunted ruin' (595). In view of this episode from *The Brides' Tragedy*, the phrase 'haunted ruin' carries a strongly self-critical charge. His own drama, published to critical acclaim three years earlier is subject to literary hauntings; and his dramatic composition since that time, particularly in the unfinished works of 1823, is 'ruined' in the sense of growing piecemeal by a process of fragmentary accumulation.

Macbeth or Hamlet in soliloquy capture the immediacy of sensation, and the drama of psychological change; their speeches in solitude do not so much report on the present disposition of the character and analyse it, but *are* that character, mapping its orientation. Macbeth, like Hamlet, is a paradigm of modern subjectivity, gradually assembling and defining 'himself' in the interface between various performances. Here, in Beddoes's Hesperus, there is a singular absence of this kind of narrative progression. His soliloquies have a luridly static quality; and Beddoes signals this by having his protagonist directed at once by his own hand and by the force of accumulated tradition. Hesperus's 'dagger scene', therefore, is a travesty of dramatic development in that it takes its form and motif from a dramatic representation of psychic upheaval and makes of this a (heavy-handed) performance, and an attraction for its literate readers.

The phantom dagger of Macbeth has an afterlife as a pictured dagger rising as though conjured from the tapestry, moving the speaker's hand unconsciously to the real dagger at his belt. The exorcism of an object from pictorial art and on to the 'stage' signals the summoning up of old dramatic forms to be re-embodied in the new text. The fact is, of course, that the 'stage' on which *The Brides' Tragedy* is played is a 'closet', or 'mental' stage, rather than a material theatre; and the elusive location of the late Romantic stage further dissipates the energetic drive towards individuation.[6] The image of 'gnawing a secret from the heart' suggests the attempt to dig up elusive information, and an encounter between matter and spirit. The style of the speech also 'doth blush and steam' with the self-consciousness and risk of the revival, and the embarrassment of trumpeting the literariness of the new drama.

The very pertinent question '*Who* placed this iron aspic in my hand?' (my emphasis) suggests that Beddoes is alive to the operation of what we would now call the ghost in the text, and the question is not easily answered: the hand of Hesperus is directed by the hand of Shakespeare and by the hand of Beddoes, who are in uneasy collaboration in the formation of this protagonist, as *Macbeth* and *The Brides' Tragedy* meet in dialogue in this scene. The presence of other hands may also be felt here — the hands of the writers who mediate between Beddoes and his mentor, and the hands of the readers of the closet drama who constitute the silent audience of this encounter. Hesperus, then, is not his own man. He is directed by divided authorities, his speeches split between registers which are differently authored. One implication of the resultant half-life of the character is that 'character', in the sense of a fictional self, is not developed in these speeches at all. The lurid poise between authors and idioms gives Hesperus's pronouncements on mortality and immortality the broken form of a hybrid existence. And the gnawing away at the paradigmatic force of the Shakespearean protagonist enacts a strategic erasure of Shakespeare's power, even as Shakespeare is simultaneously resuscitated as Beddoes's master. In this way, Beddoes is able to perform both a surrender *to* and an escape *from* powerful influence, and to assert a qualified independence for himself in the context of his admiration for Shakespeare.[7]

Beddoes's letters and poems of the 1840s reflect ironically on his early career in the '20s, which had been a time of extraordinarily fertile composition and brief public acclaim. He wrote to Kelsall from the Continent in November 1844 of the poverty of contemporary English poetry, connecting literary and national regeneration: '20 years ago I was so overrated, that of course I must fall short of all reasonable and unreasonable expectation. Times are much changed, it is true' (676–77). Twenty years previously, with the fêting of *The Brides' Tragedy* by George Darley, Bryan Waller Procter and others, Beddoes was for a short time treated to considerable fame in a literary scene of which even then he held a low opinion, or at least affected to.[8] By 1844 he has connected his increasingly miserable frustration at the revision of *Death's Jest-Book* with this early over-praise. Beddoes's reflection on the homespun mediocrity of English poetry has an aggressive edge; he is apt to characterize the present generation by referring to the blandness of Bernard Barton and 'L .E. L.' (Letitia Landon), two poets of whom he thought little. But, from his self-imposed exile in Germany and Switzerland, he had less idea of what was popular in England and of the literary scene in general than he may have realised. The letter continues in a note of semi-serious prophecy:

> Verily, verily, I say unto you amid the lyrical chirpings of your young English sparrows, shall come an eagle, and fetch fire from the altar Miltonic to relight the dark-lanterns of Diogenes and Guy Fawkes. As to the who, where, and when of the prophecy, axe Moore of the almanac. Few are called this day, and none are chosen (677).

The slumber of contemporary poetry in the doldrums of mediocrity has become a malaise of nationality. The sinister misquotation of Matthew's gospel ('few are called [...] and none are chosen') projects regeneration beyond the present generation. The Miltonic may symbolize epic stature as well as republicanism.

Diogenes, a strange allusion, stands perhaps for a robust contempt for the merely decorative or musical in poetry and other things of comfort, and an ascetic concentration on practical good; Beddoes seems to invoke the Cynic as an ally in the despondent search for true illumination and integrity. Guy Fawkes stands for violent rebellion (in spite of Beddoes's strong aversion to Roman Catholicism). All suggest new criteria for literary regeneration as expressly political; and all locate the imagined recapture of poetic fertility beyond some vaguely conceived violent upheaval.

But the said relighting of 'the dark-lanterns' is particularly interesting here. The expression 'dark-lantern' or 'dark-lanthorn' had long been associated with furtive nocturnal activity, but in the early nineteenth century had acquired specific associations with the robbing of graves. A dark-lantern was the usual name for a lamp used by 'resurrectionist' grave-robbers, masked so as to give a limited and subdued glow and avoid attracting attention.[9] With the use of a dark-lantern, the resurrectionist could go about his business without the interference of the local beadles. A dark-lantern might therefore be the emblematic illumination of belated-generation poets such as the Beddoes of 1826, who tried to resurrect and galvanize Melpomene, the subdued light in which macabre negotiations with the past were carried out. The implication is that antiquarian revivalism is regarded with suspicion; renewal of the literary state will take more than the morbid experiments of the 1820s. It will require, in fact, the removal of this generation of poetic grave-robbers. A new poetic republic will be founded with 'fire from the altar Miltonic', uncomfortably exposing the resurrection men with its brilliance. The passage indicates Beddoes's own complicity with the age of petty 'chirping' in English poetry; his early success with *The Brides' Tragedy* may have been instrumental in making English taste grow accustomed to praising the mediocre, and making greatness of it. It is symptomatic of a tendency in Beddoes's late letters to express distaste for self and for himself, and to look ahead suicidally to a future generation given the necessary space and silence by the death of his own.

The greatest poets are absent, resurrect them though we will in our words; the central section of Beddoes's last major text, 'Lines written in Switzerland', is wilfully given over to another poet in an act of theatrical ventriloquism:

> The voice, the voice! when the affrighted herds
> Dash heedless to the edge of the craggy abysses,
> And the amazed circle of scared eagles
> Spire to the clouds, amid the gletscher clash
> When avalanches fall, nation-alarums —
> But clearer, though not loud, a voice is heard
> Of proclamation or of warning stern (35–41).[10]

Written in the pre-revolutionary climate of Europe in 1848, the style of this passage is clearly an attempt to capture the revolutionary and prophetic voice of Shelley; and the use of Shelley here corresponds closely to the 'altar Miltonic' prose passage. After years of isolation and disappointment in Germany, Beddoes's lifelong ardent admiration for Shelley lends his verse a headlong bitterness and desperation. Always a champion of Shelley, and always ready to resent the fame of Byron for eclipsing that of Shelley, Beddoes makes a desperate plea for a poetic and political apocalypse which will set the record straight. Approaching with increasing explicitness a confession of his own failure as a poet, Beddoes extinguishes his own voice in favour of his hero; if Beddoes's day is done, as it seems to be, at least the day of Shelley may return with renewed vigour. The passage at large is written in Beddoes's performance of the style of Shelley; and yet the clear pronouncement of 'the voice' within it also has a Shelleyan character: Beddoes has placed Shelley both inside and outside the passage. Beddoes's unmistakably Shelleyan prophecy is thus made all the more powerful and desolate by the poet's apparent attempt to have the voice of Shelley prophesying itself — the deafening absence of the trumpet of a prophecy. Beddoes looks to his own absence, apparently willing to exchange states with Shelley, and he resolves not to break silence in print for any 'vainglorious motive' (44). Shelley's ghostly presence is welcomed into the dying texts of his disciple; Beddoes shows himself to be imbued with unacknowledged influence, as all must be in the generations of 'owl-season'. A career as a ghost-writer and raiser of ghosts has made Beddoes part of a damaging complacency of taste; therefore he will be absent, like the shaping absence of Shelley (but unlike Shelley the immortal 'luminary'), and provide the space for new voices to inhabit.

*   *   *

Writing to Kelsall in 1868, Robert Browning considers raising Beddoes from the literary grave:

> Don't fear but that your zeal and the marvellous power of the man will eventually raise up the whole Beddoes again out of the Luz, the bookful of beauty & something beyond, which you have rescued out of that 'rough sketch of beginning Adam'.[11]

Browning is alluding to Beddoes's favoured myth of resurrection, the Cabbalistic doctrine of the indestructible bone (*Luz*), the seed from which the resurrection body will grow. The doctrine appears in the third act of Beddoes's drama *Death's Jest-Book*, in which an actual resurrection takes place 'on stage':

> *Duke.* What tree is man the seed of?
> *Ziba.*   Of a ghost.
> Of his night-coming, tempest-waved phantom:
> And even as there is a round dry grain
> In a plant's skeleton, which being buried
> Can raise the herb's green body up again;
> So there is in man, a seed-shaped bone,
> Aldabaron, called by the Hebrews Luz,
> Which, being laid in the ground, will bear
> After three thousand years the grass of flesh,
> The bloody, soul-possessed weed called man (III. 3. 445–54).

In his letter to Beddoes's literary executor, Browning implies a method of reading fragmented remains not by attempting to re-assemble the extinct whole, but by projecting an absent whole. Beddoes is to be raised as a resurrection totality, not disinterred and fumbled over in the furtive glow of the dark-lantern. In effect Browning is attempting here to re-separate the sacred and profane senses of 'resurrection' which Beddoes has cynically allowed to become conflated. By suggesting a constitutive reading of this troublesome inheritance, Browning intriguingly misquotes an already unreliable text. The line '*Like the red outline of beginning Adam*' appears as a fragmentary epigraph to the *Love's Arrow Poisoned* (1823) fragments in Donner's edition, and is authenticated by Kelsall's recollection alone; no text was available to the editor, nor had there been one for some years, but Kelsall believed he remembered it and was loath to let it go to waste.

Browning rewrites 'red outline' as 'rough sketch'. If this is a deliberate comment by Browning, it is a brilliant one; if the slip is accidental, it is no less fortuitous in demonstrating the ghostly interface between generations. Browning misquotes an already highly fallible fragment of text, as a 'rough sketch', contextualizing the raising anew of the 'marvellous' Beddoes with an ironic acknowledgement that readers who perform this kind of resurrection must acknowledge themselves to be constructing or 'authoring' the author. The readers of these troublesome texts in the next generation must have the strength to read alone, and self-sufficiently, if they are to resist the stigma and contamination which Beddoes himself has attached to 'reanimation'.

This view of Beddoes as an unreliable text and indeterminate presence, reliant for any future resurrection upon readerly experience, echoes closely some of Browning's comments on his own poetry, for example, in a letter to John Ruskin of 10 December 1855, in which the words 'outline' and 'rough' also appear, and which anticipates the emphasis on the graphic which characterizes his letter to Kelsall:

> I cannot begin writing poetry till my imaginary reader has conceded licences to me which you demur at altogether. I *know* that I don't make out my conception by my language; all poetry being a putting the infinite within the finite. You would have me paint it all plain out, which can't be; but by various artifices I try to make shift with touches and bits of outlines which *succeed* if they bear the conception from me to you. [...] But I write in the

blind-dark and bitter cold, and past post-time as I fear. Take my truest thanks, and understand at least this rough writing.[12]

Browning's closing complaint that he is writing *in the dark* reinforces a hint of frustration at being asked for explicitness by literal-minded readers of his works. A more perfect reader would not begrudge him the freedoms of rough writing, and be granted for this generosity a greater illumination; but this reader is 'imaginary'. For Browning here the reader has 'imaginary' status in his poetry at the point of writing, and he implies that the relationship between a writer and a reader is a relationship between imaginary projections. The conditions Browning attempts to give for the right reading of his own poetry answer eloquently to the critical stagnation that has been Beddoes's lot since the mid-nineteenth century. And Browning is implicated in this state of affairs: Kelsall bequeathed the Beddoes papers to him, eagerly anticipating a magisterial edition, and imagining that the Browning endorsement would secure immortality for his dead friend. But Browning tired of the Beddoes project, notwithstanding his admiration for the poetry, and even in the letter to Kelsall quoted above, one can observe the gradual stagnation of a reputation; 'Don't fear', he writes, 'eventually' Beddoes will be raised.

A corpus of work which consists to such a great extent of outlines and rough writing requires the activity of the liberated reader which Browning valorizes so lightly and so definitely, or, in Beddoes's phrase, 'a bold trampling fellow – no creeper into worm-holes'. It is by a combination of editorial accident and writing design that the texts of Beddoes are in such a notoriously fragmentary condition. The transmission of his texts has been fraught with many problems: the disappearance of the 'Browning Box' of manuscripts, while in the possession of Browning's son 'Pen', left the incomplete corpus which is now extant, consisting largely of transcriptions made by James Dykes Campbell to supplement Kelsall's edition of 1850–51. Due to a combination of factors, including a willingness in both poet and executor to suppress material, Beddoes is *the* Romantic poet of fragments.

Beddoes's drama *The Last Man*, according to a letter of February 1824, was once substantial enough for him to submit it to the judgement of Procter:

> I have finished the first act of a play; oh! so stupid. Procter has the brass to tell me that he likes that fool The last man. I shall go on with neither; there are now three first acts in my drawer: when I have got two more I shall stitch them together, and stick the sign of a fellow tweedling a mask in his fingers, with "good entertainment for man and ass" understood (580).

The jesting tone conveys a bitterly ironic self-awareness in Beddoes of the opportunism of his fragmentary writing method. Again to Kelsall, Beddoes writes from Göttingen in October 1827:

> I can really send you nothing of my own: I have a pretty good deal in fragments which I want to cement together and make a play of — among them is the last Man. They will all go into the Jest book — or the Fool's Tragedy [...] I have dead game in great quantities, but when or how it will be finished Aesculapius alone knows (636).

Beddoes's statement of intention to pillage his drama so ruthlessly is consistent with Campbell's descriptions of the manuscripts from between the publication of *The Brides' Tragedy* (1822) and his departure for the Continent (1825). One of Beddoes's composition notebooks is said by Campbell to have contained an index to the accumulating fragments, so that an apt conceit could be located and withdrawn for cannibalistic use elsewhere.[13] Dead matter from one text is plundered to fuel its successor: in statements of this kind Beddoes confesses to a fragmenting, even editorial method of writing. Images of patching, stitching and pasting in relation to the management of his texts abound in his letters from this time up until the 1840s, and throughout these years he indulges the macabre comedy of making analogies between corpus and corpse.

Beddoes's writings are obtrusively 'fragmentary', both in terms of their textual disarray, and in terms of the erratic rhythms of his writing, so often apt to pursue a knotty conceit at the expense of overall cohesiveness. There is an unclear relationship between this fragmentariness and the state of the poet's reputation, his standing on the margins of the Romantic canon.[14] The fragment *topos* is now so well established in Romantic studies that textual disarray might be expected to be an incentive rather than a disincentive to the reading and study of Beddoes. The critic Fiona J. Stafford has written on Beddoes *en passant*, as one of the Romantics who treated the 'last man' myth:

> The apparently fractured work [has] the inescapable coherence of a nightmare. [...] The inability to create *The Last Man* was [...] inherent in the subject itself. [...] The sense of experiencing the catastrophe — of all form being torn apart — was captured more successfully by Beddoes than any of his contemporaries, but the logical consequence of his vision was a broken work which was to prove an emblem of his own, tragic life.[15]

Stafford is complimentary about the paradoxical coherence she observes in Beddoes's treatment of the 'last man', which now exists only as a loose association of fragments in blank verse. But the transfer from textuality to biography is made with some smoothness here. This glancing reference to Beddoes in a much wider study may be representative of how the cult of the fragmentary can be brought to bear on Romantic texts. Contemporary criticism tends to privilege the fragmentary text in order to enlist it in a wider discourse of fracture and defacement. The reader of a fragment can have no ultimate recourse to the author's supposed intention, since the text is by definition deficient in determined closure, and even a small fragment can be a powerful ally in theoretical debate. The combination of the extreme fragmentariness of Beddoes's texts with this tendency in current critical practice might be expected to give him a certain timeliness at present.

With the loss of so many major manuscripts, Beddoes may never be edited from first principles again. Donner's 1935 edition will in all likelihood continue to be the main point of reference. In this sense, the 'dark-lantern' reading of piecemeal re-construction is no longer possible; Beddoes must now be read by 'bold trampling fellows' and 'raised out of the Luz, the bookful of beauty & something beyond'. The writings of Beddoes provide a greater concentrated richness of unfinished texts than those of almost any other Romantic poet. The readerly resurrection of projecting the absent whole, so finely captured in Browning's urbane hesitation, must now operate whenever Beddoes's writings are opened.

The example of Beddoes as a haunted and a haunting poet serves to emphasize the part played by a certain necessary element of suppression in the achievement of literary succession, and it foregrounds the liberated reader. Harold Bloom writes in the *apophrades* chapter of *The Anxiety of Influence*: 'Perhaps all Romantic style, at its heights, depends upon a successful manifestation of the dead in the garments of the living, as though the dead poets were given a suppler freedom than they had found for themselves'.[16] Beddoes establishes the macabre supernatural deliberately as a trope for the elusiveness and intricacies of poetic indebtedness, and develops this trope system with an intensity that anticipates the 'ghost' of modern critical practice. But he is also the poet who, making a virtue of defeat at the hands of the Bloomian precursor, can turn this idiom on its head: rather than parading in his borrowed robes, he steals the clothes of past and future and buries them back in the grave to await the true resurrection of a transforming reading.

Far from being *merely* a grave-robber, Beddoes develops the language of anatomy and disinterment to embrace a wide variety of shifting relationships with the literary past. The 'last Elizabethan' and 'prince of morticians' views of Beddoes allow for only a fairly straightforward use of the 'grave-robbing' analogy, and fail ultimately to take into account the intensity and depth of Beddoes's self-consciousness in developing this vocabulary: they suggest, respectively, that he somehow reproduced exactly the conditions of Elizabethan drama, and that he was purely passive in his necrophile devotion to Renaissance literature. Neither does justice to the amplitude of the anatomy language in Beddoes. The patterns of morbid intertextuality in his works display an active and subtle engagement with literary forebears of various ages, and his suicidal projection into the emptiness of the future is bold, defiant and dignified. Beddoes, of course, pre-empts the modern canon's queasy uncertainty about his works and status. If the present canon of 'Romanticism' is somewhat less open and volatile than we have been led to believe, and if at the last there is no very obvious welcome for Beddoes, this state of affairs will hold few surprises for the poet who so energetically sought to remove himself from the poetic landscape in the 1840s in favour of his beloved Shelley. Similarly, it is with Beddoes's ironic prompting that we see him as a transitional poet, standing midway between Shelley and Browning. It strikes a different kind of irony, however, that a body of work so dominated by and given over to the currently empowered *topoi* of ghostly transition and fragmented remains, is still dug up so rarely.

---

[1] Strachey writes of Beddoes's letter on the revival of the drama ('these reanimations are vampire-cold' (January 1825); all quotations from Beddoes are taken from *The Works of Thomas Lovell Beddoes*, ed. by H. W. Donner (London: Oxford University Press, 1935; repr. NY: AMS Press, 1978), p. 595): 'The words [...] are usually quoted by critics, on the rare occasions on which his poetry is discussed, as an instance of the curious incapacity of artists to practise what they preach. But the truth is that Beddoes was not a "creeper into worm-holes," he was not even a "reviver"; he was a reincarnation', 'The Last Elizabethan' (1907), in *Books and Characters, French and English* (London: Chatto and Windus, 1922), pp. 225–52 (p. 239). Pound calls Beddoes's dialect 'purely archaistic', 'Beddoes and Chronology', 1917, in *Selected Prose, 1909–1965*, ed. by William Cookson (London: Faber and Faber, 1973), pp. 348–53 (p. 351). The epithet 'prince of morticians' is from Canto LXXX, *The Cantos of Ezra Pound* (London: Faber and Faber, 1964), p. 531.

[2] 'Stanzas from the Grande Chartreuse', ll. 85–86, *The Poems of Matthew Arnold*, ed. by Kenneth Allott, 2nd edn, rev. by Miriam Allott (London and NY: Longman, 1979).

[3] *Blackwood's Edinburgh Magazine*, 14 (1823), 639–46 (p. 646). For the author of this article a 'goblin' is very similar to a 'ghost', but Beddoes treats the words as synonyms throughout his writings; these lines are spoken by Mandrake in *Death's Jest-Book*: 'They all live jollily underground and sneak about a little in the night air to hear the news and laugh at their poor innocent great-grandchildren, who take them for goblins, and tremble for fear of death' (III. 3. 11–14).

[4] *The London Magazine*, 9 (1824), 253–56.

[5] A good example of this style is the review of Beddoes's *The Improvisatore* in *The Monthly Review; or Literary Journal, enlarged*, 95 (1821), 218–19.

[6] For a recent discussion of the vexed question of Romantic 'mental' theatre, and Beddoes's place in this context, see Alan Richardson, *A Mental Theater: Poetic Drama and Consciousness in the Romantic Age* (University Park, Penn. and London: Pennsylvania University Press, 1988), especially '*Death's Jest-Book*: "Shadows of Words"', pp. 154–73.

[7] Beddoes yields to no-one in his 'bardolatry': '"A star" you call him: if he was a star, all the other stage-scribblers can hardly be considered a constellation of brass buttons. I say he was an universe, and all material existence with its excellencies and defects was reflected in shadowy thought upon the chrystal waters of his imagination, ever-glorified as they were by the sleepless sun of his golden intellect' (3 March 1824, p. 581). The same letter gives some detailed commentary on the stage-craft of Macbeth (p. 581).

[8] See, for example, Bryan Waller Procter's review in *The London Magazine*, 7 (1823), 169–72; 'On Ancient and Modern Tragedy', *The Album*, 3, 5 (1823), 1–31; the review in *The Gentleman's Magazine*, 93, 2 (1823), 347; George Darley (as 'John Lacy'), 'A Sixth Letter to the Dramatists of the Day', *The London Magazine*, 8 (1823), 645–52; John Wilson's review in *Blackwood's*, 14, 723–29.

[9] Ruth Richardson documents this specific sense of the term with reference to the biography and autobiography of nineteenth-century medical men: 'Probably the best extant description of grave-robbers' techniques is to be found in the memoirs of a Victorian President of the BMA, Sir Robert Christison, which contain detail so precise as to suggest the author had been an eyewitness/accomplice in his youth. The bulk of the work was done at night, using wooden shovels where noiselessness was crucial, and a "dark-lanthorn" – a device commonly used by burglars: designed to shed light where necessary, but not to attract attention', *Death, Dissection and the Destitute* (London and NY: Routledge and Kegan Paul, 1987), p. 59; Richardson finds references to 'dark lanterns' in *The Life of Sir Robert Christison, Edited by His Sons* (Edinburgh: [no pub.], 1885–86), p. 175, and B. B. Cooper, *The Life of Sir Astley Cooper* (London: John W. Parker, 1843), p. 357. Cooper was a pre-eminent figure in the London hospitals at the time of Keats's medical training. The term 'dark-lantern' has other applications (for example, the *OED* cites 'the Servant or Agent that Receives the Bribe', 1700), but it is highly likely that Beddoes, his father an eminent medical man, and apt himself to boast of his skill with the dissector's scalpel, would be aware of this usage and find the connection with theft and morbid anatomy both appealing and expedient. The studied flippancies 'resurrectionist' and 'resurrection man' for a procurer of 'things for the surgeon', were both in well-established use by Beddoes's time.

[10] *Gletscher* is the German word for glacier, imported into English from the Swiss dialect in the sixteenth century, but generally rare; in using the word, Beddoes indicates the specifically Swiss, rather than generally Germanic, environment of the poem.

[11] *The Browning Box: or, the Life and Works of Thomas Lovell Beddoes as reflected in letters by his friends and admirers*, ed. by H.W. Donner (London: Oxford University Press, 1935), 19 June 1868, p. 111.

[12] W. G. Collingwood, *The Life and Work of John Ruskin with Portraits and Other Illustrations*, 2 vols (London: Methuen, 1893), pp. 200, 202. I am grateful to Catherine Maxwell for drawing my attention to this letter.

[13] Dykes Campbell's description of the 'Adye' notebook is quoted in 'Appendix A' to *Works*, pp. 691–95.

[14] I argue elsewhere for the relationship between fragmentation in Beddoes and the occult subject matter of his most substantial work, and comment more fully on the use made of the idea of fragmentation by modern critics, including Fiona J. Stafford, Thomas McFarland and Marjorie Levinson; see *Scattered Limbs: The Making and Unmaking of 'Death's Jest-Book'* (Belper: Thomas Lovell Beddoes Society, 1996).

[15] *The Last of the Race: The Growth of a Myth from Milton to Darwin* (Oxford: Oxford University Press, 1994), pp. 214–16.

[16] *The Anxiety of Influence: A Theory of Poetry* (NY: Oxford University Press, 1973), p. 143.

Ghastly Visualities: Keats and Victorian Art

Sarah Wootton

Stephen Prickett hails Keats as 'the most potent single influence upon the art of the Victorian era'.[1] As literary subjects became increasingly commercial within the High Victorian art market, poets such as Keats and Tennyson supplied painters with a rich source of original, easily visualized, source material. Keats's poetry had a profound effect upon nineteenth-century art from the beginnings of the Pre-Raphaelite Movement to the last Romantics of the 1920s and 30s. The Romantic poet's presence was fundamental to the formation of the Brotherhood; representations of his work are key to our understanding of the Pre-Raphaelite aesthetic and the respective fortunes of its founder members. The main celebrity of the Brotherhood, Dante Gabriel Rossetti, fostered an almost sacred reverence for Keats, yet felt unable to complete a work based on his extensive readings of the poet. I shall be attempting to determine the reasons underlying this painter's tortured and complex anxiety of influence in the light of his colleagues' pronounced productivity, whilst also examining the attraction of Keats's verse for these artists. The first two sections of this essay explore visual interpretation from the perspective of individual motivations and aesthetic principles. The third part broadens in scope to incorporate the analysis of an art movement, not struggling against subjective spectres, but confronted with the corporeal horrors of the First World War. Cultural investment in Keats's work continued during a time of rapid destabilization when connections with Victorianism were being severed. Each section of this essay will focus on a different aspect of the varied spectrum of Keats-based art.

PART 1

The picture has always told me another story, however[2]

In early 1848 Keats's poetry still failed to attract public popularity; demand for reprints of his work remained negligible and Monckton Milnes's definitive Victorian biography was yet to be published.[3] However, a young aspiring artist, William Holman Hunt, had acquired an edition of the poet's verse in 1847, in 'book-bins labeled "this lot 4d."'; he acquainted his new associate, John Everett Millais, with this 'discovery' and began work on the first Hunt-Keats collaboration, 'The Eve of St. Agnes'.[4] Even though Hunt claims the painting was 'hung somewhat high up in the Architectural Room' of the Royal Academy, it received a prize of seventy pounds and the attention of a fellow Keats enthusiast. Hunt recalls,

> Rossetti came up to me, repeating with emphasis his praise, and loudly declaring that my picture of "The Eve of St. Agnes" was the best in the collection. Probably the fact that the subject was taken from Keats made him the more unrestrained (Hunt, 106).

Hunt claims that 'our common enthusiasm for Keats brought us together', forging an intimacy between unlikely allies with disparate views on artistic execution and purpose (105). George H. Ford states that this Keatsian kinship provided the catalyst for the formation of the Pre-Raphaelite Brotherhood, 'a group in which an admiration for Keats was almost a badge of membership'.[5]

The representation of Madeline and Porphyro, in the painting, captures the caution of the lovers in the denouement of Keats's poem, and, in the contorted pose of the Porter, his 'uneasy sprawl'.[6] Hunt also incorporates 'the bloated wassailers', seen through the framed recesses on the left-hand side of the composition, who by the penultimate stanza of Keats's poem have already drunk themselves into oblivion (346).[7] Hunt's manipulation of his source, his rearrangement of Keats's narrative order, creates a climactic moment which encapsulates more of Hunt's didactic interpretation of the poem: 'the sacredness of honest responsible love and the weakness of proud intemperance' (Hunt, 85). Therefore, Hunt is re-fashioning the Keatsian scene after his own moral vision, circumventing the sensuality at the poem's epicentre. Julie F. Codell perceives the painting as a deliberate misreading: 'Hunt's selection of the escape scene avoids the poem's complex emotional responses and counter-responses of the bedroom and any direct depiction of the topics of sexual desire, consummation, and seduction'.[8] Codell cannot, however, penetrate beyond the artist's imposed meaning to the painting's 'hidden' agenda. Whilst Codell suggests that Pre-Raphaelite employment of Keats provided a means to 'explore the subject of transgressive desire through painterly conventions', she also creates an image of Hunt as too 'squeamish' to engage directly with Porphyro's voyeurism and seduction (341, 351). An analysis of Hunt's 'The Eve of St. Agnes' evokes a rather different, less confused, picture of the artist and his work; the physical proximity of the lovers forges a suggestive intimacy, whilst sexual energy is also generated by the phallicism discernible in the hero's clasped hilt and the belt dangling between his thighs.[9] The colour of Madeline's gown is also suggestive of carnal intent, confirming another kinship between Hunt and Keats in their passion for purple: 'in his pained heart / Made purple riot; then doth he propose / A strategem, that makes the beldame start' (137–39).[10] Subconsciously or not, Hunt's painting responds to the sexual display of Keats's verse rather than an imposed morality or mystical worship of beauty; his appreciation of Keats does not consist of distant reverence but a complete sensuous immersion: a consummation with the poet's aesthetic, awakening him to the ambiguity inherent within the text.

A further contradiction in Codell's argument emerges when she maintains that Hunt utilized Keats to 'carry the message of rebellion', but subsequently states that the painter's finished product remained 'conventional'; even his early work, the Isabella drawing and both versions of 'The Eve of St. Agnes', 'were all tied to market expectations' (Codell, 363). The original Pre-Raphaelites, however, shared strong idealistic convictions, and, if Hunt's initial motivations were based on personal gain, the formation of the rebellious Brotherhood could only be viewed as a misguided blunder. Pre-Raphaelite paintings were anything but popular during the early, turbulent years and, as Hunt's autobiography attests, the money raised by each sale was of vital importance in saving the artist from virtual destitution. To the despair of his family, Hunt passed up the prospect of a secure job in the City to devote himself entirely to painting and, unlike Millais and Rossetti, he had no middle-class background to fall back upon. However, Hunt's fortunes markedly improved, as did those of Millais, when the artist finally capitulated to market forces: in 1860, 'The Finding of the Saviour in the Temple' was sold to Gambart for a staggering five and a half thousand pounds (the highest price yet paid to a living artist). Hunt's return to Keats's verse, in the form of 'Isabella' (1868), also proved lucrative, bringing the artist two and a half thousand pounds: a figure as significant to our reading of the painting as the heroine herself. The aesthetic value of this work is overshadowed by the artist's accommodation of middle-class tastes: the solecisms of Keats's verse now circumvented to achieve mainstream acceptability.[11]

Unlike Hunt's earlier sketch based on this poem, concerned with issues of social hierarchy and injustice, 'Isabella' embodies the sombre mood of the heroine towards the denouement of Keats's work.[12] Death's pervasive presence is reflected in the dark gloom of the chamber and the skull-head handles adorning the majolica pot. Hunt emphasizes the luxuriance of Lorenzo's decomposition in the rich ornamentation of the painting and the thriving bush which has germinated out of his murder. His severed head is indeed a 'prize' which Isabella sensuously tends with her caressing fingers ('Isabella', 402). Her opulent hair not only drapes, as in Keats's poem, but intertwines with the nutrient rich soil. In this painting, death is paradoxically equated with fertility; Hunt's heroine is not constantly weeping or anorexically self-consumptive but, like the basil plant, she is thriving: here, Isabella is a robust woman in stark contrast to the pale, retiring maids figured in Hunt's and Millais's earlier conceptions.[13]

The patterned rug which has slipped from her waist provocatively reveals a transparent dress through which we can discern both her dark pubic hair and the radiance of her skin's texture, whilst the scattering of roses and the passion flowers on the exquisitely crafted altar-cloth contribute to the feeling of an illicit sexual communion. The viewer is invited to penetrate the dark recesses of private bereavement, and directed to the necrophilic union hinted at in Keats's poem. After the early inhibitions of the lovers are dissolved by Lorenzo's death, thus releasing them from social conventions, Isabella nurtures her sexual supplement; the sensual description of the silken scarf, to enwrap Lorenzo's member in 'odorous ooze', represents a displaced allegory for sexual intercourse (399–411). Such perverse pleasures stimulate Isabella's distraught nerves whilst gradually consuming her vitality: unlike Hunt's painting in which Lorenzo's death generates an invigorating eroticism that 'fleshes out' the heroine. Keats's Isabella remains an ambiguous figure whose paradoxical fruition necessitates a disquieting and undiagnosable wasting disease, whilst Hunt's comely belle circumvents such semantic perplexity by merely satisfying the voracious appetite of a consumer clientele: 'Isabella' is served as a healthy object for the cannibalistic voyeur. The awkward friction of early Pre-Raphaelitism has dissipated into conventional contentment: personal success producing a rather suspect subtext of stylistic and sexual satiation.

PART 2

the wind blows cold out of the inner shrine of fear[14]

Whether we view Hunt's work with Keats's poetry as either aesthetically or economically productive, semantically regenerative or perversely parasitic, the artist engaged creatively with the precursor throughout his lengthy career. In contrast, Rossetti remained either unable or unwilling to respond to the visuality he also admired in Keats's verse. Rossetti predicted on several occasions that the next Keats would be a painter, presumably putting himself forward as an ideal candidate, but the prestigious mantle was never to be awarded to this devotee. During his lifetime, Rossetti produced a number of preparatory sketches from Keats, none of which were developed further, and a half-finished oil work. A biographer of Rossetti, Alicia Craig Faxon, excuses the incompletion of this large scale oil painting, 'Mnemosyne' (derived from the female figure in Book Three of *Hyperion*, plate 11), on the basis that 'he was a seriously ill man [who] surmised that he had not long to live'.[15] Rossetti was undeniably unwell during this period (although it is difficult to discern between genuine illness, hypochondria and the effects of completely severing the chloral that fed his addiction) yet as Thomas Hall Caine states, 'Weak as he was in body, his intellect was as powerful as in his best days, and he was just as eager to occupy himself'.[16] As Rossetti's letters of this time attest, he was intellectually engaged with the forthcoming publication of *Ballads and Sonnets* and had completed the immense canvas of 'The Daydream'. Faxon asserts that 'Mnemosyne' was 'the last painting that Rossetti completed before his death', yet the work was never finished and sold in its incomplete state to Leyland in 1881, whilst Rossetti subsequently saw 'The Daydream' through to its final stage and extensively reworked the composition after all mention of 'Mnemosyne' had ceased.[17] When we examine previous abortive attempts to interpret Keats, 'Mnemosyne' does not represent an uncharacteristic instance of painter's paralysis but one example in a lifelong pattern which can be traced back to a rough sketch of *La Belle Dame sans Merci*, drawn by Rossetti in the mid 1850s (plate 12).

The drawing of *Belle Dame* incorporates a verse from the source text, beginning 'I set her on my pacing steed' (21). Rossetti has selected the stanza in which the hero appears most active in a poem which predominantly portrays the languidity of the knight; this conveys the artist's confidence in producing a positive interpretation within an unnaturally inhibiting environment. In contrast, the 'lady' looks startled by her companion's physical closeness, representing the converse side of Rossetti's secured masculine empathy. If nothing else, this drawing provides an early example of Rossetti's disturbing schizophrenia when faced with the task of interpreting Keats. However, the most productive approach to this sketch does not lie in a semantic reading of its encoded subtext but in an analysis of its failure as a piece of precursory art work. Compositionally it is weak: unlike Hunt, Rossetti was not proficient in animal drawing, and the arrangement of his human figures is equally deficient. The hero and heroine appear to belong not only to the different planes of existence in Keats's poem, but to independent pictures: note the stiff straightness of the knight awkwardly juxtaposed against the curving lines of the lady, and the wind blowing her tresses into a stream of locks which does not touch his hair.[18] Admittedly, this is just a drawing, a setting down of ideas on paper, but when we compare it to sketches worked on at the same time, the difference in quality becomes undisguisably problematic; for example, 'Hamlet and Ophelia' is a far more detailed, accomplished and symbolically rich piece, and even its hastily executed understudy is structurally stronger. By contrast, *Belle Dame* is a singularly lacklustre, half-hearted attempt to capture some of the beauty and sexual potency of a poem so dearly prized by the artist.

However, as noted at the beginning of the first part of this essay, Rossetti's exuberant enthusiasm for Keats forged a bond between Hunt and himself. Hunt audaciously proclaimed that his 'The Eve of St. Agnes' was the first visual representation of Keats's poetry when Rossetti had previously produced an earlier version of *Belle Dame* for the Cyclographic Society of which both Hunt and Millais were members. Codell adds,

> Some scholars speculate that Rossetti, who had first suggested Keatsian subjects for a series of drawings for the Cyclographic Club, was perhaps the originator of the idea of using Keats as a subject (342).

Arthur C. Benson claims that it was Rossetti who 'discovered' Keats at the age of eighteen, two years prior to the formation of the Brotherhood: 'At this time [1846] Rossetti's intellectual ardour was very great. He read Shelley and Keats with profound admiration', but, Benson adds, 'In 1847 he discovered Browning, and everything else sank into the background' (12).[19] Perhaps this explains Rossetti's lack of artistic engagement with the Romantic poet, yet Rossetti's copious correspondence on the subject of Keats refutes such a supposition. As Doughty and Wahl's comprehensive edition of Rossetti's letters attest, Keats remained a regular item on the aesthetic agenda of the painter until his death. His correspondence with Buxton Forman, editor of *The Poetical Works and Other Writings of John Keats*, displayed such an extensive knowledge of Keats's entire body of work that it was privately published in a slim volume shortly after World War One. Rossetti's letters on this subject justify George Milner's claim that the painter was 'something of a specialist' on this Romantic poet, but they are equally revealing of the reasons why he felt unable to transform his impressive understanding into art.[20]

Rossetti prefaces his correspondence with Buxton Forman by asserting that he is a 'lover of Keats', and certainly the Romantic poet functions as partner to the painter, shadowing his thoughts and comments on art.[21] Keats becomes a standard by which all contemporary poetry is judged: friends are seen as a 'Keatsian sort of bard', William Morris is a 'dreary romantic [who] goes back to Keats with a little modification', and portraits of Chatterton are valued for having a 'savour of Keats in them'.[22] His correspondence with Hall Caine, during the last years of his life, reveals the extent of Rossetti's preoccupation with Keats: an obsessive urge to prove that the Romantic poet was indeed 'the one true heir of Shakespeare' (23 November 1879).[23] Rossetti dwelt upon Keats and revered him to such a degree that it disabled his own working practice; the brilliance of what Rossetti perceived as artistic 'perfection', blinded his own painterly vision (13 July 1881). His conviction in the unadulterated excellence of Keats's poetry harboured distinct moral overtones; and the pedestal upon which he placed the 'flawless gift' of the precursor's verse proved too sacred a shrine to be stained by his own sensual emulation (11 June 1880).

Following Buchanan's devastating attack on the salaciousness of Rossetti's verse, in the infamous essay 'The Fleshly School of Poetry', the artist revises the nature of his appreciation of Keats: he is newly enraptured by the simplicity of the narrative poems, and, in particular, the chastity of his favourite poem, *La Belle Dame sans Merci*. At the same time as Rossetti omits a ballad from his 1881 volume of poetry because 'it deals trivially with a base amour', he asks Buxton Forman to refrain from publishing Keats's poem 'Sharing Eve's Apple', because its ignoble expression of sexual passion is 'rather vulgar [...] and gives no idea of his true nature'.[24] Rossetti is also saddened by the publication of Keats's love-letters: 'they add nothing to one's idea of his *epistolary* powers' (1 April 1880, my italics). Yet, another letter to Buxton Forman reveals suggestive slips in his 'cover story'; he relates that he has been 'greatly pained by the perusal of the Keats-Brawne letters', but also 'greatly interested'.[25] Even though Rossetti deems some of the letters to be 'markedly passionate', the book should still be 'obtainable as a literary treasure', presumably to admit his own, private access to the letters whilst preserving the carefully constructed reputation of Keats.[26] The sanitized image of Keats, as the idol of wholesomeness and moral purity, facilitates a vision of his own work in which Rossetti can claim: 'I deal with nothing but what is healthy' (25 October 1880); Rossetti is projecting onto the life and works of the precursor a self-reflexive discourse of artistic wish-fulfilment.

William Henry Marquess also comments on this facet of Rossetti's poetic criticism:

> Clearly, Rossetti not only pities and praises but also identifies with these martyrs of English song. Indeed, the composite portrait's psychological lineaments may resemble those of its author more than the features of any one of the subjects. This is an artistic re-creation of biography, following a model made after the writer's own image (63).

However, the construction of such an elaborate framework of denial is undermined by the actual practice of artistic emulation.[27] Rossetti's sensual kinship with Keats can barely be contained in his elegiac tribute; he lingers on the Romantic poet's 'reverberant lips', whilst the daisies grow profusely from his grave: 'Their fragrance clings around thy name', but when confronted with reproducing a Keatsian voluptuousness in paint, self-deception founders and a series of thwarted desires are revealed. Rossetti was evidently interested in the 'sweet moan' of sexual communion in *Belle Dame*, as is apparent in his final drawing on this theme in which the lovers are bonded through sexual tension alone (20). His later rendition of Keats's figure, Mnemosyne, represents a characteristic tribute to the abundant flesh, copious curls, wide eyes and full, red mouth of the Rossettian image of Jane Morris, with the suggestive inclusion of a phallic chalice upheld by the model which appears to be emitting a white glow from its teat-end, resembling seminal discharge. Mnemosyne was the goddess of poetry and painting, providing a fitting tribute to the word-painting precursor, yet, as with the equally troublesome social study 'Found', whilst the subject remained absorbing to the artist over a period of years, resolution became increasingly elusive. The symbolic nature of 'Mnemosyne', encapsulating the essence of Keats's twofold artistic influence, suggests a reason for such pronounced procrastination; within this ultimate conjoining of the arts lies a further source of anxiety: 'ekphrastic fear'.[28] As well as being haunted by the Bloomian spectre of belatedness, the ekphrastic artist, in responding verbally to an existing visual medium or vice-versa, is necessarily relegated to the uncomfortable status of Other in deference to the Self of original conception. Rossetti's 'Mnemosyne' represents one painting in a series of beautifying battles with the sexual Other, and also exhibits the 'resistance and counterdesire' which W. J. T. Mitchell identifies as a by-product of this illicit union of the arts (151). Grant F. Scott even suggests that ekphrasis has historically been stigmatized and associated with the unnatural relations of incest.[29]

To summarize, Rossetti was anxious to avert both the revelation of sensuality in his Keatsian art and the disintegration of his imposed discourse of spiritual purity; he feared both the private and public exposure of hypocrisy, insincerity and ingenuousness (the humiliating denunciation of the fake). The imbalanced mind of the artist also provides the focus for Lucy Newlyn's essay, 'The Anxiety of the Writing Subject', in which the precursor is perceived as a two-headed monster paralysing the present-day poet.[30] Lurking beneath the luxury of an easy empathy lies the spectre of recognition, the ghastly reflection of the Self in the Other. As Jonathan Bate put it, 'In no other case are you enjoined to achieve and at the same time to try at all costs, *not* to follow closely what you admire ... The arts stutter, stagger, pull back into paralysis and indecision before such a conflict of demand'.[31] The pressure to simultaneously 'kindle and restrain' the influence of the precursor creates a 'double burden of anxiety' which distracts, and ultimately develops into a blockage (Newlyn, 623). An even more discrediting fate is the guilty fear of repetition, and the shameful feelings of fraudulence and plagiarism it engenders lead inevitably to the figurative death of the artist, or what Newlyn refers to as 'extinction' (623). The prospect of the phantom-like twin mocking his mirror image may have haunted Rossetti to the unbearable degree that the literary painter could not work from his poetic hero.

Newlyn also argues in her essay that there exists an ever present, murky middle ground between the overshadowed interpreter and his mentor that can prevent creative contact, acting as an unbridgeable gulf, which remains unaccountable and genuinely 'ghostly' (622). Perhaps Rossetti's increasingly frequent bouts of paranoia and neurosis, towards the end of his life, developed out of the self-knowledge that he had fallen from his chosen path and become lost in this limbo-like state; he required the precursor to aid him on his quest for pure Beauty, yet his Keats-based art realized only subconscious images of sexual fetishism. Rossetti's consciously noble intentions were perverted by the very medium he had chosen to illuminate his ideal, ensnaring the painter in a realm of hesitation and self-doubt. Or, maybe it is simply the case that he did not endeavour, in marked contrast to the Bloomian compulsion, to discredit and expel the influence of the forefather; Rossetti preferred an alternate, and more congenial, form of uncritical worship which led to a frustrating imbalance between emulative desires and a disabling impotency.

PART 3

> It is hardly surprising, then, that many literary figures [at the turn of the century] felt that they were living between two worlds, one dead and the other struggling to be born.[32]

Rossetti's inability to react positively to Keats's visuality is, however, singular, deriving from individual inhibitions. Whilst Rossetti abandoned his creative tribute to *Belle Dame*, many artists subsequently produced stimulating and insightful interpretations on this theme, following the Pre-Raphaelite movement's popularization of Keats as an artistic source. As Pre-Raphaelitism was gradually absorbed into mainstream art, Keats underwent a similar transformation from radical to middle-class icon, his poetry becoming a legitimate and lucrative source of imitative images. Almost guaranteed a buyer, paintings with ostensibly Keatsian themes crowded the walls of late nineteenth-century art exhibitions; most merely sentimentalized a scene from a narrative poem, but some artists still perceived visual potential and poignancy in his verse.

Waterhouse's *fin-de-siècle* interpretation of *Belle Dame* evokes the dark atmosphere pervading the lovers' pairing (plate 13). As in Keats's poem, the Self through which we perceive the story enters the alien environment of the Other, wherein he becomes entrapped and begins to wither. Waterhouse's knight is merely a shadow of his former being, awaiting his place in the nightmare procession of 'death-pale' warriors (38). The paleness of Belle Dame's skin, highlighting her red lips, suggests a vampiric encounter in which her conquest is drained of his vital life forces, yet Waterhouse's woman is no typical *femme fatale* like Rossetti's harsh, unyielding portraits of the Siren (for example, 'Lady Lilith'). This version of Belle Dame is sensitive and wistful; she is the soft, delicate maiden who woos Keats's knight with 'sweet moan', entices him with the sensual delights of 'fragrant zone', 'honey wild, and manna-dew', as well as capturing the hint of remorse, 'And there she wept and sighed full sore', before the climactic consummation (18–26). This 'faery's child' is not intended to represent the threatening Other: it is the knight, with his spectral pallor, who disconcerts the viewer (14). His ghastly monotones of grey and brown contrast with the girl's luminescent purples and blues which sparkle with the gems, pearls and flowers of her wood. This permits a reading of the lovers in terms of symbolic binary oppositions: the knight represents the twilight of the fading day in comparison to Belle Dame's colourful dawn, and he embodies the end of Autumn when 'the harvest's done' and the stark glare of Winter withers the sedge from the lake (8), to her fresh Spring. The warm blood of life animates her veins whereas the despondency of death seeps through his, not through any cannibalistic consumption, but because the newly evolving embryo of the twentieth century favours her above the spectres of a passing era.[33]

In Frank Dicksee's *Belle Dame* the close, foreboding wood and sinister gloom of Waterhouse's painting has cleared to reveal a picturesque landscape and bright, radiant sunset (plate 14). This Siren is beautiful: she is enjoying her sensuality and revelling in an undisguised sexual power. In direct contrast to

Rossetti's configuration, it is Dicksee's heroine who has actively taken charge of the knight's steed (literally and metaphorically holding the reins) whilst he is left stranded, passive and 'woe-begone' (6). She embodies movement in the flow of her dress and the fall of her hair as opposed to her counterpart who is stationary, encased in restrictive armour. She is carefree in comparison with the heroines in Dicksee's most famous work; for example, 'Chivalry', in which traditional gender stereotypes are reinforced: masculinity is triumphant, conquering his combatant and claiming the sexuality proffered as reward by a rather fearful femininity. Such scenes, featuring male heroism and female bondage, were commonplace during the 1870s and 80s: Walter Crane's 'The Laidly Worm' was exhibited four years before 'Chivalry' and Edward Burne-Jones's 'Perseus Slaying the Serpent' also appeared at this time, highlighting Dicksee's *Belle Dame* as a rather subversive divergence from the norm.

    A similar instance of uncharacteristic gender role reversal can be discerned in Russell Flint's early twentieth-century *Belle Dame* (plate 16). Like Dicksee's work, the figures partake of the Victorian, and Keatsian, vogue for ornate medievalism: there is more than a suggestion that the hero and heroine represent Lancelot and Guinevere. The work is light, the heroine playful, as the water-colours merge to provide soft, gentle hues: yet, concealed within this delightful ditty of a painting, lurks a disconcerting strangeness. Guinevere is poised above the vulnerable figure of the slumbering knight; one can imagine her creeping stealthily into a position of power, reflecting, perhaps, Flint's fears over the progressive, but increasingly militant, demands of women's suffrage. However, the viewer cannot help but fear for the knight basking in his post-orgasmic somnolence and clutching the sword, his final phallic emblem of masculinity, which disturbingly forms an inverted cross with the erect lance. The landscape appears to be conspiring against him: one tree entwines the knight's shield, his material mode of defence against the enemy, whilst the other tree houses the most unsettling corner in literary painting. The overall mood and style of the work does not prepare the viewer for the host of ghostly faces peering out of the foliage, the most disturbing aspect of which is the indefinite number of eyes prying into the lovers' intimate scene. One explanation for the presence of these eerie spectres would be to suggest that they represent the all-pervasive public sphere of the Arthurian court intruding into the privacy of its subjects: an alternative reading is that the ghosts of chivalry, the spirits of knights past, have come to witness the final, symbolic defeat of a doomed era. Via the 'safe' medium of the past, Flint is able to contribute to the historically specific discourse of women's rights as it arose out of the crumbling infrastructure of the Victorian male hierarchy.

One of the chief characteristics of Keats's verse is the examination of such semantically provocative fault-lines in which the overshadowed new struggles to separate itself from the inheritance of the old.[34] Before the legacy of the precursor can be completely eradicated, old and new are forced to coexist. Keats probes the emotional experience of these potentially volatile social junctures in his narrative poems; for example, 'The Eve of St. Agnes' juxtaposes the principles of pre-arranged marriages with the impetuosity of pre-destined, romantic love. Codell reads this poem as the dramatic 'collision of dying feudalism with emerging capitalism', an interpretative model which can also be applied to 'Isabella' (Codell, 350). This represents a fraction of the thematic battles enacted throughout Keats's poetry; a particularly relevant facet of the Keatsian discourse for the cultural climate of the early twentieth century. The popularity of *La Belle Dame sans Merci*, amongst painters of the 1880s to the 1930s, results from the sexualized dichotomies which structure the composition: liberation and enslavement, alien and socially specified normality, Self and Other (anima); but it is also within the rich seams, which supposedly separate these opposing factors, that complex, creative criticism is generated. The poet's ambiguities and ambivalences, cocooned within an archeologized past, admitted even the most conservative painters to explore the slippery blisses of the Keatsian subtext and produce their own startlingly re-evaluative interpretations.[35]

The suggestive power of Keats's verse could also sustain a spectrum of female representations: from the maiden modesty beloved by Waterhouse, the object of the scopophilic gaze, to the invulnerable vanquisher. Anne K. Mellor suggests that out of the male Romantic poets only Keats presents the reader with powerful and autonomous women (like Moneta) who do not merely represent fodder for the all-consuming male poetic ego.[36] Keats's artistry shows evidence of sympathy for the mother figure and empathy with 'feminine' Romanticism, yet his ideological cross-dressing is constantly undermined by the fear of being branded effeminate, his narratives smokeable and compared to 'the drawling of the blue stocking literary world'.[37] Mellor firmly states that Keats can be considered a transvestite but not a transsexual: in the case of *La Belle Dame sans Merci*, the woman is empowered, yet simultaneously stereotyped as a cold, cruel 'bitch' by the ghostly group of warriors who represent the collective voice of masculinity.[38] The story is told from a perspective which, as Karen Swann suggests, appropriates and silences the female.[39]

Nevertheless, as we observe in Frank Cadogan Cowper's 1926 version of *Belle Dame*, Keats's poem can alternatively afford a positive image of re-birth: this Siren represents the result of the metamorphosis from sexual subject to vibrant Self (plate 15). From Rossetti's sketch, showing the vigour of masculinity encircling its prey, and Waterhouse's depiction, in which the ghastly knight of the past looms over the fairy's blossoming spirit, Cowper's heroine appears resplendent above the defeated knight. Like Dicksee's lady, this Siren is visually stunning, but here her gown has graduated from pretty pink to a startling crimson, whilst passionate playfulness has matured into an awesome self-confidence. Upon closer examination of the painting, we observe that its visual discourse is not consumed by the habitual one of domination or conquest, the rather well worn war of the sexes, but reflects a new ideology arising Phoenix-like from the corpse of the old. Time is the knight's symbolic adversary, casting aside male mythologies and petrifying its victims. An elaborate network of cobwebs veils the knight's face; history has spun its sentence over the ancient relic of chivalry.

To set this reading in its historic context, Asa Briggs states that by the end of 1914 the dead included six knights and eighty-four sons of knights: Lord Beaverbrook, owner of the *Daily Express*, proclaimed 'The public had no heroes'.[40] Cowper's knight suffers the emblematic blow of his age, but what Keats's ballad admits is the Other side of the masculine Self, an heroine who can re-emerge as a positive icon. Cowper's Siren embodies the vital essence of her time in a dynamic of stylish grace and Charlestonesque frivolity: a propitious victor in this social revolution. From the *fin-de-siècle* onwards, the Siren shed her suffocating skin of binary oppositions and cast off the stigma of servitude to generate alternative modes of expression. Through this succession of paintings, even though framed by a masculine perspective, is the materialization of a strong, bold and forceful female sexuality gaining social credence.

Keats's poetry, with its delicious ambiguity sustained through a precarious balancing of opposites, demanded both artistic ingenuity and poetic insight from painters who sought a transference of meaning from the page to the canvas. Some artists recreated the tense essence of his work with varying degrees of daring, subtlety and success, whilst others produced only poor imitations; and Rossetti, always a singular example, knew the pleasure of a personal communion, engaging himself to such an extent with the light of his worship that his creativity was consumed by its dehabilitating glare. Keats could animate or extinguish, elucidate or inhibit, or, alternatively, forge a curious intermixture of suppression and expression on the painter's canvas, furnishing a fortuitous window for the sylvan ahistoricism and preternaturally precise social comment of the late Romantics. Either way, Keats's influence was decisive in determining the credibility of a work and its artist, and the proficiency of the interpreter in adapting poetic imagery to the changing cultural discourses of a fragmenting society. The shadow of Keats's life and work looms large over the last century and beyond, his spectre inspiring some of the most semantically rich, provocative and illuminating examples of Victorian art.

Reproduced by permission of the author and The Folio Society, London.

[1] Quoted in Cedric Watts, *A Preface to Keats* (Hong Kong: Longman, 1985), p. 66.

[2] Letter from Thomas Hall Caine to William Michael Rossetti, dated 27 September 1879, in reference to Arthur Hughes's painting 'Music Party' (1864) which was accompanied by a quotation from 'Ode on a Grecian Urn', see note 22.

[3] For almost twenty years after the poet's death, not a single reprint of his poems appeared in England: 'I should like to print a complete Edition of Keats's Poems', Taylor wrote on 9 January 1835, 'but the world cares nothing for him — I fear that even 250 copies would not sell'. At about the same time, Keats's friend, Charles Brown, abandoned the idea of a biography following an unprofitable lecture in Plymouth. At last, in 1840, *The Poetical Works of John Keats* appeared as a paperback in William Smith's *Standard Library* series. See *Keats: The Critical Heritage*, ed. by G. M. Matthews (London: Routledge and Kegan Paul, 1971), p. 9.

[4] Hunt's discovery of Keats and the reception of 'The Eve of St. Agnes' are recalled by the artist in his autobiography, *Pre-Raphaelitism and the Pre-Raphaelite Brotherhood*, 2 vols (NY: AMS Press, 1967), I, pp. 105–07.

[5] George H. Ford, *Keats and the Victorians: A Study of His Influence and Rise to Fame, 1821–1895* (London: Archon Books, 1962), pp. 107–08.

[6] 'The Eve of St. Agnes', l. 363. All references to Keats's poems are taken from *John Keats: The Complete Poems*, ed. by John Barnard, 3rd edn (London: Penguin, 1988).

[7] The archways in Hunt's painting create a picture within a picture, thereby suggesting the increasing insubstantiality of the revellers; taken out of Keats's narratorial sequence, the hordes become little more than artificial embellishments.

[8] Julie F. Codell, 'Painting Keats: Pre-Raphaelite Artists Between Social Transgressions and Painterly Conventions', *Victorian Poetry*, 33 (1995), 341–370 (p. 352). Judith Bronkhurst also aligns herself with this argument in her catalogue entries to *The Pre-Raphaelites*, ed. by Leslie Parris (London: Tate Gallery, 1984). Analytic arguments on the Keats-based paintings of the Pre-Raphaelites include: Paul Barlow, 'Pre-Raphaelitism and Post-Raphaelitism', in *Pre-Raphaelites Re-Viewed*, ed. by Marcia Pointon (Manchester: Manchester University Press, 1989), pp. 69–77; Wayne Cook, 'John Keats and the Pre-Raphaelite Brotherhood: Pictorial Poetry and Narrative Painting', *HSL*, 20 (1988), 1–23; Lynne Pearce, *Woman/Image/Text: Readings in Pre-Raphaelite Art and Literature* (Exeter: Harvester Wheatsheaf, 1991).

⁹ Codell refers to the 'phallic power' of the piece and suggests that 'The rich setting and revelry are also reminiscent of Keats's sensual language', but such factors merely serve to highlight the monolithic theme of 'moral dilemmas' which safeguard the 'bitter chill' ('The Eve of St. Agnes', l. 1) of rigid saintliness from the dangerous contaminants of desire (Codell, pp. 352–53). From this perspective, both Keats's poem and Hunt's interpretation can be reduced to a series of conventional binary oppositions including light versus dark, purity versus vice.

¹⁰ William Morris purchased Arthur Hughes's 'April Love' (1855–56) soon after completion because of his association between purple and desire: for further discussion of this subject see K. E. Sullivan, *Pre-Raphaelites* (London: Brockhampton Press, 1996), p. 55 and Grant F. Scott, *The Sculpted Word: Keats, Ekphrasis, and the Visual Arts* (Hanover and London: New England University Press, 1994), p. 91.

¹¹ For a discussion of the mid to late Victorian art market, the emergence of the West End art dealer and wealthy industrialists, and subsequent shifts in public taste see Bernard Denvir, *The Late Victorians: Art, Design and Society, 1852–1910* (London and NY: Longman, 1986).

¹² See Parris, for further details on Hunt's sketch, 'Lorenzo at his Desk in the Warehouse' (1848–50). This early drawing contrasts with both Hunt's and Millais's later representations of Keats's work, which supplied the ever increasing demand for lewd portraits of women; the prominent, columnar figure of a semi-clad female is discernible in Strudwick's 'Isabella' (1879) and two works flagrantly eroticizing 'The Eve of St. Agnes': Maclise's 'Madeline After Prayer' (1868) and Millais's 'The Eve of St. Agnes' (see Pearce for a feminist reading of Millais's voyeuristically inviting version). The success of this compositional form greatly influenced the artists of the Classical Movement; for example, Poynter produced such a work entitled 'The Vision of Endymion' (1902).

¹³ Judith Bronkhurst also comments on the heroine's healthy physique in Hunt's rendition, in contrast to Keats's pale waif who withers like autumnal leaves (Parris, p. 217).

¹⁴ Arthur C. Benson, *Rossetti* (London: Macmillan, 1904), p. 90.

¹⁵ Alicia Craig Faxon, *Dante Gabriel Rossetti* (NY, London and Paris: Abbeville Press, 1989), p. 213.

¹⁶ Thomas Hall Caine, *Recollections of Rossetti*, 2nd edn (London: Cassell, 1928), p. 236.

¹⁷ William Michael Rossetti's table of his brother's art works states that the oil version of 'Mnemosyne' occupied Rossetti from 1876 to 1880, and lists twelve other oils commenced after that time, including 'The Salutation of Beatrice' and 'Desdemona's Love Song', see William Michael Rossetti, *Dante Gabriel Rossetti as Designer and Writer* (London: Cassell, 1889), pp. 288–89.

[18] With regards to artistic awkwardness, John Beer reminds us that 'One of the most common effects of everyday anxiety is a disturbance of fluency', see John Beer, *Romantic Influences: Contemporary-Victorian-Modern* (NY: St. Martin's Press, 1993), p. 51.

[19] Rossetti produced a design based on Browning's 'Pippa Passes' which was turned into a watercolour and an oil-painting; also, he visited his new found idol on several occasions during the mid 1850s.

[20] George Milner, 'On Some Marginalia Made by Dante Gabriel Rossetti in a Copy of Keats's Poems', *Englische Studien*, 61 (1929), 211–219 (p. 212).

[21] D. G. Rossetti, *John Keats: Criticism and Comment* (London: Thomas J. Wise, 1919), 10 February 1880, p. 6.

[22] These three letters are part of the Hall Caine archive which is housed in The Manx Museum on The Isle of Man (15 March 1881, 11 June 1880, July 1880). As the letters between Rossetti and Hall Caine are unpublished and uncatalogued all future references to the letters between Rossetti and Caine will come from this collection unless otherwise indicated. The unlikely correspondence began when Thomas Hall Caine, later to find fame as a popular Victorian novelist, wrote to Rossetti after giving a lecture in defence of his poetry. Despite differences in age and experience the two men wrote to one another regularly, mainly on literary matters, before Hall Caine moved in with Rossetti at 16 Cheyne Walk, London. For further discussion see the aptly named 'A Boswell from the Isle of Man', in William Gaunt, *The Pre-Raphaelite Tragedy* (London: Jonathan Cape, 1942), pp. 215–24 and Vivien Allen, *Hall Caine: Portrait of a Victorian Romancer* (Sheffield: Sheffield Academic Press, 1997).

[23] Hall Caine dramatically proclaims that Keats has become 'the sole tyrannt of my desires' when conducting research on the Romantic poet for his compendium of analysis, *Cobwebs of Criticism* (9 March 1880).

[24] Rossetti, 1919, 9 and 19 May 1881, 191, pp. 15–16

[25] Rossetti, 1919, 9 May 1881, pp. 12–13

[26] Later Pre-Raphaelite interpretations of Keats's poetry, and prominent figures such as Richard Monckton Milnes (Lord Houghton) and Harry Buxton Forman, were instrumental in the sanitization of the life and work of the Romantic poet. See Ford, 1962; William Henry Marquess, *Lives of the Poet: The First Century of Keats Biography* (University Park, Penn. and London: The Pennsylvania State University Press, 1985); Matthews, 1971; Robert G. Stange, '1887 and the Making of the Modern Canon', *Victorian Poetry*, 25 (1987), 151–168; Robert Woof and Stephen Hebron, *John Keats* (Kendal: The Wordsworth Trust, 1995). See also the bibliographical debate

over *La Belle Dame sans Merci* which incorporates much interesting comment on the role of the Pre-Raphaelites and Monckton Milnes in the popularization of the 1848 edition of the text.

[27] To emulate literally means to 'attempt to equal or surpass [...] to rival or compete with' (*OED*). In the case of Rossetti, however, I have determined no instance of envy, jealousy or rivalry in his relationship with Keats, and although this close kinship is not positively productive (in terms of artistic output), it cannot be read as antagonistic. Bloom's theory of literary history, based on the disordered misreadings between a poet and his forefather in the inextricable battle of artistic autonomy, posits an Oedipal combat never to be won by the inheritor. He is inevitably self-slain by the strength of his precursor's originality. Exhausted and defeated, the poet dies, leaving his legacy on the negative path of poetic diminishment. See Harold Bloom, *The Anxiety of Influence: A Theory of Poetry* (NY: Oxford University Press, 1973) and René Giraud, *Deceit, Desire & the Novel: Self and Other in Literary Structure*, trans. by Yvonne Freccero (London: Johns Hopkins University Press, 1961). Whilst I do not adhere to Bloom's apocalyptic reading of literary history, he raises some interesting points in regard to the conflict between art and the artist's self-image:

> Arnold's elegiac poetry uneasily blends Keatsian style with anti-Romantic sentiment, while Hopkins' strained intensities and convolutions of diction and Rossetti's densely inlaid art are also at variance with the burdens they seek to alleviate in their own poetic selves (p. 12).

[28] See, for discussion of ekphrasis and the Other, W. J. T. Mitchell, *Picture Theory: Essays on Verbal and Visual Representation* (London: Chicago University Press, 1994), p. 151.

[29] See also Bryan Wolf, 'Confessions of a Closet Ekphrastic: Literature, Painting and Other Unnatural Relations', *Yale Journal of Criticism*, 3 (1990), 181–204.

[30] Lucy Newlyn, 'Reading After: The Anxiety of the Writing Subject', *Studies in Romanticism*, 35.4 (1996), 609–628.

[31] Quoted in Beer, *Romantic Influences*, p. 52.

[32] Sandra M. Gilbert and Susan Gubar, *The Norton Anthology of Literature by Women: The Tradition in English*, 2nd edn (London: W. W. Norton, 1996), p. 961.

[33] Anthony Hobson suggests that the crucial difference between Waterhouse and his Pre-Raphaelite precursors is in his depiction of women as 'individual, sensitive and warm-blooded', as opposed to Edward Burne-Jones's 'anonymous and anaemic' girls, in *J. W. Waterhouse* (London: Phaidon, 1989), p. 9.

[34] Andrew Bennett discerns such solecisms in the linguistic form of Keats's poetry: 'These are some of the uncertain polarities which generate form out of the sparks which fly from an intense

conjoining and unsettling of incommensurable difference'. Andrew Bennett, *Keats, Narrative and Audience: The Posthumous Life of Writing* (Cambridge: Cambridge University Press, 1994), p. 1.

[35] This paraphrases Codell's comments on the framing of the modern subject, p. 350.

[36] See comments on Keats's feminization in Anne K. Mellor, *Romanticism and Gender* (London: Routledge, 1993), pp. 171–86.

[37] Quoted in Mellor, 1993, p. 181. Mellor entitles her chapter on Keats, 'Ideological Cross-Dressing', and she defines the concept of 'feminine' Romanticism in her introduction, 1993, p. 4.

[38] This is Mellor's use of 'modern parlance', 1993, p. 184.

[39] Karen Swann, 'Harassing the Muse', in *Romanticism and Feminism*, ed. by Anne K. Mellor (Bloomington: Indiana University Press, 1988), pp. 81–92.

[40] See the chapter 'The Divides of War', in Asa Briggs, *A Social History of England*, 2nd edn (London: Penguin, 1987), pp. 292–317.

Sinister Romance:

A Twist of the Tale in *The Turn of the Screw*

Hazel Hutchison

Dangerous Supplements

'Good ghosts,' writes Henry James of *The Turn of the Screw* (1898), 'make poor subjects, and it was clear,' he goes on,

> that from the first my hovering prowling blighting presences, my pair of abnormal agents, would have to depart altogether from the rules. They would be agents in fact; there would be laid on them the dire duty of causing the situation to reek with the air of Evil [...] This was exactly my central idea; so that, briefly, I cast my lot with pure romance.[1]

It is absorbing, especially in the light of the critical dust storm which still blows around James's celebrated ghost story, to glance back over the author's own impressions of how his tale was germinated. In particular, James's insistence on the playfully artificial genesis of his spectres appears to undercut those later readings of the novel which offer psychological explanations for the dreadful spooks whom the Governess stalks through the corridors of Bly. He seems in his preface not only to be looking back to the construction of his tale a decade previously, but also to be aligning that tale to a tradition of earlier ghost stories, of 'sinister romance' and old legend (37). The Edenic setting of Bly suggests that we are dealing with a moral and spiritual fable. The figures of the two orphaned children and the wicked servants imply a magical tale. The imaginative and impressionable Governess and James's own preference for seeing the tale as a 'romance', also introduce echoes from the Romantic movement. *The Turn of the Screw* appears at times, as we shall see, to borrow explicitly from Charlotte Brontë's *Jane Eyre* and Jane Austen's *Northanger Abbey*. And as with much of James's work it contains lexical echoes from Milton, Nathaniel Hawthorne and Edgar Allan Poe. But anyone tempted to look to James's introductory remarks for an explanation of this disturbing little work or a catalogue of its sources is likely to find the preface as teasing and contradictory as the novel itself.

James's prefaces are famously tangential, often preferring 'the story of one's story' to the story itself.[2] But here James, perhaps rather archly, insists on the simplicity of his supernatural tale. It is a 'fable', a 'fantasy', a 'fairy tale pure and simple', 'an *amusette* to catch those not easily caught' (38). Elsewhere he describes it as a 'potboiler' and a '*jeu d'esprit*'.[3] But to read the story of the young Governess sent to Bly by a dashing London bachelor to look after his niece and nephew, is to be made aware of its deep complexity. Her tale strains the limits of credibility, begging the question of whether the ghosts of Jessel and Quint, with whom she believes she wrestles for the souls of the children, are real or imagined.

This central question however is neatly side-stepped by James's preface. Instead of offering definition, the preface stands beside *The Turn of the Screw* like a Derridean supplement, augmenting yet also undermining the work of fiction that it claims to extend, apparently filling but also highlighting its gaps, its lacunae. In *The Truth About Painting*, Derrida borrows from Kant the term *parergon* to describe such a supplementary object.[4] It need not be a literary preface. Picture frames, columns on buildings, the wheelchair which carries and confines an invalid, the drapery on a classical statue, all these carry qualities of conflict and extension in relation to the work that they simultaneously support and oppose. The parergon is:

> neither work (ergon) nor outside the work [*hors d'ouvre*], neither inside nor outside, neither above nor below, it disconnects any opposition but does not remain indeterminate and it gives rise to the work. It is no longer merely around the work. That which puts it in place, the instance of the frame, the title, the signature, the legend *etc.* — does not stop disturbing the internal order of discourse (2).

James's preface is not the only rendering of *The Turn of the Screw* which disturbs the internal order of the story's discourse. For a hundred years it has been increasingly entangled in a thorny hedge of conflicting criticism, much of which has attempted (and failed) to close down its ambiguity, but has only succeeded in multiplying its possible readings. The Governess's account is also jostled and displaced by the novel's frame narrative, which, like the Derridean picture frame, simultaneously sets her account in place but also calls it into question. As the introductory prologue explains, the Governess's haunting and tragic tale is first told and then passed on at her death to a young admirer, Douglas, who years later reads the manuscript to a circle of friends in time-honoured Gothic style round the fire on a winter's night. Later, before he dies, Douglas sends the old red-bound volume to the narrator of the frame narrative, who transcribes it for the reader.

There is an intriguing tension in this between the modes of speech and writing and experience: each time the text is passed on it changes shape and form, and each step seems to be prompted by desire or affection, and attended by death. It is also difficult to say whether the assurances of credibility given by each of the successive narrators make us more likely or less to suspend our disbelief in the fantastic tale they tell. Thus the repeating of the story at once preserves and distorts it. Each version becomes a supplement and a substitute for the one before. This not only invites us to trace back, as best we can, along the infinite chain of composition and reference by which the tale trickles down to us, it also calls into question the very operation of language.

Derrida sees in the action of the sign, grasping at the thing it seeks to represent, an almost Gothic attempt at possession. Such a haunting, brooding dislocation at the centre of all discourse renders every story in its own way a ghost story, a tale of presences now absent:

> We are dispossessed of the longed for presence in the gesture of language by which we attempt to seize it [...] The speculary dispossession which at the same time institutes and deconstitutes me is also a law of language. It operates as a power of death in the heart of living speech: a power all the more redoubtable because it opens as much as it threatens the possibility of the spoken word.[5]

In his exploration of the tension between the written and the spoken word from which this passage is lifted, Derrida challenges the traditional hierarchy which sets speech (notionally closer to the speaker's intention and experience) above writing. Derrida points out that all attempts to engage with language are simply reworkings of words already used and overlaid with complex associations and diversions. Speech is, he argues, especially insidious in its apparent promise of an immediate meaning which it cannot in reality provide, while writing at least has the virtue of recognizing its dislocated nature. The relationship of writing to speech is therefore complementary but also subversive, the 'dangerous supplement' which undermines as it extends (141). This argument seems pertinent, both in the light of the transmigration of the Governess's tale through its various forms of verbal speech and written word, and in the light of James's appropriation of earlier texts. It is also important to note the two sides, or effects, of Derrida's idea of supplementarity; the necessary recourse to something auxiliary to the work in order to glimpse its most vital essence, and the impossibility of ever replacing or representing one thing completely by the other (experience by speech, speech by writing, novel by preface). These effects, far from offering answers to the myriad questions thrown up by *The Turn of the Screw*, allow us to probe but deeper into the problems of its language and its revision of stories already told and texts already written.

A Train of Associations

It is, of course, no revelation that James is a deeply intertextual writer. The densely allusive and metaphorical language of his mature novels, known rather architecturally as the Late Style, feeds off references to and derivations from James's wide reading experience.[6] James seems to have had difficulty disentangling the processes of reading and writing and to be aware that many of his works are in a measure *re*writings:

> Lo and behold the subject isn't [...] 'given' at all — I have doubtless simply, with violence and mutilation, *stolen* it. It is of the nature of that violence that I'm a wretched person to *read* a novel — I begin so quickly and concomitantly, *for myself*, to write it rather — even before I know clearly what it's about! The novel I can *only* read I can't read at all! (26 July 1899, 110).

James also seems to have had trouble reading his own books without rewriting them; he revised many of his novels, including *The Turn of the Screw,* for the New York Edition of his work (1907–9). But Jamesian critics have also fallen over themselves, not to mention each other, in the search for definitive outside sources, literary and anecdotal, for *The Turn of the Screw*. James's preface and his notebooks cite the inspiration for the tale as 'the shadow of a shadow' of a ghost story told by Archbishop Edward White Benson in January 1895 (36).[7] But intriguingly Benson's children later denied ever having heard the story, or anything like it, from their father.[8] James himself recalls that the Archbishop's thumbnail sketch of a ghost story was itself a retelling of a tale told to Benson by a woman who had heard it years before. James's preface, in this matter as in others, cancels out the outline that it appears to draw, leaving the story suspended without a traceable history of its own. Shoshana Felman writes of the preface that:

> It is like a Prologue to the Prologue, an introduction to the introduction, as if to make up for the missing origin or beginning, but succeeding only in repeating once again the tale of the constitutive loss of the tale's beginning.[9]

The tale's absolute beginning is beyond view, concealed in the chain of references, perhaps in the 'train of associations' which James sees attached to it (*Turn of the Screw*, 39). But it is still possible, even at times fruitful, to trace its links to other works of literature, seeing these not so much as sources of identity but as supplementary texts, extending, delineating and challenging the boundaries of the story.

Certainly James's novella appears at times to be visibly flirting with the plot of *Jane Eyre*.[10] The overlaps of circumstance and expression between the two works are striking. Alice Hall Petry catalogues their similarities: a clergyman's daughter, hired as governess by an attractive bachelor known as the Master; a brooding mystery in an isolated mansion; the bookishness and morbidity of both heroines and their tendency towards theatricality which leads them to feed off danger and difficulty.[11] Petry points to the story told by Blanche Ingram, Mr Rochester's supposed fiancée, of an affair between her own governess Miss Wilson and her brother's tutor Mr Vining, as a possible source for James (*Jane Eyre*, 201). Petry goes on to offer a reading of *The Turn of the Screw* as comic parody, claiming that James's Governess, with her head full of too many Gothic romances, has a fancy to play out the part of Jane Eyre and invents the whole supernatural drama to gain the attention and affection of the Rochester-like Master in London.

It is always a relief in dealing with *The Turn of the Screw* to come across any viewpoint that allows one to escape, even fleetingly, from the debate over whether the ghosts are real or not, or whether the Governess is mad, but there are some problems with such a precise source and such a prescribed reading as those suggested by Petry. Apart from the fact that it ignores what James has to say about the silent, unnamed malevolence at the centre of his tale (we never do find out what it is that the dead servants are meant to have done that is so dreadful) and the singularly unfunny death of Miles, Petry's insistence on a comic reading of the tale rather fancifies some important structural parallels. She also moves towards a closing down of the list of possible referents for James's allusive language, whereas the author's receptive mind and extensive reading would suggest that he may have borrowed from a longer list of authors and genres, Gothic Romance being just one.

James was not shy about lifting ideas, forms and turns of phrase from other writers: 'I take liberties,' he once boasted 'with the greatest' (20 August 1902, 238). And *The Turn of the Screw* borrows its title, as well as some of its atmosphere from Dickens's *Bleak House*.[12] Milton's *Paradise Lost* echoes in many of the garden scenes at Bly and in the sinister, appealing fascination of Peter Quint. The novel's curious mix of supernatural possibilities with domestic practicalities recalls Hawthorne's *The House of the Seven Gables,* and there are various allusions to fairy tales and the Bible. The Governess's question as to 'whether there was a secret at Bly — a mystery of Udolpho or an insane, an unmentionable relative kept in unsuspected confinement?' not only confirms a link with *Jane Eyre*, but also with Ann Radcliffe's *The Mysteries of Udolpho* (1784) and with the many imitations it inspired (166).

And if one wants Gothic parody, is not *Udolpho* the very book that gets Catherine Morland into such trouble in *Northanger Abbey*?[13] If Petry is right that James's over-read Governess believes herself to be living out the part of Jane Eyre or some other Gothic heroine, her actions would be not at all unlike Catherine's fanciful invention of a gruesome secret at Northanger, the supposed murder or imprisonment of Henry's mother. Petry rightly points out that the Governess has a voracious appetite for reading, often staying up with one of the books from the library at Bly: 'last-century fiction some of it, which, to the extent of a distinctly deprecated renown, but never so much as that of a stray specimen, had reached the sequestered home and appealed to the unavowed curiosity of my youth' (194). Like Catherine, the Governess is a young woman whose unfolding experience of life away from home is paralleled by the discovery of sensational eighteenth-century fiction. Indeed Catherine Morland is recalled by the frame narrative's introduction of the Governess as the daughter of a 'country parson' an 'anxious girl out of a Hampshire vicarage' (149). This is a description which also fits Jane Austen herself and, as we shall see, each of these three heroines demonstrates authorial (though sometimes simply self-dramatizing) tendencies. Then again, the middle-class governess and the clergyman's daughter are familiar figures in the nineteenth-century novel. Indeed the Victorian governess frequently was a clergyman's daughter. Pat Macpherson's study of the figure of the governess points out that clergymen often educated their daughters to a high standard, but were unable to put them in a position to marry into educated families.[14] Many vicarage daughters found themselves caught between class categories, poor and yet intellectual. The post of governess could provide employment and the opportunity to rub shoulders with the wealthier classes, though, as Jane Eyre and James's Governess both discover, this often simply led to a different kind of isolation. They belonged neither to the employer's family nor to the servant community. But this anomaly created an appealing character for the Victorian novel: socially mobile, perceptive and articulate, commanding the reader's sympathy in the face of that same aristocratic snobbery of which Catherine Morland is a victim. So, while it is tempting to make much of the parallels between these three young women, any suggestion of a source for a work of James's should probably be just that — a suggestion not a solution.

In her investigation of James's appropriation of classic texts, Adeline Tintner warns against restriction in linking sources to his novels.[15] Appropriation for James, she claims, is a high form of criticism and an unlimited extension which allows his work to resonate with unexplained echoes and associations, and to expand its boundaries into other genres, other periods, other cultures, in a receding chain of literary reference:

> The reader cannot say where his fiction ends or his criticism begins but when a classic by another writer has been encoded within James's story a process of extended literary relations begins that seems to be endless. By the analogy produced, the limits of the tales James tells are extended, for the pleasure of the reader as well as the creator [...] James's complex relation to the absorbed text produced another work of art — his own — which justified the theft (xxii).

Or as James puts it himself:

> To criticize is to appreciate, to appropriate, to take intellectual possession, to establish in fine a relation with the criticized thing and make it one's own. The large intellectual appetite projects itself thus on many things, while the small [...] projects itself on few.[16]

The ideas of projection and possession are of course deeply resonant when labouring anywhere near the field of Gothic fiction, but this statement is just as absorbing for its emphasis on the pleasure of the task, on the idea of multiplicity, and the diverse, fly-paper nature of the intelligent mind. James appears to be implying in his use of other texts not a direct line of source or influence, nor even a Bloomian struggle for ascendancy over his precursors, but an intricately woven pattern of allusions, a clever dance that touches, connects, admires, turns and changes partners. Derrida also acknowledges that the business of tracing the ancestry of a text is fraught with detours and contradictions:

> And if a text always gives itself a certain representation of its own roots, those roots live only by that representation, by never touching the soil [...] To say that one always interweaves roots endlessly, bending them to send down roots among the roots, to pass through the same points again, to redouble old adherence, to circulate among their differences, to coil around themselves or to be enveloped one in the other, to say that a text is never anything but a *system of roots*, is undoubtedly to contradict at once the concept of system and the pattern of the root. But in order not to be pure appearance, this contradiction takes on the meaning of a contradiction, and

receives its 'illogicality' only through being thought within a finite configuration — the history of metaphysics — and caught within a root system which does not end there and which as yet has no name (Derrida, 1974, 101).

In the way that *The Turn of the Screw* is a novel with many sources and connections and yet no defined beginning, so even the attempt to trace such sources and beginnings belongs to a larger or earlier, infinitely variable and unsolvable pattern and history. In James's unfinished novel, *The Sense of the Past*, the hero Ralph Pendrel experiences the precursive past in his imagination as 'a chain of open doors through which endless connections danced'.[17] Or as he writes elsewhere with a rather Gothic image: 'Experience is never limited, and it is never complete; it is an immense sensibility, a kind of huge spider-web of the finest silken threads suspended in the chamber of consciousness, and catching every airborne particle in its tissue'.[18] And surely James's tendency to annexe Gothic conventions in his continual search for images which illuminate the inner world of the mind is one of the strongest trails that leads us back from *The Turn of the Screw* to *Jane Eyre*. As Robert Heilman claims, what Charlotte Brontë is aiming for in her novel is not the cheap thrill of supernatural romance but an attempt to engage with the nature of consciousness, through a use of symbolism and psychology, which he sees as a radical development in the Gothic genre: 'She instinctively finds new ways to achieve the ends served by old Gothic — the discovery and release of new patterns of feeling the intensification of feeling [...] Charlotte is plumbing the psyche, not inventing a weird *decor*'.[19] This 'New' Gothic, which at times functions as anti-Gothic, at times as Gothic internalized and psychologized, seems not unlike James's use of the genre in *The Turn of the Screw*. Through the Governess's fear that she may be mad, through the assumption by many critics that she is, and through her unnatural, grasping bid to save, almost to possess Miles and Flora, the grim horror of the tale is displaced from the external to the psychological. Like James's ghosts, this kind of Gothic departs from the rules. This is, to corrupt a phrase from Derrida, a kind of *Gothic under erasure*, appealing to the terminology and associations of the genre without endorsing or submitting to it (Derrida, 1974, 60). As with Austen's *Northanger Abbey*, the Gothic is called up only to be questioned, is summoned only to be undermined, is at once present and absent. It is also possible to see James further pushing out the boundaries of the Gothic theme, connecting it to the process of expression, and highlighting the dangers, the evils, the sinister hauntings and possessions that operate at the heart of language.

Blighting Presences

The problem of presence and absence in *The Turn of the Screw* is apparent from its first pages. Initially even the tale is absent, present only in Douglas's mind; he will not tell it until he has sent to London for the written copy. The old volume operates as a representation of the Governess, as well as a tangible reminder of her loss. The barriers between speech and writing, between absence and presence, almost between characters, are blurred as Douglas reads her words: he speaks 'with a clearness that was like a rendering to the ear of the beauty of his author's hand' (151). This pattern of absent presences repeats itself throughout the tale. There is the absence of Miles and Flora's lost parents, the absence and silence of their uncle in London, and the sensible presence of Jessel and Quint who ought to be absent but are not quite. The story also resonates with absent presences of a more thematic and structural variety. James co-opts the Gothic convention of the disturbing silence, and places it at the very heart of the novel, refusing to name the blight at the story's centre, leaving it rather to the reader's imagination. 'Make him think the evil,' writes James, 'make him think it for himself' (42). Of course the silence, the lacuna, the vacuum this creates can be filled by as many different things as there are readers. In being forced to imagine the evil, the reader becomes implicated in it. As Felman says, 'There is no such thing as an innocent reader of this text' (97). They run not simply a moral risk, but also that of being possessed by the fundamental dishonesty of the text, of being caught in the web of signs, which suggest and imply meaning but which ultimately do no more than circle around a deliberate silence. 'My values,' writes James in his preface, 'are positively all blanks' (42). This constitutes a danger perhaps but, as Alan Gardner Smith points out, it also is the very means by which reading is possible, by which the story becomes open to us:

> If the text risks failure of communication, it has nevertheless the advantage of a plurality of possible interactions. Further we may say that what is present in the text points always to what is absent, as figure implies ground. Therefore the act of revealing is also an act of concealing, the signifier implies the absence of the signified and the co-ordinates of discourse plot a secret geography of the unspoken.[20]

As the frame narrative dramatizes the impossibility of presence, so James's text is most effective in what it refuses to say. And with so much duplicity, so many valid perspectives, and so many possible voices from moral fable to parody, it becomes clear that this is a text which is impossible to define or to nail down to any single meaning or reading. Indeed this seems to be one of the few things on which critics of James's novel can agree, that it invites and sustains divergent and opposing readings. Indeed the most rewarding way to read it seems to be, as Felman advocates, to read its ambiguity, to allow it to remain unresolved, to preserve its deeply Gothic uncertainty about the divide between reality and illusion, to leave it on its knife-edge between the supernatural and the rational; that knife-edge which Todorov describes as the essential experience of the Fantastic.[21]

This is the kind of hesitation that is also required in order to read Austen's *Northanger Abbey*. In this case no one seems able to decide whether the novel upholds parody or realism. As Tara Ghoshal Wallace says, each view of the text is incomplete, is supplemented and undermined by the opposite view: '*Northanger Abbey* refuses to yield a stable vision, either moral or aesthetic. What it *does* yield, what it insists upon, is an awareness of the reader's participation in narrative strategies'.²² This is perhaps most evident in its closing chapter with Austen's final abandonment of authority over the text. Her final appeal to narrative conventions and the reader's own preference, closes the book with an open option: 'I leave it to be settled by whomsoever it may concern, whether the tendency of this work be altogether to recommend parental tyranny, or reward filial disobedience' (219).

All this is not so very different from James's preference for making the reader 'think the evil, make him think it for himself'. Austen's silence has, of course, a different quality; it is the silence of modesty, of virtue and of self-restraint.²³ In this instance it is even a silence of authorial self-erasure. Its operation is similar however in that it permits infinite expansion, and forces readers to supply or construct their own meaning to meet the author's deliberate lacuna. Thus, like parody, silence provides an ambiguity which allows that hesitation between possible readings which is the experience of the Fantastic; it undermines not just the novel's ability to carry meaning, but the ability of language to carry significance, and even the reliability of one's own senses.

This indeed, seems a more convincing parallel between these three novels. Like *Northanger Abbey*, both *Jane Eyre* and *The Turn of the Screw* are 'attempting to pose important and difficult questions about the links between fictional and actual worlds'.²⁴ Each on its own level engages with the problem of silence and the haunting nature of expression. Catherine Morland is often lost for words in a world whose follies and whose fiction Austen attacks with parody. But the self-effacing Austen seems also to undermine the very use of parody as a weapon for dealing with these. The frustration of not knowing what around her is serious and believable, especially in the discourse of Henry and his family, frequently leaves Catherine too agitated 'for any endeavour at discourse' (167). The gap in her knowledge of Henry's dead mother and all-too-real father prompts her to compose her Gothic fantasy. And later she finds herself in the 'silence and sadness' of a broken heart, from which she can only be rescued by Austen's appeal to fictional convention (209). Jane Eyre's autobiographical narrative moves her into the role of story-teller, defying (or perhaps simply fulfilling) Mrs Reed's injunction that 'until you can speak pleasantly, remain silent' (13). Jane's married life with the blinded Rochester also increases her traffic with language. Her role as a kind of speaking eye for him, translating sight into language, casts her as a frame for his perception of reality. He sees 'through' her, much as the reader relies on her description: 'He saw nature — he saw books through me; and never did I weary of gazing for his behalf, and of putting into words the effect of field, tree, town, river, cloud, sunbeam — of the landscape before us' (500). James's Governess also breaks the Gothic spell of isolation when she breaks her silence in the act of sharing her story with Douglas. At Bly, she is forbidden from contact or speech with the Uncle in London. And silence is, in her meeting with the ghostly Peter Quint, the thing that provides 'the whole horror, huge as it was, its only note of the unnatural' and then becomes the palpable 'element into which I saw him disappear' (196). At the novel's close, Miles's spoken confession, the naming of Quint, is the thing that saves the boy's soul — or so the Governess believes. But there is perhaps a darker irony attached to the process by which, in the action of writing, she slides into the role of the haunter rather than the haunted. Her control of language is what represents her, almost physically but disembodied, at the fireside as Douglas reads with that fine clearness of the beauty of her hand.

This movement of our three heroines from silence to language, shows not just their own necessity of expression to supplement experience, but that of their authors. As James puts it:

> The effort to see and really to represent is no idle business in the face of the *constant* force that makes for muddlement. The great thing is indeed that the muddled state too is one of the very sharpest of realities, that it also has colour and form and character, has often in fact a broad and rich comicality, many of the signs and values of the appreciable (*Literary Criticism*, 1164).

His Governess then is perhaps no more mad than anyone who attempts to express sensation in language — like Jane Eyre and Catherine, like Austen and Brontë themselves — to order the fragmented chaos of experience into discourse. The attempt twists and turns towards resolution, towards primacy without ever arriving. It is a pattern of absent, blighted presences and tangible, flawed losses. Derrida describes this spectre-like quality of language itself as: 'Somewhat like the architecture of an uninhabited or deserted city, reduced to its skeleton by some catastrophe of nature or art. A city no longer inhabited, not simply left behind, but haunted by meaning and culture'. [25] All writing is then, to a measure ghostly, tracing a presence no longer living, which, in turn, casts all authors in the somewhat ambiguous role of the 'ghost writer'. Derrida's idea of the ghost writer extends the common use of the phrase, the speech writer who 'composes speeches for use by litigants, speeches which he himself does not pronounce, which he does not attend, so to speak, in person, and which produce their effects in his absence'. Such a writer, he goes on, constructs words that he would never say, frames thoughts that he would probably never even think, therefore becoming 'the man of non-presence and non-truth'.[26] Ultimately, he insists, all writers are like this. Language then, at its very core, carries a sinister measure of duplicity and illusion that presents, but fails to penetrate the constantly muddled state of things; it speaks in a web of infinitely complex reference and allusion, circling but never revealing or defining some source or intention at its centre. Its values remain 'positively all blanks', and thus the end of the text (as in its direction and purpose) is lost, very much like its beginning, in an unresolvable ambiguity which can only be ridden out, or settled by the individual imagination of 'whomsoever it may concern'. Thus, in borrowing from the already written, James simply repeats on a larger, more literary scale the everyday operation of language, which constantly recycles and reiterates, chases and connects. Good ghosts may indeed make poor subjects, as James points out, but such haunting lexical echoes of other texts, such disturbing reworkings of borrowed themes, such shadowy traces of familiar ideas, do make, in their own way, sinister and convincing ghosts.

---

[1] Henry James, Preface (1909) to *The Turn of the Screw* (1898; repr London: Penguin, 1986) p. 41. All page numbers for quotes are taken from this text.

[2] Henry James, Preface (1909) to *The Ambassadors* (1903; repr. London: Penguin, 1986), p. 38.

[3] Henry James, *Letters IV 1895–1916*, ed. by Leon Edel (Cambridge, MA: Harvard University Press, 1984), 9 December 1898, p. 86. All future references to James's letters come from this edition.

[4] Jacques Derrida, *The Truth in Painting*, trans. by Geoff Bennington and Ian McLeod (London: University of Chicago Press, 1987).

[5] Derrida, *Of Grammatology*, trans. by Guyatri Chakravorty Spivak (Baltimore: Johns Hopkins University Press, 1976), p. 141.

[6] See Nicola Bradbury, *The Later Novels* (Oxford: Clarendon Press, 1979).

[7] Henry James, *The Complete Notebooks*, ed. by Leon Edel and Lyall H. Powers (Oxford: Oxford University Press, 1987), p. 109.

[8] E. F. Benson, 'The Genesis of *The Turn of the Screw*', in *Henry James: Interviews and Recollections*, ed. by Norman Page (London: Macmillan, 1984), pp. 72–74: 'The contents of the family story-box are usually well known to the members of the circle, and it seems very improbable that we should all have forgotten so arresting a tale, if it was ever told to us' (p. 73).

[9] Shoshana Felman, 'Turning the Screw of Interpretation', *Literature and Psychoanalysis: The Question of Reading Otherwise*, Yale French Studies, 55/56 (1977), 94–207, (p. 122).

[10] Charlotte Brontë, *Jane Eyre* (1847; repr. London: Penguin, 1996). All future quotations are taken from this text.

[11] Alice Hall Petry, 'Jamesian Parody, *Jane Eyre* and *The Turn of the Screw*', *Modern Language Studies*, 13 (1983), 61–78.

[12] Charles Dickens, *Bleak House* (1853; repr. London: Collins, 1953). Chapter 34 carries the title 'The Turn of the Screw' (p. 433).

[13] Jane Austen, *Northanger Abbey* (1818; repr London: Penguin, 1995), p. 36. All future references are taken from this text.

[14] Pat Macpherson, *Reflecting on Jane Eyre* (London: Routledge, 1989), p. 4.

[15] Adeline Tintner, *The Book World of Henry James: Appropriating the Classics* (London: UMI Research Press, 1987).

[16] Henry James, Preface (1907) to *What Maisie Knew*, in *Literary Criticism: European Writers and the Prefaces to the New York Edition*, ed. by Leon Edel (NY: The Library of America, 1984), p. 1169.

[17] Henry James, *The Sense of the Past* (London: Collins, 1917), p. 45.

[18] Henry James, 'The Art of Fiction' (1884), in *The House of Fiction: Essays on the Novel*, ed. by Leon Edel (London: Rupert Hart-Davis, 1957), p. 31.

[19] Robert Heilman, 'Charlotte Brontë's "New" Gothic in *Jane Eyre* and *Villette*' (1958), in *Charlotte Bronte: Jane Eyre and Villette: A Casebook*, ed. by Miriam Allott (London: Macmillan, 1973), pp. 195–205, (p. 196).

[20] Alan Gardner Smith, 'The Occultism of the Text', *Poetics Today*, 3.4 (1982), 5–20 (p. 8).

[21] Tzvetan Todorov, *The Fantastic: A Structural Approach to Literary Genre*, trans. by Richard Howard (London: Press of Case, Western Reserve University, 1973), p. 25.

[22] Tara Ghoshal Wallace, *Jane Austen and Narrative Authority* (London: Macmillan, 1995), p. 29.

[23] Joseph Kestner, *Jane Austen: Spatial Structure of Thematic Variations* (Salzburg: Universität Salzburg, 1974), p. 90.

[24] Michael Williams, Jane Austen: Six Novels and Their Methods (London: Macmillan, 1986), p. 12.

[25] Jacques Derrida, 'Force and Signification', in *Writing and Difference*, trans. by Alan Bass (London: Routledge, 1978), p. 5.

[26] Jacques Derrida, *Dissemination*, trans. by Barbara Johnson (London: The Athlone Press, 1981), p. 68.

Mediumistic Shelley Sonnets in the Netherlands

Kris Steyaert

In his early twenties, Willem Kloos (1859–1938) was without doubt the most accomplished poet of his generation in the Netherlands. Yet, when his lover Albert Verwey (1865–1937) told him in 1888 about his forthcoming engagement, Kloos suffered a major blow. He became an alcoholic, suffered severe fits of delirium, attempted to commit suicide on several occasions and was eventually locked away in an Utrecht asylum from which he was released a broken man in 1896. Soon afterwards, he too got married and assumed the life of a thoroughly respectable man. Kloos more or less regained his mental and physical health but had to pay for it with the dramatic loss of his poetic powers. He was anxious, however, to be considered the most important and most influential poet and critic of his day and continued to proclaim himself as such for the rest of his life. Since his literary output gave little reason for such reverence, Kloos had to devise other means to boost his reputation. More precisely, in his attempts to exhume the literary self which had been buried during his stay at the mental institution, he turned to his profound admiration for Shelley.

On 23 March 1921 Willem Kloos wrote a rapturous letter to Jacob ('Co') Reyneke-van Stuwe, his brother-in-law, who lived in Wimbledon:

Dear Co, you will probably not believe this. You will say: Willem is dreaming, or joking. Yet, I can assure you that I am telling the naked truth when I claim that, yesterday evening, I became the owner of a hitherto unpublished and [...] unknown manuscript letter written by Shelley.[1]

Outbidding a considerable number of prospective buyers from Britain and the United States, Kloos acquired what he called 'the holy document' for the hefty sum of five hundred and fifty guilders. Naturally, Kloos was enraptured to have a truly unique and tangible Shelley relic in his possession, and one coveted by many, as the auction had made manifest. He continued his letter to 'Co' with unmitigated enthusiasm: 'I am overjoyed with this unique document from which Shelley's own psychic essence seems to be emanating'.[2] It was Kloos's fervent desire to inform the public in England about Shelley's newly discovered letter thereby giving him the opportunity to assert his ownership. To this end, a transcript, accompanied by a note made by 'Co' with much proprietorial signposting on behalf of 'Mr. Willem Kloos, the Dutch poet', was sent to the *Times Literary Supplement* where it was duly published.[3]

Kloos had the precious document framed between two sheets of glass, and hung it in a prominent place in his study which had been gradually turned into a shrine to Shelley. Around that time, his personal library of Shelleyana had taken on impressive proportions and contained well over one hundred titles of works by or on Shelley. Amongst them was a rare 1859 imprint of *Queen Mab* as well as a complete set of *The Liberal*, the short-lived radical periodical set up by Leigh Hunt, Byron and Shelley in Pisa in 1822. As his eyes roamed over his new, proudly displayed treasure, Kloos must have felt the need to express his euphoria in a more lasting and more public form than in his private correspondence with Co. With such a potent charm close at hand, Kloos now found himself in a position to conjure up some spectres of the past and make them totally subordinate to his command. Indeed, shortly after the acquisition of the letter and with all the propitiousness of a self-fulfilling prophecy, he experienced a visitation from

Shelley's ghost. This event inspired him to write a series of poems which took the form of a self-contained sonnet cycle. With a distinctive flair for theatricality, Kloos contrived to turn the sequence into a grand public gesture to reclaim his significance as a man of letters. The sonnets are nothing less than Kloos's attempt to capture Shelley's own volatile 'psychic essence' which had been brought into the house with the manuscript letter, and have the poet's spectre secure Kloos a place amongst the Eternal.

The series of twelve sonnets was dedicated to 'Co' and appeared under the heading 'Percy Bysshe Shelley, by Willem Kloos' in the journal Kloos edited, *De Nieuwe Gids [The New Guide]*.[4] With the whole set tightly constructed, each sonnet is given a separate title, pointing towards a progressive and logical narrative: I. 'Proem', II. 'Premonition', III. 'The Murder', IV. 'Shelley's Death', V. 'Confession of the Murderer', VI. 'Shelley's Apparition', VII. 'Continued', VIII. 'Continued', IX. 'Answer from Me', X. 'Continued', XI. 'Shelley's Judgement', XII. 'Conclusion'. The main title summarizes at once the whole agenda behind the set of poems: the reader is presented with an image of Shelley as seen *by* Kloos, and as Kloos wants it to be perpetuated. Indeed, Kloos appoints himself the trustworthy intermediary through whom the reader is allowed to enter a heavenly kingdom where he can behold a splendid, and above all, authentic, vision of 'the divine genius' (II. 14).

Given the underlying motivation and the importance of the issues at stake, it was imperative for Kloos to preclude all readings in which his Shelley persona could be interpreted as an entirely fictionalized character with little or no bearing on the historical figure. The illusion of historical veracity is achieved by the inclusion of footnotes commenting on a few factual details in the poems, such as the names of Shelley's sailing companions when the poet made his fateful journey from Livorno to Lerici, and the title of the volume of Keats's poetry which was found on his body. These references are devised to underpin Kloos's premise about the events of Shelley's final hours. Indeed, the point of departure for the cycle relates to the precise circumstances of Shelley's death, which according to Kloos was unquestionably the result of a cruel felony: 'Shelley perished at sea through murder' (I. 14). In the ten-page prose explanation following his poems, Kloos sums up some evidence to substantiate the claim that his account of the deliberate collision at sea between a pirate vessel and Shelley's *Ariel* 'can be called historical' (710). He paraphrases some 'reports' in 'the English press' about an unnamed Italian sailor who allegedly confessed to the crime half a century after the tragic events in the Gulf of La Spezia. The original notice had caused quite a stir when it appeared in *The Times* of 1 December 1875. It was written by W. M. Rossetti acting on the request of Trelawny whose daughter had picked up the sensational news in Italy. At the time, the leading Dutch periodical *De Nederlandsche Spectator*, which tried to keep up with literary developments abroad, deemed the story remarkable enough to devote a whole column to it.[5]

It is easy to see how the idea of a violent death would have appealed to Kloos. Presented as a martyr, Shelley could be appropriated as the redeemer of all future poets and invested with the authority to salvage Kloos and recognise him as one of the elected. As such, the sonnets evince how much Kloos relied on this spurious image of Shelley to reconstruct his own public persona. In a much earlier sonnet ('Moisa') published in 1888, when he was at the height of his poetic powers, and which can be read as another address to Shelley, Kloos had written: 'Comest thou, while I fall ... Soul of my Soul / Who art nothing but dream ... I appeal to thee: O, come'.[6] In the sonnet cycle, Kloos's incantation has at last become successful. In order to silence his critics, who had many misgivings about his remaining capacities as a poet, Kloos now has himself acknowledged by Shelley as one who has taken to 'the road, trodden by all poets' (VIII. 12). The 'greatest [poet] of the nineteenth century' is thus promoted to the rank of personal Paraclete, comforting Kloos with the prospect of a just reward in an existence yet to come (719).

The cycle has many distinct religious overtones with its concentration on the transitory states of life and death, and the permeable boundaries of the hereafter. Shelley, the notorious atheist, is said to reside with the 'First Principle' (VIII. 6), 'the imagined Centre of this Chaos' (XII. 14), and with the 'All-Essence' (X. 2). Contemporary reactions to Shelley's death at sea had been of a rather different nature. In August 1822, the correspondent of *The Courier* commented: 'Shelley, the writer of some infidel poetry has been drowned; *now* he knows whether there is a God or no'.[7] The outspoken mysticism of Kloos's cycle, however, was a prerequisite to turn the visitation of Shelley's spectre into an existential possibility. At the same time, it renders Shelley an innocuous creature seemingly invested with divine, and hence indisputable, authority. Each sonnet represents, as it were, a Station which the reader has to visit with Kloos himself as the experienced guide. Starting with Shelley's premonition of his imminent death, the narrative continues with his subsequent murder, resurrection and, finally, his pentecostal apparition to his most devout apostle. Shelley is indeed presented as a Christ figure throughout. When his boat is sinking, Shelley wonders: '"Is this Death? receive me ..." and gliding wilfully / He falls into the deep, [...] with arms spread' (IV. 13–14). As in St Matthew's version of the Gospel where the two thieves crucified with Jesus are given a voice to speak, Kloos's fifth sonnet consists of the confession of one of Shelley's alleged slayers who, on his deathbed, is haunted by Shelley's spirit and begs for forgiveness.

All this seems to be designed to inspire the reader with religious awe and reverential solemnity. Such a mood was imperative to minimize as much as possible the reader's potential scepticism before being confronted with the dialogue between Shelley and Kloos in the second half of the sonnet cycle. Having described Shelley's murder, Kloos now concentrates on the visitation of Shelley's spirit which duly informs him of his own redemption. Shelley's status of apocalyptic angel is suggested by the title of the penultimate sonnet ('Shelley's

Judgement') in which the apparition paints a very bleak picture of the future indeed:

> 'Soon poets will be living in barracks,
> To where they will be driven,
> — After having dug and delved —
> By the rifle-butts of vile, Bolshevist Cossacks (XI. 5–8).

For the modern reader, it is simply impossible to associate such pronouncements with Shelley's anarchism and humanitarian concerns. As an iconoclastic radical and advocate of the reformist cause, Shelley had much more in common with the revolutionary convictions of the Bolsheviks, whom Kloos identifies as the arch-enemies of all poets, than with Kloos's own self-centred aestheticism and reactionary tenets. The lines, however, are entirely consistent with Kloos's perception of Shelley's character and art. After all, Shelley had to be depoliticized and presented as an inoffensive creature so that the effects of Kloos's claimed allegiance to the poet could only be perceived as beneficial. Incidentally, the outcast status of the poet who in life has to endure, like Christ, 'the burghers' taunting' (I. 13) and the 'mockery of fools' (VIII. 2) would become the leitmotif of many of Kloos's later, self-aggrandizing poems. Pairing himself with Shelley, Kloos lifts all 'personal Suffering' to a higher plane, giving it a cathartic significance (X. 10). The underlying philosophy is simple: Kloos discerns in Shelley's martyrdom and subsequent canonization as a poet of world stature a foreshadowing of his own fate.

Granting Shelley's spectre the faculty of speech Kloos objectifies his personal conviction of his own superior qualities as a poet. Shelley has in effect become the vindicator of Kloos's artistic calling and of the way in which he responds to it. The second sonnet of the apparition sequence opens with the bold and all-revealing assertion: 'Thus I felt: Shelley spoke it' (VII. 1). In other words, Shelley has been fully absorbed by Kloos and turned into his mouthpiece. Similarly, the sonnet in which Shelley informs Kloos of his redemption, despite the unhappy fate lying in store for all future poets, starts with the phrase: 'Yet Shelley's voice said' (XI. 1). Like the ill-fated nymph Echo in Greek Antiquity, the historical Shelley is deprived of his bodily self to become the sounding board for Kloos's authoritarian voice.

When 'Shelley trod towards [him]' (VI. 1), the spectral form was barely visible. Yet, Kloos does not need to see in order to comprehend what befalls him ('I scarcely saw', VI. 2) during the Annunciation. He shows no signs of fear or even surprise. This suggests that all along Kloos had been waiting in silent anticipation for Shelley's spirit to pluck like a 'breeze' the chords of his inner being (VI. 7). This moment is also described in the prose explanation appended to the cycle: 'when I felt these verses stir within me, I have, while listening very carefully, put onto paper what was dictated to me by my most inner Being' (717). Kloos certainly did not assume a passive role in this process. The phrase he uses in the commentary explicates that he was, above all, listening to and transcribing his own voice. Hence, the Shelley *simulacrum* can be interpreted as a subdivision of Kloos's self, speaking in accents which bear the stamp of the Dutch poet's typical diction and ideological make-up.

Even the spatial element which Kloos allows the apparition to traverse reflects the former's monopolistic intentions. From the start, Kloos makes it quite clear that Shelley is now residing in that starlit abode where the eternal are. Yet, in order to observe these heavenly constellations, it does not suffice to raise one's eyes at night. In an astonishing act of interiorization, Kloos turns his vision inwards. He believes that 'when we climb deep into our thoughts / Towards the spots visible on the black azure', to the realm where all those who 'created that which never can decay' dwell 'in immortality', we may be granted the same astral vision he has been privileged to see (I. 1–2, 11, 9). Having invested Shelley with his own beliefs, Kloos looked for Shelley *inside* himself and found him present there, not only as a burning beacon, but as the 'Soul of [his] Soul'.

Revealing Shelley both as the ally and ministering spirit in his literary pursuits, the sonnet cycle was a strongly assertive gesture towards a certain group of poets who opposed Kloos's hyper-individualistic writings. Their most important spokesman was Albert Verwey, Kloos's erstwhile lover, which made the rivalry all the more bitter. Verwey himself was an ardent admirer of Shelley's work, yet one much more responsive to its hortative, political undercurrent. From his articles on Shelley, as well as from Kloos's pronouncements, it emerges that nothing less than the rightful 'ownership' of Shelley was at stake. This culminated in a translation battle fought on the pages of *De Nieuwe Gids*, Kloos's periodical, and *De Beweging [The Movement]*, edited by Verwey. Though Kloos himself did not produce any translations himself, he supervised those made by his loyal disciple and protégé K. H. de Raaf, and wrote polemical prefaces or congratulatory reviews to promote them. Verwey tried his hand at several important Shelley poems, and supported his pupil Alex Gutteling in his attempts to render *Prometheus Unbound* and *Adonais* into Dutch. The result was a string of Shelley translations published over a short period of time: 'Mont Blanc' and 'Hymn to Intellectual Beauty' (1904, Verwey), *Alastor* (1905, De Raaf), *Epipsychidion* (1906, De Raaf), *The Cenci* (1908, De Raaf), *Prometheus Unbound* (1909, Gutteling), *Alastor* (1909, Verwey), and *Adonais* (1914, Gutteling).

This proliferation of Dutch Shelley texts externalizes the strong interactive forces at work between both groups of writers. One anecdote will suffice to illustrate the level of intensity with which this battle of literary territoriality was fought. When Gutteling's *Prometheus Unbound* translation was issued, Kloos found fault with many specific renditions. He singled out Gutteling's translation of the word 'ruin' as 'prooi' [prey] in line 618 of the first act to state his case, and had no qualms about charging the translator with gross incompetence. A reply swiftly followed, urging Kloos not to rely on the Shelley edition most readily at hand. If Kloos had used an uncorrupted text, he would have noticed instead that Shelley had written 'ravin' and not 'ruin', so the rebuttal ran. Such a frontal attack on someone who claimed to be the foremost authority on Shelley in the Netherlands could, of course, not fail to generate a strong reaction. An aggressive tit-for-tat discussion ensued with each party refusing to yield. Kloos took the matter so personally and was so bent on proving himself right that he resorted to drastic measures: in June 1916 he instructed the ever obedient 'Co' in London to contact the renowned, but by then terminally ill, Shelley scholar and editor Harry Buxton Forman, and ask him for his expert opinion. Eventually, Buxton Forman confirmed Kloos's 'ruin' reading. This is hardly surprising, however, since it was his edition which Kloos had used for the comparison of Gutteling's translation with the original text. A mildly embarrassing squabble over one single word thus took on ridiculous proportions as it was spread out over no less than seven articles in *De Nieuwe Gids* and *De Beweging*.

In order to assess Kloos's later appropriation strategies in the poetic record of the Shelley visitation, the following phrases taken from the first of his articles on the ruin-ravin controversy, prove particularly revealing.[8] There, Kloos pontificated that Shelley 'ought to be sacrosanct [...] to all translator[s]' as they are dealing with the 'angelical and yet real-visionary beauty' of his verse (134, 138). In other words, Shelley had not been a real denizen of this world and his poetry should be approached as holy writ. By failing to display the appropriate amount of reverence in his Dutch rendition of *Prometheus Unbound*, Gutteling had only himself to blame for incurring the wrath of the Shelley 'expert and friend' par excellence, namely Willem Kloos (137).

In the later sonnet sequence, Kloos tries to account for his privileged relation with 'the divine genius' (II. 14) by asking Shelley's spirit whether he, perhaps 'in an earlier Existence' as his 'playmate', has been running 'freely through the undulating English countryside?' (IX. 11–12). Preposterous as these lines may sound, it would be a mistake to think that Kloos was not in complete earnest. They are indicative of his genuine desire to be seen by the public as an artist whose being was physically and spiritually interconnected with Shelley's life and works. Kloos was well aware that Shelley had the reputation of being a poet's poet: his own self-advertised affinity with the English writer would lift him to the same literary heights. The lines may also help the present-day reader to comprehend the marked intolerance Kloos showed towards anyone who seemed to pose a threat to the exclusivity of his personal 'friendship' with Shelley. The informal word 'playmate' shows at once the degree of familiarity Kloos allowed himself in making his intimate bond with Shelley totally explicit. Incidentally, Kloos wrote many sonnet cycles as tributes to deceased friends, including the composer Alphons Diepenbrock, the painter and photographer Willem Witsen, and the critic and poet Hein Boeken. By writing a poetic in memoriam for Shelley, Kloos clearly sought to incorporate the poet among the pantheon of his close personal friends.

After the grim depiction of the fate of future poets quoted above, Shelley's spectre suddenly appears to be in a similarly congenial mood. The apparition urges Kloos:

'O, friend, fly with me, as a light feather;
'Tis bliss here above, where in the boundless
Ether, azure spheres are spinning around us!' (XI. 12–14)

Like Matthew Arnold's 'ineffectual angel', or like his own air-borne sky-lark, Shelley is portrayed as most at ease in the aethereal heights of heaven, far away from the dealings of 'Mankind' (XI. 13, I. 12). The sonnet cycle therefore can be read as Kloos's ultimate translation of Shelley. Not restricting himself to the textual level as his literary rivals had done before him, he has seized on Shelley's persona as the subject of his translation activities. In the *OED*, 'to translate' is also defined as 'to remove the dead body or remains of a saint, or, by extension, a hero or great man, from one place to another', and more specifically as 'to carry or convey to heaven'; this is exactly what Kloos has done here. However, since Kloos's heaven, or 'black azure' exists only within his 'own inner Being', the 'translation' becomes paradoxically a more radical interment than before (I. 2). Like another Ariel, Shelley's servile sprite is firmly locked up within the confines of Kloos's manipulative mind, waiting to execute its master's commands.[9] Kloos was undoubtedly familiar with the inscription from *The Tempest* on Shelley's tomb at the Protestant Cemetery in Rome: 'Nothing of him that doth fade / But doth suffer a sea-change / Into something rich and strange'. There could be no more appropriate paraphrastic translation (in its conventional sense) of Kloos's cycle; he has made the sea give up its dead, and suffered the mortal clay to change into an unearthly spirit rich with qualities quite strange to the historical Shelley.

The picture of an otherworldly, endearingly absent-minded poet pervades the entire cycle, but is most explicit in the sonnet which describes the actual collision at sea. Though the tempest is gathering in strength, threatening to topple the boat, 'Shelley lay stretched out / and read' (IV. 1-2). While his companions Edward William and the boatswain Charles Vivian are in utter distress trying to steady the vessel, Shelley is engrossed in his self-centred activities. These can be interpreted as a translation away from the sphere of reality to the ideally, and even solipsistically, fictional: 'He just read, read, until he did see naught' (IV. 8). It is with equally blissful composure that Shelley finally embraces the luxury of death. The supramundane quality as well as the sentimentality evoked by Kloos in his representation of the English poet's final moments pervade many nineteenth-century Shelley hagiographies. Nevertheless, Kloos was by no means the only writer of the twentieth century to depict a wistfully acquiescent Shelley in the face of death. Timothy Webb, in his study *Shelley: A Voice not Understood*, quotes a few lines from Thom Gunn's *Fighting Terms*, a collection of poetry published in 1954: 'Shelley was drowned near here. Arms at his side / He fell submissive through the waves'.[10] Though Kloos's Shelley, in accordance with Christian iconography, has his arms outstretched after the boat is rammed, the gesture of resignation, or even eagerness to be engulfed and erased for ever, is very similar.

Webb's observations on Gunn's account are therefore equally applicable to Kloos's representation:

> Such a death and such a posture imply an unwillingness to bare the knuckles, to counter the assaults of life in vigorous fighting terms. Where Thom Gunn suggests Shelley lacked the pugilistic muscle which might be expected of a true poet in a violent time, the nineteenth century critics spoke of his effeminacy and his 'lack of robustness' (2).

To interpret Kloos's collusive Shelley image as a belated exponent of nineteenth-century mawkishness would be too reductionist a reading though. When George Bernard Shaw, one of the more recalcitrant members of the Shelley Society fulminated against the 'conspiracy' and disingenuous attempts by many of his contemporaries 'to make Shelley a saint', his aim was to expose the ideological differences between the bourgeois values of most of the members and Shelley's political radicalism.[11] In this respect, Kloos, who was one of the only three non-Anglo-Americans to join the Society in the year of its foundation (1886), would not have stood out among the majority of genteel members with his stereotypical notion of Shelley. It can also be safely assumed that he agreed with the tenor of the inaugural address by the Reverend Stopford Brooke which was reproduced in the Society's *Notebook* and in which the speaker enthused about Shelley's 'fancies [...] woven of ether and fine fire'.[12] Yet, if Kloos can be seen as heavily drawing on the Victorians' conception of Shelley as a quixotic sprite or 'ineffectual angel', the fallacy of his representation served a far more significant and personal purpose. It was inconceivable for Kloos to tolerate a blot on Shelley's reputation because he identified so strongly with his idol. If he represented Shelley as a seditious troublemaker, Kloos would by implication lose the respectability for which he had battled since his release from the Utrecht asylum in the 1890s. He would also be forced to concede a major, irreconcilable difference in character between the English poet and himself, which would render the identification an impossibility. Consequently, Kloos had no choice but to manipulate, misrepresent or withhold essential facts during his careful reinvention of Shelley.

This sanitization process is perhaps most conspicuous in the concluding paragraph of the prose commentary following the sonnet cycle:

> Shelley, who was in the early years of his youth a revolutionary, though this revolutionary zeal was totally distinct from the present one, more reasonable and respectable, Shelley, I say, after having fully developed his mental faculties and having witnessed the true nature of humanity in its excesses of unwisdom, soon withdrew from politics and devoted himself from the age of twenty-three to studying and to art. [...] Hence, and from then onwards, he portrayed his inner self, the splendour of his idealism, into the expressive music of his immortal creations, and became one of the greatest poets, yes, for many, the greatest of the nineteenth century (718–19).

Of course, this is an instance of devious biographical falsification. No matter how much Kloos would like to have it otherwise, it is beyond dispute that during 'no period in his life was Shelley completely indifferent to political issues and events'.[13] One does not need a keen historicist eye to contest Kloos's outrageous claims: a cursory glance at a list of Shelley's works, written after 1815 and chronologically arranged, is more than sufficient. Even if the most overtly political poems, such as 'The Mask of Anarchy' or 'Song to the Men of England' were not published during Shelley's lifetime, they were readily available to Kloos in any edition of the collected works.

'Shelley's tragic death has been much mythologized,' Michael O'Neill concludes in his critical biography, and what many seem to have conveniently forgotten, and these include Kloos, was that Shelley's death 'occurred while he was returning from a visit whose purpose was to help establish *The Liberal*'.[14] To the last, the English poet was acting according to his passion for reforming the world. Surveying her husband's writing career, Mary Shelley, unlike Kloos, acknowledged that Shelley's radicalism had not abated after his twenty-third birthday; it had simply taken on another guise: 'Hitherto [until 1815], he had chiefly aimed at extending the political doctrines, and attempted so to do by appeals in prose essays to the people, exhorting them to claim their rights; but he had now begun to feel that the time for action was not ripe in England, and that the pen was the only instrument wherewith to prepare the way for better things'.[15] It is a well known fact that Mary Shelley herself did not shrink from depoliticizing Shelley's work. Yet, even her moderate views could not be shared by Kloos who sought to isolate his hero still further from such mundane considerations as parliamentary reform.

Bent on convincing his readers of Shelley's rarefied sensibilities and delicate constitution, Kloos uses the lengthy 'Commentary' which follows the sonnets to 'translate' Shelley once more from 'society [...] which was to him, at best, an inevitable horror' (715). By dint of a radical displacement, Kloos hopes to assume absolute control over Shelley's insubstantial world, ensuring that nothing in this realm exceeds his capacity of endurance. The poet's favourite pastime, so the reader is informed, was 'to roam the countryside [...] all by himself'. At this point in the epilogue, Kloos describes yet another Shelley apparition: 'I see that great artist so clearly before me, as he must have lain [underneath a tree]' reposing after his solitary wanderings (715). This mental picture reminds Kloos of some eighteenth-century engravings

> where an ideal shepherd is playing the flute underneath a tree on the sloping banks of a river. The broad straw hat lies next to him in the grass. He keeps his flock of sheep around him by the music of his lips and by his hands playing the flute (715).

The idyllic atmosphere evoked by this pastoral *tableau* is again grossly misleading: it suggests Shelley's intentional seclusion from the political turmoil in his country which, in reality, proved to be the germ from which some of his greatest poetry had sprung. Kloos's mental picture is nonetheless reminiscent of an existing Shelley portrait made by Joseph Severn, who had nursed the dying John Keats in Rome. The sentimental painting, entitled 'Shelley composing

Prometheus Unbound in the Baths of Caracalla' shows the poet among the ruins of the Baths in a rather languid, meditative pose, his large straw hat resting on the gnarled roots of a picturesque tree.[16] The representation, however, is as imaginary as Kloos's, for Severn painted it in 1845, twenty-three years after Shelley's death. Severn's prettified portrait would lead few to suspect how awkward the start of his acquaintance with Shelley had actually been. Back in 1817, his introduction to Shelley had made for a memorable evening at Leigh Hunt's Hampstead cottage. At this meeting, Severn had sided himself with the painter Benjamin Robert Haydon in a passionate defence of Christianity against Shelley's outpouring of abuse on 'that detestable religion'.[17] When, in his preface to *Adonais*, Shelley later referred to 'Mr Severn, a young artist of the highest promise', Severn's family were absolutely 'horrified to find his name in the writings of that "atheist, republican and free-liver"'.[18] Severn had a difficult time afterwards trying to reassure his kin that Shelley's ideologies had no effect on him. To convince the world of Shelley's, and indeed his own, respectability, Severn produced a very inoffensive picture indeed. Little can be less threatening than the effeminate, innocent-looking youth in his painting. This ought to be seen in the larger context of Severn's determination to suppress the more militant sides of Shelley's character. The similarities between his and Kloos's image-management are plain. What distinguishes both Kloos and Severn from all those others whose 'obsessive retelling of Shelley's life [...] operates [...] insidiously as a censoring or silencing of his work' is that their motives to do so were primarily based on self-preservation.[19]

In 1876, Severn urged Harry Buxton Forman to include the portrait in his edition of Shelley's collected works, at the same time assuring the editor that Shelley was 'the only *really* religious poet of the age'. He therefore hoped that Buxton Forman would '*omit* [the Notes to *Queen Mab*] for they do not contain anything but blasphemy of the most virulent nature'.[20] By then, Severn had already been engaged in a religious make-over of Keats, who had frustrated all attempts at conversion on his death-bed. In his 'On the Adversities of Keats's Fame' (1861), Severn recorded how he, during the poet's final days, had 'Prayed by him'. Twelve years later, in 'My Tedious Life' (1873), this had become 'Prayed with him'.[21] Likewise, Severn appears to have offered his tendentious painting to Buxton Forman in order to gloss over Shelley's heterodox beliefs.

Besides Severn's canvas, Kloos's pastoral description seems to draw on another fanciful source: 'One can think these sheep away,' Kloos completes his mental picture, 'and put in their stead the truly grandiose imaginings of Shelley's brain which must have dwelt around him' (715). It is not unlikely that this refers to a passage in *Adonais*, where Shelley mourns for Adonais's

> quick Dreams,
> The passion-winged Ministers of thought,
> Who were his flock, [and now] [...]
> Wander no more, from kindling brain to brain (73–75, 78).

Just as Shelley perpetuated the image of Keats in *Adonais* as the frail poet-boy killed off by acerbic reviews, Kloos presents a vision of Shelley as a martyred, introspective lyricist in his fictionalized elegy. Shelley deployed his homage to Keats in order to shame the hostile critics of whose abuse he himself had first-hand experience. He flouted their admonitions to abandon all literary pursuits by producing a substantial poem in what is arguably the most poetic of English metres: the Spenserian stanza. Kloos used his composition to deride his critics by transforming their blunt attacks into marks of distinction: the wounds to be inflicted by the critics' vicious 'rifle-butts' will be turned into venerable stigmata, similar to Shelley's 'ensanguined brow' in *Adonais*, and single out Kloos as one of the blessed (305).[22]

After the publication of his sonnet cycle, Kloos could claim success. Several Dutch writers wrote to him in person to congratulate him on his achievement. With Kloos's acquisition of the Shelley letter and the subsequent report in the *Times Literary Supplement*, the British also became rather intrigued by this Shelley enthusiast in the Netherlands. For instance, John Foxworthy, a minor Glaswegian poet, paid Kloos a visit in The Hague and wrote a sonnet on the occasion: 'Shelley: Written after Seeing Mr. Kloos' Study'. In it, he seems to have adopted the same spiritistic overtones of the Dutch sonnet sequence and endorses retrospectively the past communication 'Beyond all life' (4) between the 'Godhead' Shelley (4) and 'Friend' Kloos (1):

> Most love their poets: but one Friend I knew
> Loved nigh to ecstasy this Spirit pure
> Of fire Promethean: a love to endure
> Beyond all life, love for a Godhead due.
> The portrait there! enshrined in sadness rich,
> With just at hand a letter proudly hung,
> Writ by this deathless hand, featured among
> A facade set in books: a sainted niche,
> Hallowed beside an oracle of prayer.
> Around there seemed to burn a rubrous light,
> Imaging the portrait in a feeble gloom,
> Which seemed to lean so sad unto the air,
> Longing to whisper to this acolyte,
> That all seemed sanctuary and not a room.[23]

More than thirty years earlier, Shaw had warned against the 'conspiracy' to 'make Shelley a saint'. Not only has Foxworthy done just that, but he allows Kloos to bask in the serene aura of the English poet's holiness. It must have been with immense satisfaction that Kloos had Foxworthy's sonnet printed in his own periodical *De Nieuwe Gids*.

One year after Kloos's death in 1938, James Anderson Russell dedicated his survey of the Dutch Romantic revival, in which Kloos had once played a dominant part, to the poet's memory. Russell too was prone to having visions:

> I was privileged to enjoy friendship with [Kloos] right up to the time of his death [...]. I see him yet. He stood in that long, double, book-lined study in which his days were passed, just beside his innumerable English editions and the letter of Shelley's [...] of which he was so justifiably proud — a tense, waiting, almost sinister, figure in the shadows. Then I caught the

light shining in those eyes, wild yet reflective; and I knew immediately that here was the almost traditional poet and seer. It was not Shelley any longer, of course, that I could detect in him — he was too old, too subdued, too sage-like for that; there was but one poetic figure to whom I felt I could truly liken him — and that was the venerable, the laureated, Wordsworth.[24]

If Kloos was capable from the hereafter to cast his eyes on Russell's labour of love, he may have been unable to suppress a contented smile. Perhaps he did not quite leave the sublunary world as another Shelley, but a respectable, mature and level-headed Wordsworth will have struck him as no bad second choice.

PERCY BYSSHE SHELLEY

BY
WILLEM KLOOS [25]

For Co R. v. S.

I. Proem

Sometimes, when we climb deep into our thoughts
Towards the spots visible on the black azure,
The distant nebulas, many light-centuries away,
Whose magic shimmering fades by slow degrees,

We long, where everything sparkles and glows,
To stretch out rapidly both arms
In mighty sweep, as if decked out with wings,
Which will take us to where, on the further horizon,

The palace rises where dwell in immortality
All those who lived on earth in Uncorrupted Beauty
And created that which never can decay.

Ah! mankind rewarded them for their excellence ...
Aeschylus had to flee the burghers' taunting,
And Shelley perished at sea through murder.

II. Premonition

Who went, with hasty steps, slim, and with slightly

Bent head, along the murmuring beach?
Suddenly he lifts his Countenance and with eyes,
Dim and yet clear, he scans the brink,

The farthest seam of the horizon, where birds
Are flying, like specks on the crystalline screen
Of the endlessly wide heavens, and his hand,
Like a bird, swings itself upwards.

He seemed so small, standing in the vast universe,
The immortal Shelley ... With heavy, deep, loud breathing,
— An animal roaring at unreachable loot —
The sea bellows, beating wave on wave:

These know it well, for, ah, only a few hours later
The divine genius lay far, deep in the water, a corpse.

III. The Murder

The boat's slender body (shooting from
The harbour, suddenly, like a gull, with full
Sails, which billow hurriedly and with fervour)
Skims over sea-foam, where, at wild speed

(The mysteries of the Abyss sounding the death-knell)
She aspires to meet the oncoming gale,
While, behind and alongside, two equally wild
(Like, ah! slaves sent out to rob and murder)

Barques speed on. Then Darkness falls:
Mist lies low on the water: an infernal
Noise, just the horns are hooting ...
The hollow, muffled sound of a crash: one guesses,

Through dense whiteness, a pair of weak and stifled screams*
And nothing else but ... Death, the deeply silent one.

* Captain Williams, Shelley's friend, and Charles Vivian, the boatswain.

IV. Shelley's Death

Headlong, in the ship's hold, Shelley lay stretched out

And read.* The wild waves were beating
Louder and louder at the sides, pushing upward
The fragile boat, with the wail

Of shrill, whizzing screech through rigging and stay,
All crunching. Did he not hear how the others ran
Hither and thither, sighed, shouted, moaned?
He just read, read, until he did see naught.

Then he rose, in wonder; everywhere clouds of mist
Pressed forward, and suddenly ... a dark, threatening block
Jumps towards him through these mists ...
He reels at the thundering shock ...

'Is this Death? receive me ...' and gliding willfully
He falls into the deep, in silence, and with arms spread.

* Keats's 'Eve of St. Agnes', which was found opened in his pocket.

V. Confession of the Murderer

We were young savages: o, the curse
Of having to be young and foolish: not knowing,
And yet doing the deed ... soon it is forgotten ...
But later ... later ... ah! I am tired, I search

For words, to salve my conscience,
Though find none ... Look there, in that corner,
There He stands and smiles: seems to measure
The distance to my bed ... give me that handkerchief,

I have to cough again: 'tis blood: I feel it, as if devils
Were racing through my chest: I will confess it quickly,
For my breath now almost fails me ... and I die:

Once, in the stormy billows of Tuscany ...
Absolve, absolve me or I am doomed ...
I ran over a small English boat for money.

VI. Shelley's Apparition

All was silent when Shelley trod towards me ...

I scarcely saw him, but I felt his near
Supernal breath caress my head,
So softly, as if on an outer path

Where no-one walks, a gentle wind goes by: no leaf
Moves: one only notices in mild contentment a
Strange refreshing breeze steal across one's temples ...
Respectfully I waited where I sat, motionless:

'Listen to thy Soul, which thou knowest well, which rocks
Within, far behind the earthly play of shadows,
On the depths of thine own life, where love
Flies endlessly around the Eternally-Beautiful,

'As in the Universe, around the Sun of Suns, never
To be known, all other suns are orbiting.'

VII. Continued

Thus I felt: Shelley spoke it, and peace
Of secure knowing penetrated my entire
Being into my deepest soul, which I heard
Play from afar, in silence and alone on the wide

Meadows of infinity, before it began to chant again
Very deep within, its prayers to be one
With the All-Being, like so many
Had done since their earliest, saddest years ...

Yet Shelley laughed and exclaimed, while he shook
His young head — his laughing seemed like silver bells: —
'Thou must no longer torture thy Self so cruelly,
Thou never walkedst with the muted herd

'Of those who wanted to dissolve, through Death, into Nothingness:
Thou art Thyself, strictly free from Appearances or Lies.'

VIII. Continued

'Like me, thou didst not know of wincing or retreating,
Thou ne'er tookst heed of the mockery of fools,
But went, held back by nothing, from an early age,
Thine own true way towards the highest Fulfillment ...

'The Deepest descent and the Farthest reach,
Towards the unmentionable First Principle, Infinite guessing
And, though carrying Thought's eternal burthen,
Yet never didst succumb, not even for a second.

'To be wise, not to hope, but to fear neither
Whilst continuing to press forward, driven silently,
On the path, shown to thee by thy deepest Being ...

'That was the road, trodden by all poets,
Who did not sing for their own sake, but for their Soul ...
So remain, what thou always aspired to be: one of these.'

IX. Answer from Me

Master! ... forgive me that I call Thee so in diffidence,
But with a deep and all-supernal joy,
Since I learned, as a vague, touching after-pleasure
Of exquisite dreams long since gone,

Which suddenly appear before us in cold daylight,
Thy name — o how I recall that moment! —
With devotional affection
In the very first stages of my youth;

I saw him ... read him ... did not know what befell me ...
Did a far recollection rekindle within me
How I, in an earlier Existence, with Thee as playmate,
Ran freely through the undulating English countryside?

O, is all Mankind, which here appeared on earth,
One varied blossoming of the deep Eternal-Oneness?

X. Continued

Does all that one experiences, reflect back to the Great,
To the Infinitely-deep All-Essence (behind the appearances
Of this and that and something else again, Thine and mine)
To the Eternal Thought, from where, in continual blows

Of No on Yes, of Small against Great,
Under pains always suffered beyond reprieve,

In which the Fragile and the Tender perish,
Life's Riddle sprang forth?

Should we then, comforted thus, away from all futile
Complaints about all trivial, personal Suffering,
— The All-unique, eternally-existing, generous,

The God-named, always good-taking
Powerlessly honouring — continue in well-living
Coldness to do Good, and avoid Evil?

XI. Shelley's Judgement

Yet Shelley's voice said, sounding like the waves
Of the wind through slender-topped poplar-branches:
'The earth became the haunt of weaned wolves,
Which grab all with their young teeth.

'Soon poets will be living in barracks,
To where they will be driven,
    — After having dug and delved —
By the rifle-butts of vile, Bolshevist Cossacks.

'Mankind is like Nature, where all battle,
Robbing goes on eternally: it comes and goes,
This one wins, then the other, but 'tis to the detriment of both.
O, friend, fly with me, as a light feather;

''Tis bliss here above, where in the boundless
Ether, azure spheres are spinning around us!'

XII. Conclusion

Then I laughed. 'Master, in these high domains,
To where my dreams flew in my childhood,
When I lay staring for long evenings
Whilst all stars gazed on me, like eyes ...

'I, who am but a mortal, feel so heavy,
And do not belong there as much as Thou doest.' Like a pale
Moonbeam, broken by some moving leaves,
Shelley, as a mirage, was suddenly gone ...

'Illusion, didst thou go?' I said softly. 'Where didst thou stay?
Musical breath from better spheres,
Which once, for one brief moment, camest to dwell
On earth, only to flee, also too soon then ... Doest thou

'Aspire through the infinity of Space, to meet again
The imagined Centre of this Chaos which we greet ...?'

---

[1] Quoted from Harry G. M. Prick, 'Willem Kloos als Eigenaar van een Brief van Shelley' [Willem Kloos as Proprietor of a Letter by Shelley], *Juffrouw Ida*, 11 (April 1985), 11–21 (p. 12). All translations from Dutch sources are my own.

[2] Prick, p. 15. The text of Shelley's letter is reproduced under number 15 of Frederick L. Jones's standard edition, *The Letters of Percy Bysshe Shelley*, 2 vols (Oxford: Clarendon Press, 1964), I, 14–15. Jones records that the original is 'not traced'. Kloos bequeathed the holograph to the Dutch Royal Library in The Hague where it is still kept today (signature 69 F 21).

[3] J. R. van Stuwe, 'A Shelley Letter', *TLS*, 2 February 1922, 76.

[4] Willem Kloos, 'Percy Bysshe Shelley', *De Nieuwe Gids*, November 1921, 698–719. My English translation of the sonnets can be found on pp. 216–222.

[5] L. [A. C. Loffelt], 'Shelley's Dood' ['Shelley's Death'], *De Nederlandsche Spectator*, December 1875, p. 403.

[6] Quoted from *Willem Kloos: Verzen*, ed. by P. Kralt, Alfa Series (Amsterdam: Amsterdam University Press, 1995), p. 26 (ll. 13–14).

[7] Quoted from Newman Ivey White, *Shelley*, 2 vols (NY: Knopf, 1940), II, 391.

[8] Willem Kloos, 'Literaire Kroniek', *De Nieuwe Gids*, May 1912, 901–11. The remarks on the 'holiness' of Shelley's texts follow some disparaging remarks on *Queen Mab* which is called a 'juvenile product' riddled with 'empty rhetoric' (p. 903). However, the presence of the 1859 edition of the poem amongst Kloos's Shelleyana demonstrates that his unequivocal dislike of Shelley's alleged youthful lapse did not interfere with his collector's instinct.

[9] Two years after Kloos's sonnet sequence, André Maurois published his *Ariel, ou la Vie de Shelley* (Paris: Grasset, 1923) which contains such phrases as: Shelley 'avait acheté une maison dans la charmante bourgade de Marlow. Ariel consentait enfin à habiter une demeure humaine' (p. 214); 'Le Roi des Elfes mari[a] [...] la très réelle Mary [Godwin]' (p. 248); 'Jane et Edward [Williams] étaient Ferdinand et Miranda, le beau couple princier, et Shelley leur fidèle Ariel [...] l'esprit captif et pur' (p. 273); 'Quittant la terre pour un monde de formes plus fluides et plus pures, il avait rejoint ces beaux fantômes, ces cristallins palais, ces transparentes vapeurs qui avaient longtemps été pour lui la seule réalité' (p. 301). The fairy tale approach to Shelley's life is

made even more specific in the title of the English translation of Maurois's work: *Ariel: A Shelley Romance*, trans. by Ella D'Arcy (London: The Bodley Head, 1924).

[10] Timothy Webb, *Shelley: A Voice Not Understood* (Manchester: Manchester University Press, 1977), p. 2.

[11] G. B. Shaw, 'Shaming the Devil about Shelley', *The Albermarle Review*, September 1892. Reproduced in *Pen Portraits and Reviews*, 2nd edn (London: Constable, 1942), pp. 236–46 (p. 241).

[12] Stopford Brooke, 'Inaugural Meeting', *Notebook of the Shelley Society*, 2nd edn (London: Reeves and Turner, 1888), I, 1–8 (p. 3).

[13] P. M. S. Dawson, *The Unacknowledged Legislator: Shelley and Politics* (Oxford: Clarendon Press, 1980), p. 166.

[14] Michael O'Neill, *Percy Bysshe Shelley: A Literary Life*, Macmillan Literary Lives (Houndmills and London: Macmillan, 1989), p. 157.

[15] *Shelley: Poetical Works*, ed. by Thomas Hutchinson, corrected by G. M. Matthews (Oxford and NY: Oxford University Press, 1971), p. 528.

[16] The oil painting is now kept at the Keats-Shelley Memorial House in Rome. The central scene has graced the cover of several imprints of Thomas Hutchinson's edition of Shelley's *Poetical Works* for Oxford University Press.

[17] Quoted from Richard Holmes, *Shelley: The Pursuit* (London: Weidenfield and Nicholson, 1974), p. 361. For Severn's later reinterpretation of this incident, see William Sharp, *The Life and Letters of Joseph Severn* (London: Sampson Low and Marston, 1892), pp. 116–17.

[18] All references to Shelley's poetry are taken from *Shelley's Poetry and Prose*, ed. by Donald H. Reiman and Sharon B. Powers, Norton Critical Edition (NY and London: Norton, 1977), p. 392. The Severn family's response is quoted from Sheila Birkenhead, *Illustrious Friends: The Story of Joseph Severn and His Son Arthur* (London: Hamish Hamilton, 1965), p. 76.

[19] Leela Gandhi, 'Future Poetics: Sri Aurobindo's Reception of Shelley', in *P. B. Shelley: An Anthology of Recent Criticism*, ed. by N. P. Singh, New Orientations (Delhi: Pencraft International, 1993), pp. 53–61 (p. 59).

[20] Joseph Severn in letter to H. Buxton Forman dated 21 October 1876. Reproduced in *John Keats: Letters of Joseph Severn to H. Buxton Forman*, ed. by Maurice Buxton Forman (Oxford: privately printed, 1933), p. 4.

[21] See Robert Gittings, *John Keats* (Harmondsworth: Penguin, 1979), p. 618.

[22] Though strictly speaking Shelley wrote about the 'ensanguined brow' of a 'Stranger' (303), it is generally accepted that this passage in *Adonais* can be read as a self-portrait.

[23] J. L. Foxworthy, 'Shelley: Written After Seeing Mr. Kloos' Study', *De Nieuwe Gids*, November 1928, p. 540.

[24] James Anderson Russell, *Dutch Poetry and English: A Study of the Romantic Revival* (Amsterdam: H. J. Paris, 1939), p. 167.

[25] Note to the English translation: I have opted for a close and literal rendition of Kloos's Dutch sonnets. This meant that the original metre (iambic pentameter) and rhyme scheme had to be sacrificed. A very distinctive feature of Kloos's later poetry, including the twelve Shelley sonnets, is the use of hyphenated compounds and a distorted syntax; I have retained these wherever possible in the translation (notably in sonnet X). All capitals and most punctuation marks in the English version reflect Kloos's own usage. K.S.

Bibliography

Allen, Vivien, *Hall Caine: Portrait of a Victorian Romancer* (Sheffield: Sheffield Academic Press, 1997)

Allott, Miriam, ed., *Keats: The Complete Poems* (London: Longman, 1970)

—, ed., *Charlotte Brontë: 'Jane Eyre' and 'Villette': A Casebook* (London: Macmillan, 1973)

Amis, Kingsley, *The New Oxford Book of Light Verse* (Oxford: Oxford University Press, 1978)

Anon., 'The Literati and Literature of Germany', *The Anti-Jacobin Review and Magazine*, 5 (1800), 568–80

—, 'A Chapter on Goblins', *Blackwood's Edinburgh Magazine*, 14, 83 (1823), 639–46

Ashton, Rosemary, *The German Idea: Four English Writers and the Reception of German Thought, 1800–1860* (Cambridge: Cambridge University Press, 1980)

Auden, W. H., *W. H. Auden's Oxford Book of Light Verse* (Oxford: Oxford University Press, 1938)

Austen, Jane, *Northanger Abbey* (1818; repr. London: Penguin, 1995)

Baker, Carlos, *Shelley's Major Poetry: the Fabric of a Vision* (Princeton: Princeton University Press, 1948)

Bakhtin, Mikhail, *Problems in Dostoyevsky's Poetics*, trans. by Caryl Emerson (Minneapolis: University of Minnesota Press, 1984)

Baldwin, Anna, and Sarah Hutton, eds, *Platonism and the English Imagination* (Cambridge: Cambridge University Press, 1994)

Barker-Benfield, G. J., *The Culture of Sensibility: Sex and Society in Eighteenth-Century Britain* (Chicago: Chicago University Press, 1992)

Barnard, John, ed., *John Keats: The Complete Poems*, 3rd edn (London: Penguin, 1988)

Bate, Jonathan, *Shakespeare and the English Romantic Imagination* (Oxford: Clarendon Press, 1986)

Bate, Walter Jackson, *The Burden of the Past and the English Poet* (London: Chatto and Windus, 1971)

—, *John Keats* (London: The Hogarth Press, 1992)

—, and James Engell, eds, *Biographia Literaria*, 2 vols (Princeton: Princeton University Press, 1983)

Bayley, John, *The Uses of Division: Unity and Disharmony in Literature* (London: Chatto and Windus, 1976)

Beddoes, Thomas Lovell, *The Browning Box: or, the Life and Works of Thomas Lovell Beddoes as reflected in letters by his friends and admirers*, ed. by H. W. Donner (London: Oxford University Press, 1935)

—, *The Works of Thomas Lovell Beddoes*, ed. by H. W. Donner (London: Oxford University Press, 1935; repr. NY: AMS Press, 1978)

Beer, John, *Romantic Influences: Contemporary-Victorian-Modern* (NY: St. Martin's Press, 1993)

Bennett, Andrew, *Keats, Narrative and Audience: The Posthumous Life of Writing* (Cambridge: Cambridge University Press, 1994)

Benson, Arthur C., *Rossetti* (London: Macmillan, 1904)

Benson, E. F., 'The Genesis of *The Turn of the Screw*', in *Henry James: Interviews and Recollections*, ed. by Norman Page (London: Macmillan, 1984), pp. 72–84

Bentley, G. E., *Blake Records* (Oxford: Clarendon, 1969)

Bindman, David, *Blake as an Artist* (Oxford: Phaidon, 1977)

—, ed., *Blake's Illuminated Books*, 6 vols (London: Tate Gallery and Blake Trust, 1991–95)

Birkenhead, Sheila, *Illustrious Friends: The Story of Joseph Severn and His Son Arthur* (London: Hamish Hamilton, 1965)

Blake, William, *Blake's Poetry and Designs*, ed. by Mary Lynn Johnson and John E. Grant (NY: W. W. Norton, 1979)

—, *The Complete Poetry and Prose of William Blake*, rev. edn, ed. by David V. Erdman (NY: Anchor and Doubleday, 1988)

—, *The Complete Poetry and Prose of William Blake*, rev. edn, ed. by David V. Erdman (NY: Anchor and Doubleday, 1988)

—, *Jerusalem*, ed. by Morton D. Paley, Blake's Illuminated Books (London: Tate Gallery and William Blake Trust, 1991)

—, *Milton: A Poem*, ed. by Robert N. Essick and Joseph Viscomi, Blake's Illuminated Books (London: Tate Gallery and William Blake Trust, 1993)

—, *The Early Illuminated Books*, ed. by Morris Eaves, Robert N. Essick and Joseph Viscomi, Blake's Illuminated Books (London: Tate Gallery and William Blake Trust, 1993)

—, *The Urizen Books*, ed. by David Worrall, Blake's Illuminated Books (London: Tate Gallery and William Blake Trust, 1995)

Bloom, Harold, *Shelley's Mythmaking* (Ithaca, NY: Cornell University Press, 1969)

—, *The Anxiety of Influence: A Theory of Poetry* (NY: Oxford University Press, 1973)
—, *The Anxiety of Influence: A Theory of Poetry*, 2nd edn (NY and Oxford: Oxford University Press, 1997)
Boucle, P. G., ed., *Sexuality in Eighteenth-Century Britain* (Manchester: Manchester University Press, 1982)
Bradshaw, Michael, *Scattered Limbs: The Making and Unmaking of 'Death's Jest-Book'* (Belper: Thomas Lovell Beddoes Society, 1996)
Briggs, Asa, *A Social History of England,* 2nd edn (London: Penguin, 1987)
Bromwich, David, *Hazlitt: The Mind of a Critic* (Oxford: Oxford University Press, 1983)
Brontë, Charlotte, *Jane Eyre* (1847; repr. London: Penguin, 1996)
Brooke, Stopford, 'Inaugural Meeting', in *Notebook of the Shelley Society*, 2nd edn (London: Reeves and Turner, 1888), pp. 1–8
Brow, Nathaniel, 'The "brightest colours of intellectual beauty": Feminism in Peacock's novels', *Keats-Shelley Memorial Bulletin*, 36 (1985), 91–104
Brown, John, *The Elements of Medicine*, 2 vols (London: J. Johnson, 1795)
Bürger, Gottfried August, *'The Chase' and 'William and Helen': Two Ballads from the German of Gottfried Augustus Bürger*, trans. by Walter Scott, ed. by Jonathan Wordsworth (Oxford: Woodstock Press, 1991)
Burgess, Anthony, *Abba Abba* (London: Minerva, 1977)
Burns, Bryan, 'The Classicism of Peacock's *Gryll Grange*', *Keats-Shelley Memorial Bulletin*, 36 (1985), 89–102
Burwick, Frederick, 'How to Translate a Waverley Novel: Sir Walter Scott, Willibald Alexis, and Thomas De Quincey', *The Wordsworth Circle*, 25 (1994), 93–100
Butler, James, and Karen Green, eds, *Lyrical Ballads and Other Poems* (Ithaca: Cornell University Press, 1992)
Butler, Marilyn, *Peacock Displayed: A Satirist in his Context* (London: Routledge and Kegan Paul, 1979)
Buxton Forman, Maurice, ed., *John Keats: Letters of Joseph Severn to H. Buxton Forman* (Oxford: privately printed, 1933)
—, ed., *The Letters of John Keats* (Oxford: Oxford University Press, 1952)
Bynum, W. F., and Roy Porter, eds, *William Hunter and the Eighteenth-Century Medical World* (Cambridge: Cambridge University Press, 1985)
Carlson, Julie, '"Unsettled Territory": The Drama of English and German Romanticisms', *Modern Philology*, 88 (1990), 43–56
Carlyle, Thomas, *The French Revolution: A History in Three Parts*, 3 vols (NY and London, Methuen, 1902)
Chandler, James, *Wordsworth's Second Nature: A Study of the Poetry and Politics* (Chicago: University of Chicago Press, 1984)

Christensen, Jerome, 'The Color of Imagination and the Office of Romantic Criticism', in *Coleridge's Theory of Imagination Today*, ed. by Christine Gallant (NY: AMS Press, 1989), pp. 227–42

Christian, John, ed., *The Last Romantics: The Romantic Tradition in British Art, Burne-Jones to Stanley Spencer* (London: Lund Humphries, 1989)

Clark, Bruce, and Wendell Aycock, eds., *The Body and the Text* (Texas: Texas Tech University, 1990)

Codell, Julie F., 'Painting Keats: Pre-Raphaelite Artists Between Social Transgressions and Painterly Conventions', *Victorian Poetry*, 33 (1995), 341–70

Coleridge, Samuel Taylor, *Biographia Literaria*, ed. by Walter Jackson Bate and James Engell, 2 vols (Princeton: Princeton University Press, 1983)

Collingwood, W. G., *The Life and Work of John Ruskin with Portraits and Other Illustrations*, 2 vols (London: Methuen, 1893)

Cookson, William, ed., *Selected Prose 1909–1965* (London: Faber and Faber, 1973)

Coote, Stephen, *John Keats: A Life* (London: Hodder and Stoughton, 1995)

Cowper, William, *The Anatomy of Humane Bodies* (Oxford, 1698)

—, *Myotomia Reformata* (London, 1724)

Crick, Joyce, 'Some Editorial and Stylistic Observations on Coleridge's Translation of Schiller's *Wallenstein*', *Journal of the English Goethe Society*, 54 (1984), 37–75

Curran, Stuart, *Poetic Form and British Romanticism* (NY and Oxford: Oxford University Press, 1986)

—, ed., *The Cambridge Companion to British Romanticism* (Cambridge: Cambridge University Press, 1993)

Dacre, Charlotte, *Zofloya, or, The Moor*, ed. by Kim Michasiw (Oxford: Oxford University Press, 1997)

Dawson, Carl, *His Fine Wit: A Study of Thomas Love Peacock* (London: Routledge and Kegan Paul, 1970)

Dawson, P. M. S., *The Unacknowledged Legislator: Shelley and Politics* (Oxford: Clarendon Press, 1980)

de Man, Paul, *The Rhetoric of Romanticism* (NY: Columbia University Press, 1984)

Denvir, Bernard, *The Late Victorians: Art, Design and Society 1852–1910* (London: Longman, 1986)

Derrida, Jacques, *Of Grammatology*, trans. by Gayatri Chakravorty Spivak (Baltimore: Johns Hopkins University Press, 1976)

—, *Writing and Difference*, trans. by Alan Bass (London: Routledge and Kegan Paul, 1978)

—, *Dissemination*, trans. by Barbara Johnson (London: The Athlone Press, 1981)

—, *The Truth About Painting*, trans. by Geoff Bennington and Ian McLeod (London: University of Chicago Press, 1987)

—, *Specters of Marx: The State of the Debt, The Work of Mourning, and the New International*, trans. by Peggy Kamuf (NY and London, Routledge, 1994)
de Selincourt, Ernest, ed., *The Letters of William and Dorothy Wordsworth: The Early Years, 1787–1805* (Oxford: Clarendon Press, 1967)
Dickens, Charles, *Bleak House* (1853; repr. London: Collins, 1953)
Donner, H. W., ed., *The Browning Box: or, the Life and Works of Thomas Lovell Beddoes as reflected in letters by his friends and admirers* (London: Oxford University Press, 1935)
—, ed., *The Works of Thomas Lovell Beddoes* (London: Oxford University Press, 1935; repr. NY: AMS Press, 1978)
Doughty, Oswald, and Wahl, John Robert, eds, *The Letters of Dante Gabriel Rossetti*, 4 vols (Oxford: Clarendon Press, 1967)
Duffy, Edward, *Rousseau in England* (Berkeley: University of California Press, 1979)
Earle, James, *Practical Observations on the Operation for the Stone* (London: J. Johnson, 1793)
Eaves, Morris, Robert N. Essick and Joseph Viscomi, eds, *The Early Illuminated Books*, Blake's Illuminated Books, (London: Tate Gallery and William Blake Trust, 1993)
Edel, Leon, ed., *The House of Fiction: Essays on the Novel* (London: Rupert Hart-Davis, 1957)
—, ed., *Literary Criticism: European Writers and the Prefaces to the New York Edition* (NY: The Library of America, 1984)
—, ed., *Letters IV 1895–1916* (Cambridge, MA: Harvard University Press, 1984)
—, and Lyall H. Powers, eds, *The Complete Notebooks* (Oxford: Oxford University, 1987)
Egerton, Judy, *George Stubbs 1724–1806*, exh. cat. (London: Tate Gallery, 1984)
Eliot, T.S., *Selected Prose of T.S. Eliot*, ed. by Frank Kermode (London: Faber and Faber, 1975)
Ellis, Markman, *The Politics of Sensibility: Race, Gender and Commerce in the Sentimemtal Novel* (Cambridge: Cambridge University Press, 1996)
Emerson, O. F., 'The Earliest English Translations of Bürger's "Lenore": A Study in English and German Romanticism', *Western Reserve University Bulletin*, 18 (1915), 1–120
Erdman, David V., *Prophet Against Empire*, rev. edn, (Princeton: Princeton University Press, 1969)
—, ed., *The Complete Poetry and Prose of William Blake* (NY: Anchor and Doubleday, 1988)
Essick, Robert N., *William Blake: Printmaker* (Princeton: Princeton University Press, 1980)
—, *William Blake's Commercial Book Illustrations* (Oxford: Clarendon, 1991)
—, and Joseph Viscomi, eds, *Milton: A Poem*, Blake's Illuminated Books (London: Tate Gallery and William Blake Trust, 1993)

—, and Donald Pearce, eds, *Blake in his Time* (Bloomington: Indiana University Press, 1978)

Faxon, Alicia Craig, *Dante Gabriel Rossetti* (London: Abbeville Press, 1989)

Felman, Shoshana, 'Turning the Screw of Interpretation', in *Literature and Psychoanalysis: The Question of Reading Otherwise, Yale French Studies*, 55/56 (1977), pp. 94–207

Ferguson, Frances, *Wordsworth: Language as Counter-Spirit* (New Haven: Yale University Press, 1976)

Ford, George H., *Keats and the Victorians: A Study of his Influence and Rise to Fame 1821–1895* (London: Archon Books, 1962)

Foucault, Michel, *The History of Sexuality: Volume Two* (London: Penguin, 1990)

Foxworthy, John L., 'Shelley: Written After Seeing Mr. Kloos' Study', *De Nieuwe Gids*, November 1928, p. 540

Freeman, Barbara, *The Feminine Sublime: Gender and Excess in Women's Fiction* (Berkeley: University of California Press, 1995)

Friedman, Albert B., *The Ballad Revival: Studies in the Influence of Popular on Sophisticated Poetry* (Chicago: University of Chicago Press, 1961)

Gallant, Christine, ed., *Coleridge's Theory of Imagination Today* (NY: AMS Press, 1989)

Gandhi, Leela, 'Future Poetics: Sri Aurobindo's Reception of Shelley', in *P. B. Shelley: An Anthology of Recent Criticism*, ed. by N. P. Singh, New Orientations (Delhi: Pencraft International, 1993), pp. 53–61

Gaunt, William, *The Pre-Raphaelite Tragedy* (London: Jonathan Cape, 1942)

Gilbert, Sandra M., and Gubar, Susan, *The Madwoman in the Attic: The Woman Writer and the Nineteenth-Century Literary Imagination* (London: Yale University Press, 1979)

—, *The Norton Anthology of Literature by Women: The Tradition in English*, 2nd edn (London: W. W. Norton, 1996)

Gill, Stephen, ed., *The Salisbury Plain Poems of William Wordsworth* (Ithaca: Cornell University Press, 1975)

Girard, René, *Deceit, Desire and the Novel: Self and Other in Literary Structure*, trans. by Yvonne Freccero (London: The Johns Hopkins University Press, 1961)

Gittings, Robert, *John Keats* (London: Penguin, 1968)

—, ed., *Letters of John Keats: A Selection* (Oxford: Oxford University Press, 1970)

—, *John Keats* (Harmondsworth: Penguin, 1979)

Gourevich, Victor, ed., *The First and Second Discourses Together with the Replies to Critics and Essay on the Origin of Languages* (NY: Harper and Row, 1986)

Hagstrum, Jean, *William Blake, Poet and Painter* (Chicago: University of Chicago Press, 1964)

Hall, Jean, 'The Divine and the Dispassionate Selves: Shelley's *Defence* and Peacock's *The Four Ages of Poetry*', *Keats-Shelley Journal*, 91 (1992), 139–63

Hall Caine, Thomas, *Recollections of Rossetti*, 2nd edn (London: Cassell, 1928)

Haney, David, 'Eye and Ear in Wordsworth', *Studies in Romanticism*, 36 (1997), 173–99

Hartman, Geoffrey H., 'False Themes and Gentle Minds', *Philological Quarterly*, 47 (1966), 55–68

Harvey, John, 'Blake's Art', *Cambridge Quarterly*, 8 (1977), 129–50

Hazlitt, William, *The Complete Works of William Hazlitt*, ed. by P. P. Howe, 6 vols (London: J. M. Dent, 1931)

Heilman, Robert, 'Charlotte Brontë's "New" Gothic in *Jane Eyre* and *Villette* (1958)', in *Charlotte Brontë: 'Jane Eyre' and 'Villette': A Casebook*, ed. by Miriam Allott (London: Macmillan, 1973), pp. 195–205

Henry, Thomas, *Memoirs of Albert de Haller* (Warrington: J. Johnson, 1783)

Heppner, Christopher, *Reading Blake's Designs* (Cambridge: Cambridge University Press, 1995)

Hertz, Neil, *The End of the Line: Essays on Psychoanalysis and the Sublime* (NY: Columbia University Press, 1985)

Hilton, Nelson, *Literal Imagination* (Berkeley: University of California Press, 1983)

Hobson, Anthony, *J. W. Waterhouse* (London: Phaidon, 1989)

Hogarth, William, *The Analysis of Beauty*, ed. by Joseph Burke (Oxford: Clarendon, 1955)

Holmes, Richard, *Shelley: The Pursuit* (London: Weidenfield and Nicholson, 1974)

Howe, P.P., ed., *The Complete Works of William Hazlitt*, 6 vols (London: J.M. Dent, 1931)

Huhn, Thomas, 'The Kantian Sublime and the Nostalgia for Violence', *The Journal of Aesthetics and Art Criticism*, 53 (1995), 269–75

Hunt, William Holman, *Pre-Raphaelitism and the Pre-Raphaelite Brotherhood*, 2 vols (NY: AMS Press, 1967)

Hunter, John, *A Treatise on the Venereal Disease* (London: G. Nicol, 1786)

—, *A Treatise on the Blood, Inflammation, and Gun-Shot Wounds* (London: J. Richardson for G. Nicol, 1794)

Hunter, William, *Anatomy of the Human Gravid Uterus* (Birmingham: John Baskerville, 1774)

Hutchinson, Thomas, ed., *Shelley: Poetical Works*, corrected by G. M. Matthews (Oxford and NY: Oxford University Press, 1971)

Hutchison, Sidney C., *The History of the Royal Academy 1768–1968* (London: Chapman and Hall, 1968)

Ingpen, Roger, and Walter E. Peck, eds, *The Complete Works of Percy Bysshe Shelley*, 10 vols (London: Ernest Benn, 1926–30)

Irwin, David, *John Flaxman 1755–1826: Sculptor, Illustrator, Designer* (London: Studio Vista and Christie's, 1979)
Jacobus, Mary, *Tradition and Experiment in Wordsworth's Lyrical Ballads (1798)* (Oxford: Clarendon Press, 1976)
James, Henry, *The Turn of the Screw* (1898; repr. London: Penguin, 1986)
—, *The Ambassadors* (1903; repr. London: Penguin, 1986)
—, *The Sense of the Past* (London: Collins, 1917)
—, *The House of Fiction: Essays on the Novel*, ed. by Leon Edel (London: Rupert Hart-Davis, 1957)
—, *Letters IV 1895–1916*, ed. by Leon Edel (Cambridge, MA: Harvard University Press, 1984)
—, *Literary Criticism: European Writers and the Prefaces to the New York Edition*, ed. by Leon Edel (NY: The Library of America, 1984)
—, *The Complete Notebooks*, ed. by Leon Edel and Lyall H. Powers (Oxford: Oxford University Press, 1987)
Jeffrey, Francis, review of Robert Southey's *Thabala the Destroyer*, *Edinburgh Review*, 1 (October 1802), 63–83
Johnson, Mary Lynn, and John E. Grant, eds, *Blake's Poetry and Designs* (NY: W. W. Norton, 1979)
Johnston, Kenneth R., 'Philanthropy or Treason? Wordsworth as "Active Partisan"', *Studies in Romanticism*, 25 (1986), 371–409
—, and Gilbert Chaitin, Karen Hanson, and Herbert Marks, eds, *Romantic Revolutions: Criticism and Theory* (Bloomington: Indiana University Press, 1990)
Jolles, Evelyn B., *G. A. Bürgers Ballade 'Lenore' in England* (Regensburg: Hans Carl, 1974)
Jones, Chris, *Radical Sensitivity: Literature and Ideas in the 1790s* (London and NY: Routledge and Kegan Paul, 1993)
Jones, Frederick L., ed., *The Letters of Percy Bysshe Shelley*, 2 vols (Oxford: Clarendon Press, 1964)
Jordanova, L. J., 'Gender, Generation and Science: William Hunter's Obstetrical Atlas', in *William Hunter and the Eighteenth-Century Medical World*, ed. by W. F. Bynum and Roy Porter (Cambridge: Cambridge University Press, 1985), pp. 385–412
—, *Sexual Visions: Images of Gender in Science between the Eighteenth and Twentieth Centuries* (London: Harvester Wheatsheaf, 1989)
Keach, William, 'Romanticism and Language', in *The Cambridge Companion to British Romanticism*, ed. by Stuart Curran (Cambridge: Cambridge University Press, 1993), pp. 95–120
Keats, John, *The Letters of John Keats*, ed. by Maurice Buxton Forman (Oxford: Oxford University Press, 1952)
—, *Keats: The Complete Poems*, ed. by Miriam Allott (London: Longman, 1970)

—, *Letters of John Keats: A Selection*, ed. by Robert Gittings (Oxford: Oxford University Press, 1970)
—,*Complete Poems*, ed. by Jack Stillinger (Cambridge, MA and London: Harvard University Press, 1978)
—, *The Complete Poems*, ed. by John Barnard, 3rd edn (London: Penguin, 1988)
Kelly, Gary, 'The Limits of Genre and the Institutions of Literature: Romanticism Between Fact and Fiction', in *Romantic Revolutions: Criticism and Theory*, ed. by Kenneth R. Johnston, Gilbert Chaitin, Karen Hanson, and Herbert Marks (Bloomington: Indiana University Press, 1990), pp. 158–175
Kemp, Martin, *Dr. William Hunter at the Royal Academy of Arts* (Glasgow: University of Glasgow Press, 1975)
Kermode, Frank, ed., *Selected Prose of T.S. Eliot* (London: Faber and Faber, 1975)
Kestner, Joseph, *Jane Austen: Spatial Structure of Thematic Variations* (Salzburg: Universität Salzburg, 1974)
Kiely, Benedict, ed., *The Various Lives of Keats and Chapman and the Brother* (London: Grafton Books, 1988)
King, Bruce, 'The Strategy of Carew's Wit', in *Ben Jonson and the Cavalier Poets*, ed. by Hugh Maclean (NY: W. W. Norton, 1974), pp. 540–48
Klancher, Jon, *The Making of English Reading Audiences, 1790–1852* (Wisconsin and London: University of Wisconsin Press, 1987)
Kloos, Willem, 'Literaire Kroniek', *De Nieuwe Gids*, May 1912, 901–11
—, 'Percy Bysshe Shelley', *De Nieuwe Gids*, November 1921, 698–719
—, *Willem Kloos: Verzen*, ed. by P. Kralt, Alfa Series (Amsterdam: Amsterdam University Press, 1995)
Kralt, P., ed., *Willem Kloos: Verzen* Alfa Series (Amsterdam: Amsterdam University Press, 1995)
Kreiter, Carmen S., 'Evolution and William Blake', *Studies in Romanticism*, 4 (1965), 110–18
L. [Loffelt, A. C.], 'Shelley's Dood' ['Shelley's Death'], *De Nederlandsche Spectator*, December 1875, p.403
LaBelle, Jenijoy, 'Blake's Visions and Re-Visions of Michelangelo', in *Blake in his Time*, ed. by Robert N. Essick and Donald Pearce (Bloomington: Indiana University Press), pp. 13–22
Laqueur, Thomas, *Making Sex: Body and Gender from the Greeks to Freud* (London: Harvard University Press, 1990)
Larkin, Philip, *Selected Letters of Philip Larkin: 1940–1985*, ed. by Anthony Thwaite (London: Faber and Faber, 1992)
Laws, Malcolm, *The British Literary Ballad: A Study in Poetic Imitation* (Carbondale: Southern Illinois University Press, 1972)
Levine, George, *The Realistic Imagination* (Chicago: University of Chicago Press, 1981)

Levinson, Marjorie, *Keats's Life of Allegory: The Origins of a Style* (Oxford: Blackwells, 1988)
Lewis, M. G., *The Castle Spectre: A Drama in Five Acts, Performed at Theatres of London and Dublin with Uncommon Applause* (London: J. Bell, 1798)
Liu, Alan, *Wordsworth: The Sense of History* (Stanford: Stanford University Press, 1989)
MacIntyre, Alisdair, *After Virtue* (Indiana: University of Notre Dame Press, 1981)
Maclean, Hugh, ed., *Ben Jonson and the Cavalier Poets* (NY: W. W. Norton, 1974)
Macpherson, Pat, *Reflecting on Jane Eyre* (London: Routledge, 1989)
Maddox, Donald L., 'Shelley's *Alastor* and the Legacy of Rousseau', *Studies in Romanticism*, 9 (1970), 82–98
Marquess, William Henry, *Lives of the Poet: The First Century of Keats Biography* (London: Pennsylvania State University Press, 1985)
Marshall, Tim, *Murdering to Dissect* (Manchester and NY: Manchester University Press, 1995)
Mason, Eudo C., *The Mind of Henry Fuseli* (London: Routledge and Kegan Paul, 1951)
Matthews, G. M., '"The Triumph of Life": A New Text', *Studia Neophilologica*, 32 (1960), 271–309
—, 'The "Triumph of Life" Apocrypha', *TLS* (5 August 1960), 503
—, 'On Shelley's "The Triumph of Life"', *Studia Neophilologica*, 34 (1962), 104–34
—, *Keats: The Critical Heritage* (London: Routledge and Kegan Paul, 1971)
Maurois, André, *Ariel, ou la Vie de Shelley* (Paris: Grasset, 1923)
Maxwell, Catherine, 'Not the whole picture: Browning's "unconquerable shade"', *Word and Image*, 8, 4 (1992), 322–32
Mayoux, Jean-Jacques, *Un Epicurien Anglais: Thomas Love Peacock* (Paris: Nizet et Bastard, 1933)
McFarland, Thomas, 'Field, Constellation, and Aesthetic Object', *New Literary History*, 13 (1982), 421–47
McGann, Jerome J., *The Romantic Ideology: A Critical Investigation* (Chicago: University of Chicago Press, 1983)
Mellor, Anne K., ed., *Romanticism and Feminism* (Bloomington: Indiana University Press, 1988)
—, ed., *Romanticism and Gender* (London: Routledge, 1993)
Mennie, Duncan M., 'Sir Walter Scott's Unpublished Translations of German Plays', *Modern Language Review*, 33 (1938), 234–39
Michasiw, Kim Ian, ed., *Zofloya, or, The Moor* (Oxford: Oxford University Press, 1997)
Miles, Robert, *Gothic Writing: A Genealogy, 1750–1820* (London: Routledge, 1993)

Miller, J. Hillis, 'Shelley's "The Triumph of Life"', in *Shelley*, ed. by Michael O'Neill (London: Longman, 1993), pp. 218–40

Mills, Howard, 'The Dirty Boots of the Bourgeoisie: Peacock on Music', *Keats-Shelley Memorial Bulletin*, 36 (1985), 77–88

Milner, George, 'On Some Marginalia Made by Dante Gabriel Rossetti in a Copy of Keats's Poems', *Englische Studien*, 61 (1929), 211–19

Miner, Earl, 'The Cavalier Ideal of the Good Life', in *Ben Jonson and the Cavalier Poets*, ed. by Hugh Maclean (NY: W. W. Norton, 1974), pp. 465–79

Mitchell, W. J. T., *Picture Theory: Essays on Verbal and Visual Representation* (London: Chicago University Press, 1994)

More, Hannah, *Strictures on the Modern System of Female Education* (London, 1799)

Motion, Andrew, *Philip Larkin: A Writer's Life* (London: Faber and Faber, 1993)

—, *Keats* (London: Faber and Faber, 1997)

—, *Salt Water* (London: Faber and Faber, 1997)

Mudrick, Marvin, 'Irony *versus* Gothicism (1952)', in *Jane Austen: 'Northanger Abbey' and 'Persuasion': a Casebook*, ed. by B.C. Southam (London: Macmillan,1976), pp. 73–97

Mullan, John, *Sentiment and Sociability: The Language of Feeling in the Eighteenth Century* (Oxford: Oxford University Press, 1988)

Nietzsche, Friedrich, *Untimely Meditations*, trans. by R. J. Hollingdale (Cambridge: Cambridge University Press, 1983)

O'Brien, Flann, *The Best of Myles: A Selection from 'Cruiskeen Lawn'*, ed. by Kevin O'Nolan (London: Flamingo Modern Classics, 1993)

O'Neill, Michael, *Percy Bysshe Shelley: A Literary Life*, Macmillan Literary Lives (Houndmills and London: Macmillan, 1989)

—, ed., *Shelley* (London: Longman, 1993)

O'Nolan, *The Various Lives of Keats and Chapman and The Brother*, ed. by Benedict Kiely (London: Grafton Books, 1988)

Owen, W.J.B., and Jane W. Smyser, eds, *The Prose Works of William Wordsworth*, 3 vols (Oxford: Clarendon Press, 1974)

Page, Norman, ed., *Henry James: Interviews and Recollections* (London: Macmillan, 1984)

Paley, Morton D., ed., *Jerusalem*, Blake's Illuminated Books, (London: Tate Gallery and William Blake Trust, 1991)

Panofsky, Erwin, *Meaning in the Visual Arts* (London: Penguin, 1993)

Parris, Leslie, ed., *The Pre-Raphaelites* (London: Tate Gallery, 1984)

Parrish, Stephen M., *The Art of the Lyrical Ballads* (Cambridge, MA: Harvard University Press, 1973)

Paulson, Ronald, *Hogarth's Graphic Works,* 3rd edn, (London: The Print Room, 1989)

Pearce, Lynne, *Woman/Image/Text: Readings in Pre-Raphaelite Art and Literature* (Great Britain: Harvester Wheatsheaf, 1991)
Petherbridge, Deanna, *The Quick and the Dead*, exh. cat. (London: National Touring Exhibitions, 1997)
Petry, Alice Hall, 'Jamesian Parody, *Jane Eyre* and *The Turn of the Screw*', *Modern Language Studies*, 13 (1983), 61–78
Pite, Ralph, *The Circle of our Vision: Dante's Presence in English Romantic Poetry* (Oxford: Clarendon Press, 1994)
Pound, Ezra, 'Beddoes and Chronology' (1917), in *Selected Prose 1909–1965*, ed. by William Cookson (London: Faber and Faber, 1973), pp. 348–53
Praz, Mario, *The Romantic Agony* (Oxford: Oxford University Press, 1933)
Preston, William, 'Reflections on the Peculiarities of Style and Manner in the late German Writers, whose Works have appeared in English; and on the Tendency of their Productions', *Edinburgh Magazine*, 20 (1802), 353–61, 406–08; 21 (1802), 9–18, 89–96
Prick, Harry G. M, 'Willem Kloos als Eigenaar van een Brief van Shelley' ['Willem Kloos as Proprietor of a Letter by Shelley'], *Juffrouw Ida*, 11.1 (April 1985), 11–21
Rajan, Tilottama, *Dark Interpreter: the Discourse of Romanticism* (Ithaca, NY: Cornell University Press, 1980)
—, *The Supplement of Reading: Figures of Understanding in Romantic Theory and Practice* (Ithaca, NY and London: Cornell University Press, 1990)
—, and Wright, Julia M., *Romanticism, History, and the Possibilities of Genre: Re-forming Literature 1789–1837* (Cambridge: Cambridge University Press, 1998)
Rather, L. J., *Mind And Body in Eighteenth-Century Medicine* (Berkeley: University of California Press, 1965)
Read, Bill, 'The Critical Reputation of Thomas Love Peacock with an Annotated Enumerative Bibliography' (unpublished D.Phil., University of Boston, 1959)
Reed, Mark, *Wordsworth: The Chronology of the Early Years, 1770–1799* (Cambridge, MA: Harvard University Press, 1967)
Reiman, Donald H., 'Shelley's "The Triumph of Life": the Biographical Problem', *PMLA*, 78 (December 1963), 536–50
—, and Sharon B. Powers, eds, *Shelley's Poetry and Prose* Norton Critical Edition (NY: W. W. Norton, 1977)
—, *Shelley's 'The Triumph of Life': a Critical Study, Based on a Text Newly Edited from the Bodleian Manuscript* (Urbana: University of Illinois Press, 1965; repr. NY: Octagon Books, 1979)
—, and Sharon B. Powers, eds, *Shelley's Poetry and Prose*, 3rd edn (NY: W. W. Norton, 1982)
—, ed., *Bodleian Shelley Manuscripts*, 22 vols (NY: Garland, 1986–97)

Reyneke-van Stuwe, Jacob, 'A Shelley Letter', *Times Literary Supplement*, 2 February 1922, 76

Reynolds, Joshua, *Discourses on Art*, ed. by Robert R. Wark (San Marino: Huntington Library, 1959)

Richardson, Alan, *A Mental Theater: Poetic Drama and Consciousness in the Romantic Age* (University Park, Penn., and London: Pennsylvania University Press, 1988)

Richardson, Ruth, *Death, Dissection and the Destitute* (London and NY: Routledge and Kegan Paul, 1987)

Richardson, Samuel, *Clarissa* (London: Penguin, 1985)

Ricks, Christopher, *Keats and Embarrassment* (Oxford: Oxford University Press, 1974)

—, *The Force of Poetry* (Oxford: Oxford University Press, 1984)

Rivkin, Julie, *False Positions: The Representational Logics of Henry James's Fiction* (Stanford: Stanford University Press, 1996)

Roberts, K.B., and J.D.W. Tomlinson, *The Fabric of the Body* (Oxford: Clarendon, 1992)

Roe, Nicholas, *John Keats and the Culture of Dissent* (Oxford: Oxford University Press, 1997)

Rossetti, Dante Gabriel, *John Keats: Criticism and Comment* (London: Printed for private circulation by Thomas J. Wise, 1919)

—, *The Letters of Dante Gabriel Rossetti*, ed. by Doughty, Oswald, and Wahl, John Robert, 4 vols (Oxford: Clarendon Press, 1967)

Rossetti, William Michael, *Dante Gabriel Rossetti as Designer and Writer* (London: Cassell and Company, 1889)

Rousseau, G. S., 'Literature and Medicine: The State of the Field', *Isis*, 72 (1981), 263–424

—, 'Nymphomania, Bienville and the Rise of Erotic Sensibility', in *Sexuality in Eighteenth-Century Britain*, ed. by P. G. Boucle (Manchester: Manchester University Press, 1982), pp. 96–120

Rousseau, Jean-Jacques, *Eloisa, or a Series of Original Letters*, trans. by William Kenrick (1803; repr. Oxford: Woodstock Books, 1989)

—, *The Confessions*, trans. by J. M. Cohen (London: Penguin, 1954)

—, *Reveries of the Solitary Walker*, trans. by Peter France (London: Penguin, 1979)

—, *The First and Second Discourses Together with the Replies to Critics and Essay on the Origin of Languages*, ed. and trans. by Victor Gourevich (NY: Harper and Row, 1986)

Rowland, William G., *Literature and the Marketplace - Romantic Writers and their Audiences in Great Britain and the United States* (Lincoln and London: University of Nebraska Press, 1996)

Russell, James Anderson, *Dutch Poetry and English: A Study of the Romantic Revival* (Amsterdam: H. J. Paris, 1939)

Sambrook, J., *The Intellectual and Cultural Context of English Literature, 1700–1789* (London: Longman, 1993)

Sawday, Jonathan, *The Body Emblazoned: Dissection and the Human Body in Renaissance Culture* (London: Routledge, 1995)

Scott, Grant F., *The Sculpted Word: Keats, Ekphrasis, and the Visual Arts* (London: New England University Press, 1994)

Sharp, William, *The Life and Letters of Joseph Severn* (London: Sampson, Low and Marston, 1892)

Shaw, G. B, 'Shaming the Devil about Shelley', in *Pen Portraits and Reviews*, 2nd edn (London: Constable, 1949), pp. 236–46

Sheats, Paul D., *The Making of Wordsworth's Poetry, 1785–1798* (Cambridge, MA: Harvard University Press, 1973)

Shelley, Mary Wollstonecraft [anon.], 'On Ghosts', *The London Magazine*, 9 (1824), 253–56

—, ed., *Posthumous Poems of Percy Bysshe Shelley* (London: John and Henry L. Hunt, 1824)

—, ed., *The Poetical Works of Percy Bysshe Shelley* (London: Edward Moxon, 1839)

Shelley, P. B., *The Poetical Works of Percy Bysshe Shelley*, ed. by Mary Shelley (London: Edward Moxon, 1839)

—, *The Complete Works of Percy Bysshe Shelley*, ed. by Roger Ingpen and Walter E. Peck, 10 vols (London: Ernest Benn, 1926–30)

—, *The Letters of Percy Bysshe Shelley*, ed. by Frederick L. Jones, 2 vols (Oxford: Clarendon Press, 1964)

—, *Shelley: Poetical Works*, ed. by Thomas Hutchinson, corrected by G. M. Matthews (Oxford and NY: Oxford University Press, 1971)

—, *Shelley's Poetry and Prose*, ed. by Donald H. Reiman and Sharon B. Powers Norton Critical Edition (NY: W. W. Norton, 1977)

—, *Shelley's Poetry and Prose*, ed. by Donald H. Reiman and Sharon B. Powers, 3rd edn (NY: W. W. Norton, 1982)

—, *Bodleian Shelley Manuscripts*, ed. by Donald H. Reiman, 22 vols (NY: Garland, 1986–97)

Simpson, David, *Romanticism, Nationalism, and the Revolt against Theory* (Chicago: University of Chicago Press, 1993)

Singh, N.P., *P.B. Shelley: An Anthology of Recent Criticism*, New Orientations (Delhi: Pencraft International, 1993)

Smith, Alan Gardner, 'The Occultism of the Text', *Poetics Today*, 3.4 (1982), pp. 5–20

Sontag, Susan, *Illness and Metaphor* (Harmondsworth: Penguin, 1983)

Southam, B.C., ed., *Jane Austen's 'Northanger Abbey' and 'Persuasion': A Casebook* (London: Macmillan, 1976)

Southey, Robert, *The Doctor, &c*, 7 vols (London: Longman, Rees and Orme, 1834–47)

Stafford, Barbara Maria, *Body Criticism* (Cambridge, MA: The MIT Press, 1991)
Stafford, Fiona J., *The Last of the Race: The Growth of a Myth from Milton to Darwin* (Oxford: Oxford University Press, 1994)
Stange, Robert G., '1887 and the Making of the Modern Canon', *Victorian Poetry*, 25 (1987), 151–68
Stillinger, Jack, ed., *Keats: Complete Poems* (Cambridge, MA and London: Harvard University Press, 1978)
Stokoe, F. W., *German Influence in the English Romantic Period, 1788–1818* (Cambridge: Cambridge University Press, 1926)
Strachey, Lytton, 'The Last Elizabethan' (1907), in *Books and Characters, French fand English* (London: Chatto and Windus, 1922), pp. 225–52
Sullivan, K. E., *The Pre-Raphaelites* (London: Brockhampton Press, 1996)
Swann, Karen, 'Harassing the Muse', in *Romanticism and Feminism*, ed. by Anne K. Mellor (Bloomington: Indiana University Press, 1988), pp. 81–92
—, 'Public Transport: English Romantic Experiments in Sensation', *American Notes and Queries*, 6 (1993), 137–42
Thwaite, Anthony, ed., *Selected Letters of Philip Larkin: 1940–1985* (London: Faber and Faber, 1992)
Tintner, Adeline, *The Book World of Henry James: Appropriating the Classics* (London: UMI Research Press, 1987)
Todorov, Tzvetan, *The Fantastic: A Structural Approach to Literary Genre*, trans. by Richard Howard (London: Press of Case, Western Reserve University, 1973)
Tompkins, J. M. S., *The Popular Novel in England, 1770–1800* (Lincoln: University of Nebraska Press, 1961)
Upstone, Robert, and Wilton, Andrew, eds, *The Age of Rossetti, Burne-Jones and Watts: Symbolism in Britain 1860–1910* (London: Tate Gallery, 1997)
Van Sant, Ann, *Sensibility and the Novel: The Senses in Social Context* (Cambridge: Cambridge University Press, 1993)
Viscomi, Joseph, *Blake and the Idea of the Book* (Princeton: Princeton University Press, 1993)
Wallace, Tara Ghoshal, *Jane Austen and Narrative Authority* (London: Macmillan, 1995)
Wark, Robert R., ed., *Discourses on Art* (San Marino: Huntington Library, 1959)
Watts, Cedric, *A Preface to Keats* (Hong Kong: Longman, 1985)
Webb, Timothy, *The Violet in the Crucible: Shelley and Translation* (Oxford: Clarendon Press, 1976)
—, *Shelley: A Voice Not Understood* (Manchester: Manchester University Press, 1977)
Weiskel, Thomas, *The Romantic Sublime* (Baltimore: Johns Hopkins University Press, 1976)
White, Newman Ivey, *Shelley*, 2 vols (NY: Knopf, 1940)

Williams, Michael, *Jane Austen: Six Novels and Their Methods* (London: Macmillan, 1986)

Williams, Raymond, *The Country and the City* (London: Chatto and Windus, 1973)

Wilt, Judith, *Ghosts of the Gothic: Austen, Eliot, and Lawrence* (Princeton: Princeton University Press, 1980)

Wolf, Bryan, 'Confessions of a Closet Ekphrastic: Literature, Painting and Other Unnatural Relations', *Yale Journal of Criticism*, 3 (1990), 181–204

Woof, Robert, and Hebron, Stephen, *John Keats* (Kendal: The Wordsworth Trust, 1995)

Wordsworth, Jonathan, ed., *'The Chase' and 'William and Helen': Two Ballads from the German of Gottfried Augustus Bürger*, trans. by Walter Scott (Oxford: Woodstock Press, 1991)

Wordsworth, William, *The Prose Works of William Wordsworth*, ed. by W. J. B. Owen and Jane W. Smyser, 3 vols (Oxford: Clarendon Press, 1974)

——, *The Salisbury Plain Poems of William Wordsworth*, ed. by Stephen Gill (Ithaca: Cornell University Press, 1975)

——, *Lyrical Ballads and Other Poems*, ed. by James Butler and Karen Green (Ithaca: Cornell University Press, 1992)

Worrall, David, ed., *The Urizen Books*, Blake's Illuminated Books (London: Tate Gallery and William Blake Trust, 1995)

Index

Allott, Miriam, 123, 130
Amis, Kingsley, 110–11, 114–15, 123
Amory, Thomas, 76
Anatomy, xxi–xxii, xxiv, 19–42, 154
    anatomical art, xxi, 24
    anatomy language, 154
    anatomy literature, xxii, 19
    animal anatomy, 27
    comparative anatomy, 25
Anti-Jacobin Review, 43
Ariel (Shelley's boat), 202
Aristophanes, 78
Arnold, Matthew, 140, 208
Auden, W. H., 110–13, 118, 123
    Poems, 111
Austen, Jane, 182, 188, 191–95
    Northanger Abbey, xxiv, 182, 187, 191–95

Bage, Robert, 76
Bailey, Benjamin, 123
Bakhtin, Mikhail, 57
Barker-Benfield, G. J., 5
Barry, James, 24
Barton, Bernard, 146
Basire, James, 25–26
Bate, Jonathan, 169
Bate, Walter Jackson, xix

Bayley, John, 114, 132
Beddoes, Thomas Lovell, xxi–xxii, xxiv, 139–57
    Death's Jest-Book, 146, 149
    'Lines written in Switzerland', 148
    Love's Arrow Poisoned, 150
    The Brides' Tragedy, 140–41, 143–47, 152
    The Last Man, 152
Belli, Giuseppe, 117–19
Benson, Arthur C., 166
Benson, Edward White, 185
Bentley, G. E., 69
    Standard Novels, 69
Bible, 187
Bidloo, Govard, 27, 30, 33
Bindman, David, 24–25
Blackwood's, 140
Blake, William, xviii, xx–xxi, 19–42, 45, 134
    An Island in the Moon, 25
    Descriptive Catalogue, 21, 23, 31, 37
    Jerusalem, xviii, 20–24, 28–31, 38
    Public Address, 36
    The First Book of Urizen, 21, 25–26

The Marriage of Heaven and Hell, 19, 29, 39
Bloom, Harold, xix, xxiii, 57, 68, 89, 104, 140, 154
   The Anxiety of Influence, xix, 154
Boeken, Hein, 208
Bolsheviks, 204
Brawne, Fanny, 119
Briggs, Asa, 175
Britain, 200
Brontë, Charlotte, 182, 194
   Jane Eyre, xxiv, 182, 186–87, 190, 193
Brooke, Stopford, 210
Brown, John, 25
   Elements of Medicine, 25
Browning, Robert, 149–51, 154–55, 166
Buchanan, George, 167
Bürger, Gottfried August, xxiii, 45–46, 49–50, 55, 58, 60–62
   'Der Wilde Jäger', 45, 47, 51
   'Des Pfarrers Tochter von Taubenhain', 54–55
   'Lenore', 45, 47
   'The Chase', xxiii, 47, 49–52, 55
   'The Chase' and 'William and Helen': Two Ballads from the German of Gottfried Augustus Bürger, 47
Burgess, Anthony, xxiii, 117–20, 135
   Abba Abba, 117–20, 135
Burke, Edmund, 4
Burke, William, xxii
Burne-Jones, Edward, 172
Burton, Robert, 119
   Anatomy of Melancholy, 119
Butler, Samuel, 77
Butler, Marilyn, 69, 76
Buxton Forman, Harry, 207, 213
Buxton Forman, Maurice, 166–67

The Poetical Works and Other Writings of John Keats, 166
Byron, 76–77, 112, 134, 148, 200
   Childe Harold's Pilgrimage, 76

Campbell, James Dykes, 151–52
Carew, Thomas, 125
   'A deposition from Love', 125
   'Ingratefull beauty threatned', 125
   'To a Lady that desired I would love her', 125
   'To my inconstant Mistris', 125
Carlyle, Thomas, xxiv
   French Revolution, xxiv
Castlereagh, 74
Cavalier poets, 125
Cervantes Saavedra, Miguel de, 75
Chapman, George, 120–121
Chatterton, Thomas, 122–123, 166
Chaucer, Geoffrey, 46
'Co', see Jacob Reyneke-van Stuwe
Cockney School, 83
Codell, Julie F., 161–62, 166, 173
Coleridge, Samuel Taylor, 46–47, 53, 79
   Biographia Literaria, 45–46, 63
Cowden Clarke, Charles, 115
Cowper, Frank Cadogan, 174
Cowper, William, 27–33, 38
   The Anatomy of Humane Bodies, 27–30, 33
   Myotomia Reformata, 28–29
Crane, Walter, 172
Critical Review, 47
Curran, Stuart, 68
Cyclographic Society, 166

Dacre, Charlotte, xx, 1–17
   Zofloya, or, The Moor, xx, 1–17
Dark-lanterns, 147, 156–7
Darley, George, 142, 146
De Beweging, 206–07
de Man, Paul, 97, 100–102, Shelley Disfigured', 97–98
De Nederlandsche Spectator, 202
De Nieuwe Gids, 201, 206–07, 215
De Quincey, Thomas, 45
de Raaf, K. H., 206
Derrida, Jacques, xxiii, 98, 182, 184, 189–90, 195
   Specters of Marx, xxiii–xxiv
   The Truth About Painting, 182
Dickens, Charles, 187
   Bleak House, 187
Dicksee, Frank, 171–72, 174
Diepenbrock, Alphons, 208
Diogenes, 147
Disinterment, 154
Donner, H. W., 150, 153
Doughty, Oswald, 166
Duffy, Edward, 102

Earle, James, 25
   Practical Observations on the Operation for the Stone, 25
Erdman, David V., 25
Eliot, T. S., 89, 104, 113, 115, 118
Ellis, Markman, 7
Elton Marmaduke, Isaac, 119

Fawkes, Guy, 147
Faxon, Alicia Craig, 164
Felman, Shoshana, 186, 192
First World War, 160, 166
Flaxman, John, 24, 39
Flint, Russell, 172
Ford, George H., 160
Foucault, Michel, 5

Foxworthy, John L., 215
   'Shelley: Written after Seeing Mr. Kloos' Study', 214
France, 44
Freeman, Barbara, 4
French Revolution, 97
Fuseli, Henry, 24

Galvanism, 139
Gambart, 162
Gaub, Jerome, 4
Genesis, 21
German romance, 43–46, 62
Germany, xxiv, 44–45, 47, 141, 146, 148
Gibbon, Edward, 78
Gilbert, Sandra M., 6
Gittings, Robert, 133
Godwin, William, 45, 74
   Mandeville, 74
Goethe, Johann Wolfgang von, 45
   Faust, 45
   Werther, 45
Gothic,
   male and female, 2, 3, 8,11, 15
Grave-robbing, xvii, 139, 147, 154
   Literary grave-robbing, 143
Gubar, Susan, 6
Gulielmi, Giovanni, 117, 119
Gunn, Thom, 209
   Fighting Terms, 209
Gutteling, Alex, 206–07
Guy's Hospital, 115, 121

Hall Caine, Thomas, 164, 167
Hamlet, 141, 144
Haney, David, 14
Hare, William, xxii
Harvey, John, 36
Hawthorne, Nathaniel, 182, 187
   The House of the Seven Gables, 187

Haydon, Benjamin Robert, 124–25, 128, 213
Hazlitt, William, 61, 115
   Lectures on the English Poets, 61
Heilman, Robert, 190
Henry, Thomas, 25
   Memoirs of Albert de Haller, 25
Heppner, Christopher, 36
Hertz, Neil, 4
Hilton, Nelson, 26
Hogarth, William, 24–25, 28, 37–38
   Stages of Cruelty, 24
   The Analysis of Beauty, 28, 37
Holt Monk, Samuel, 4
Hone, William, 116
Horace, 78
Horne Tooke, John, 71, 75
   Diversions of Purley, 71–72
Huhn, Thomas, 2
Hume, David, 4
Hunt, Leigh, 114–115, 124, 200, 213
   Lord Byron and Some of his Contemporaries, 114
Hunt, William Holman, xx, 160–63, 165–6
Hunter, John, xxii, 24–27, 33
Hunter, William, xxii, 24–27, 31–33, 35–36, 38
   Anatomy of the Human Gravid Uterus, 27, 31–34
Hysteria, 6

Isherwood, Christopher, 110

Jacobus, Mary, 55
Jack Tearguts, *see* John Hunter
James, Henry, xxiv, 181–97
   The Sense of the Past, 190
   The Turn of the Screw, xxiv, 181–87, 190–91, 193

Jeffrey, Francis, 61
Jesus, 203
Johnson, Samuel, 71
Johnson, Joseph, 25
Jordanova, L. J., 5, 7, 33–34
Juvenal, 78

Kant, 4, 182
Keats, George, 132
Keats, Georgiana, 132
Keats, John, xix–xxiii, xv, 2, 51, 109–37, 159–80, 213–14
   'The Cap and Bells', 114
   Endymion, 121
   'Give me women, wine, and snuff', 122
   Hyperion, 164
   'Isabella', 173
   La Belle Dame sans Merci, xv, 110, 112, 119, 129–34, 165–68, 170–74
   Lamia, 114, 134
   'Ode to a Nightingale', 111, 117
   'Over the hill, and over the dale', 122, 124–28
   'Pensive they sit and roll their languid eyes', 129–30
   'Sharing Eve's Apple', 167
   The Eve of St. Agnes, 112, 127, 173
   'To Autumn', 116, 133
   To Mrs. Reynolds's Cat, 117
   'Where be ye going, you Devon Maid', 122–25, 128
Kelly, Gary, 57
Kelsall, Thomas Forbes, 142, 146, 149–52
Kemp, Martin, 26, 32
   Dr. William Hunter at the Royal Academy of Arts, 26
King, Bruce, 125
Klancher, Jon, 69

Kloos, Willem, xix, xxii, 199–224
   'Percy Bysshe Shelley, by Willem Kloos', 201, 216–222
Knox, Robert, 24,
   Great Artists and Great Anatomists, 24
Kotzebue, August von, 45
Kreiter, Carmen S., 25–26

L. E. L., *see* Letitia Landon
La Spezia, 202
Lairesse, 27, 29–30
Lamb, Charles, 115
Landon, Letitia, 146
Laqueur, Thomas, 5
   Making Sex: Body and Gender from the Greeks to Freud, 5
Larkin, Philip, xxiii, 110–12, 121–122, 133–134
Lawrence, D. H., 110–11
Le Fage, Monsignor, 28
Lerici, 201
Levinson, Marjorie, 113–114, 116, 134
   Keats' Life of Allegory: The Origins of a Style, 113, 134
Lewis, Matthew Gregory 'Monk', 6, 9, 45
   The Castle Spectre, xviii
   'The King of the Cats', 141
   Tales of Wonder, 47
   The Monk, 6, 15
Leyland, 164
Literary Gazette, 67–68
Livorno, 201

Macbeth, 144
Macpherson, Pat, 188
Mallarmé, Stéphane, 113
Marquess, William Henry, 168
Marvell, Andrew, 113
Marx, xxiv

Matthew's Gospel, 146, 203
Matthews, G. M., 90, 92
Mellor, Anne K., 174
Michasiw, Kim Ian, 14
Michelangelo, 23, 25
Miles, Robert, 3
Millais, John Everett, 160, 162–63, 165
Milner, George, 166
Milton, John, 46, 123, 182, 187
   Il Penseroso, 113
   L'Allegro, 113
   Paradise Lost, 187
Mitchell, W. J. T., 169
Monkton Milnes, Richard, 114, 160
   Life, Letters and Remains of John Keats, 114
Moore, G., 80
   Letters and Journals of Byron, 80
More, Hannah, 44
   Strictures on the Modern System of Female Education, 44
Morris, Jane, 168
Morris, William, 166
Motion, Andrew, 110–12, 115–16, 133
   Salt Water, 116
Mozart, 75
Mullan, John, 6
Murphy, Patsy, 134

Newlyn, Lucy, 169
Newton, 29, 32
   Principia, 29
Nietzsche, Friedrich, 97, 102
   'On the Uses and Disadvantages of History for Life', 97

O'Brien, Flann, 120–21, 134
   'Cruiskeen Lawn', 120

O'Neill, Michael, 211

*p*apergon, 182
Parrish, Stephen M., 54
   The Art of the Lyrical
   Ballads, 54
Peacock, Thomas Love, xxiii–xxiv,
   67–87
   'An Essay on Fashionable
   Literature', 70
   Crotchet Castle, 80,82–83
   Four Ages of Poetry, 78–79
   Headlong Hall, 69, 71–73,
   75–76,79
   Maid Marian, 75
   Melincourt, 67, 77–78,80–83
   Memoirs of Shelley, 79
   Nightmare Abbey, 70, 74–75,
   76–77, 81
Pen (Browning's son), 151
Pemberton, Henry, 29
Percy, Thomas, 130
   Reliques of Ancient English
   Poetry, 130
Peterloo, 116
Petry, Alice Hall, 186–87
Physiology, 26
Pisa, 200
Pitt, 74
Plato, 71
Poe, Edgar Allan, 182
Pound, Ezra, 139
Praz, Mario, 15
Pre-Raphaelite Brotherhood, 159–60,
   162–63, 170
Preston, William, 44
Prickett, Stephen, 159
Procter, Bryan Waller, 146, 152
Pye, H. J., 47

Radcliffe, Ann, xx, 8, 45, 187
   The Mysteries of Udolpho, 8,
   187

Rafael, 23,28
Reiman, Donald H., 90, 96, 101, 103
Renaissance, 24
Reni, Guido, 28
Resurrectionists, 147
Reyneke-van Stuwe, Jacob, 199–200,
   207
Reynolds, Joshua, 25, 33–36, 38
   Discourses on Art, 33,35–36
Rice, James, 124, 128
Richardson, Samuel, 5
   Clarissa, 5
Ricks, Christopher, 111–12, 116,
   119–20, 134
   Keats and Embarrassment,
   112
Roberts, K. B., 27–28, 30
Romantic authorship, 57
Romantic reviewers, 44
Rossetti, Dante Gabriel, xix, 159,
   162, 164–70, 174
   Ballads and Sonnets, 164
Rossetti, William Michael, 202
Rossini, 75
Rousseau, Jean-Jacques, xv, 97–100
   The Confessions, 97, 100–101
   Essay on the Origin of
   Languages, 97–100, 102
   Julie, 97, 100
   Reveries of the Solitary
   Walker, 97, 100
Royal Academy, xxii, 20,
   24,26,32,39–40, 160
Royal Society, 27
Rubens, 23, 28
Ruskin, John, 150
Russell, James Anderson, 215

Sade, Marquis de, 7, 15
   Justine, 7
Sawday, Jonathan, 35
Schiller, Friedrich, 45
   The Death of Wallenstein, 45

Wallenstein, 45
Scott, Grant F., 169
Scott, Walter, 47
Severn, Joseph, xxii, 117, 119, 212–14
Shakespeare, William, 46, 111, 140, 145, 167
   Hamlet, xxii, 69, 143
   Henry IV, Part I, 69
   Henry IV, Part II, 69
   King Lear, 112
   Macbeth, 141, 145
   Much Ado About Nothing, 77
   The Tempest, 209
   Twelfth Night, 73
Shaw, George Bernard, 210, 215
Shelley, Mary, xxi–xxii, 45, 89–90, 93–94, 103–04, 141, 211
   'Note on Poems Written in 1822', 90, 106
   'On Ghosts', 141
Shelley, P. B., xvii–xx, xxii, xv, 15, 45, 73–74, 79, 89–107, 113, 140, 142, 148, 155, 166, 199–200, 204
   Shelley's ghost, 200, 203–04
   Adonais, 114–15, 206, 213–14
   Alastor, 206
   Epipsychidion, 142, 206
   'Hymn to Intellectual Beauty', 206
   'Lines Written in the Bay of Lerici', 93, 96–97, 99, 103
   'Mask of Anarchy', 211
   'Mont Blanc', 206
   On the Medusa of Leonardo da Vinci, 14
   Prometheus Unbound, 206–07
   Queen Mab, 200, 213
   'Song to the Men of England', 211
   St. Irvine, 14
   The Cenci, 14–15, 206
   'The Triumph of Life', xxii, xv, 89–107
   'To Jane: The Keen Stars Were Twinkling', 91–93, 95–96, 98
Simpson, David, 44
Smith, Alan Gardner, 192
Socrates, 71
Southey, Robert, xvii, 61
   The Doctor, &c, xviii
   Thabala The Destroyer, 61
Spectres, xvii–xix, 19–23, 34, 37–38, 181
   Eerie spectres, 173
   Ghosts, xvii, 140–41, 173, 181
   Macbeth's ghost, 144
   Petermännchen, 61
   Phantasms, xviii
   Phantoms, 141
   Spirits, 173
   Teutonic ghosts, 62
Spencer, W. R., 47
Spenser, 46
Stafford, Barbara, 37
   Body Criticism, 37
Stafford, Fiona J., 153
Stanley, J. T., 47
Strachey, Lytton, 139
Stubbs, George, 24
Sublime, 1–3, 9, 11, 51
   Egotistical sublime, 8, 51
   Kantian sublime, 2
   Wordsworthian sublime, 2, 8, 51
Sutton, Jim, 110–11
Swann, Karen, 174
Switzerland, 146

Taylor, William, 47, 54–55

'The Lass of Fair Wone', 54–55
Tennyson, Alfred, 159
The Ancient Britons, 23
The Courier, 203
The Examiner, 115
The Irish Times, 120
The Liberal, 200, 211
The London Magazine, 141
The Netherlands, 199, 206, 214–15
The Times, 202
Times Literary Supplement, 200, 214
Tintner, Adeline, 188
Todorov, Tzvetan, 192
Tomlinson, J. D. W., 27–29, 32
Tompkins, J. M. S., 43
    The English Popular Novel, 1770–1800, 43
Trelawny, Edward John, 202

United States, 200

Van Riemsdyck, Jan, 34
Van Sant, Ann, 7
Vargo, Lisa, 89–90
Verwey, Albert, 199, 205–06
Virtue, 3, 6–7
Vivian, Charles, 209
Voltaire, 75

Wahl, John Robert, 166
Wallace, Tara Ghoshal, 192
Ward, Aileen, 116
Waterhouse, John William, 171, 174
Webb, Timothy, 209
    Shelley: A Voice not Understood, 209
Weiskel, Thomas, 2–4, 8
    The Romantic Sublime, 2
Whytt, Robert, 4
William, Edward, 209
Williams, Jane, 90, 95–96
Witsen, Willem, 208

Wordsworth, William, xx, xxiii, 14, 43-66, 113, 216
    'Hart-Leap Well', xxiii, 46, 49–50, 52–56, 58– 62
    Lyrical Ballads, 43–66
    Salisbury Plain, 52
    'The Thorn', 49, 54
Worrall, David, 26

Zoffany, Johann, 26

OHIO UNIVERSITY LIBRARY
Please return this book as soon as you have
finished with it to avoid a fine it must
date stamped